SO-BXL-009

ACPL ITEM
DISCARDED

304.
Lavin, Michael R.
Subject index to the 1990
Census of population and

Subject Index to the 1990 Census of Population and Housing

Michael R. Lavin
Jane Weintrop
Cynthia Cornelius

Epoch Books, Inc.

Allen County Public Library
900 Webster Street
PO Box 2270
Fort Wayne, IN 46801-2270

Copyright © 1997 by Epoch Books, Inc.

All rights reserved, including the right of reproduction
in whole or part in any form.

Design and typography by:

shuffaloff press:

260 Plymouth
Buffalo NY 14213 USA

653 Euclid Ave.
Toronto ON M6G 2T6 CAN

ISBN 0-9629586-2-X

Epoch Books, Inc.
22 Byron Avenue
Kenmore, New York 14223

Contents

Preface

THE *Subject Index to the 1990 Census of Population and Housing* is the only detailed, single-source guide to the tables found in major print and CD-ROM publications of the 1990 Census. The Bureau of the Census has created various indexes to its publications, but these are limited for several reasons. The "Table Finding Guides" located in every printed Census report can be extremely helpful, but the user must first guess which report might contain the type of data he or she seeks before consulting a specific Table Finding Guide. With more than two dozen different titles in the 1990 printed series, locating the appropriate report is a daunting task for all but the most experienced Census users. Part I of the *Subject Index to the 1990 Census* resolves this problem by providing a composite index to all of the Bureau's Table Finding Guides in a single alphabet.

The Census Bureau's indexing to its CD-ROM products is similarly limited. Many of the CD-ROM discs contain a basic keyword index, but these indexes are extremely general and selective. Also, users must once again select the appropriate disc before consulting a keyword index. Part II of the *Subject Index to the 1990 Census* provides an extremely detailed composite index to the tables found in all of the *Summary Tape File* products.

The differences between Part I and Part II result from the structural differences between the printed Census reports and the CD-ROM discs. The printed reports are more difficult to deal with for several reasons. First, the table structure in each printed report is completely different from the structure of all the other reports. In contrast, the table structure and numbering in the CD-ROM products are extremely uniform and quite easy to follow. Second, most printed reports provide coverage for many different geographic levels (counties, cities, Minor Civil Divisions, etc.) in a single report, while each subfile in the CD-ROM series is limited to particular types of geographies. Third, geographic coverage in the printed reports is somewhat haphazard. Some topics may be tabulated for Census Tracts, for example, while others are not. In contrast, each subject found in the CD-ROM products is tabulated for every level of geography on the disc.

The uniform structure of the CD-ROM products, together with their limited number, enabled the creation of an extremely detailed index to the tables themselves. Users of the *Subject Index to the 1990 Census* need only consult two sections of Part II to determine the appropriate CD-ROM disc and the needed table on that disc: the guide to geographic coverage of the CD-ROM subfiles, and the subject index itself.

Unfortunately, detailed table-level indexing is not feasible for the more complex and disparate titles in the printed series. Readers should note that the composite index to the printed reports does not lead directly to the required table itself. Instead, it refers users to the appropriate report title, and it identifies which geographic levels are covered for a particular topic in each report. Users must then consult the "Table Finding Guide" within the individual report to determine an actual table number. Despite this limitation, Part I is an extremely valuable tool for locating specific Census data, and the composite index is currently being used by the Census Bureau's own Regional Offices, as well as by Census-affiliated State Data Centers across the country.

Part I and Part II each provide narrative sections which explain how to best use these indexes. They also include additional tools for using 1990 Census products more efficiently. For further assistance, readers can turn to Part III of the *Subject Index*, where they will find a brief "Glossary of Frequently Misunderstood Census Terms."

The big question at this point is, "When is it better to use the printed reports instead of the CD-ROMs?" There is no general answer to that question. Many topics are covered equally well by both formats, but many are not. Some subjects can only be found in printed reports, while others are published only on the CD-ROM discs. In many instances, printed reports offer more detailed subject breakdowns (especially in the cases of *CP-1, CP-2, CH-1,* and *CH-2*), but this is not always the case. The most sensible solution is to check both indexes and compare the results before deciding which format to consult.

The primary (and obvious) purpose of the *Subject Index to the 1990 Census* is to assist Census users in locating specific data tables quickly and efficiently. A second, less obvious application should also be pointed out. Because the indexes in Parts I and II include copious cross-references (as does the glossary in Part III), the book can be used to help identify links among related Census concepts.

An excellent example can be found in the way the 1990 Census tabulates data about children. According to the Census Bureau definition, a Child is a son or daughter by birth, adoption, or marriage (i.e., a step-child), regardless of the child's age. By this definition, a "Child" can be an adult, as long as that person is a son or daughter living with one or more parents. How does the Census user focus on the concept of young children? The Bureau employs several additional concepts to measure alternate definitions of children. The Census uses "Own Child" to count sons or daughters who are less than 18 years of age. The term "Related Child" also covers persons under age 18, but in addition to Own Children, the term includes relatives other than sons and daughters (nieces, nephews, grandchildren, etc.) living in the household. And what about young people who are not related to the Householder? Many Census tables provide data for this segment of the population, which the Census Bureau identifies simply as "Persons Under Age 18 Years." With such an array of similar terms, it is quite easy to inadvertently consult the wrong Census table-- a mistake which even experienced Census users can make.

The indexes in Part I and Part II were designed specifically to alert users to subtle differences in Census terminology, and to refer users to related concepts.

Readers should note that understanding Census concepts, terminology, and geographic constructs is an essential component to the proper use of Census data. The *Subject Index to the 1990* Census provides numerous guides to assist readers in understanding key terms and concepts, but it is no substitute for the detailed documentation found in the Census products themselves. In addition to the Census Bureau's own documentation, all Census users, whether novice or experienced, are encouraged to consult Michael Lavin's *Understanding the Census*, also published by Epoch Books. *Understanding the Census* provides in-depth explanations of every aspect of the 1990 Census, presented in a step-by-step, easy to follow format.

Michael Lavin
Jane Weintrop
Cynthia Cornelius

Buffalo, New York
February, 1997

Part I

Index to Printed Census Reports

Compiled by Jane Weintrop

Part I
Section 1

How to Use Part I

How to Use Part One: Composite Index to Table Finding Guides

Introduction

THIS IS A SUBJECT index to the printed reports produced from the *1990 Census of Population and Housing*. The index identifies the particular report(s) where each subject occurs as well as the levels of geography at which data are reported, and the amount of detail given for race and hispanic origin.

A description of the components of an entry in the index and an overview of the Census reports are included in these introductory pages. The terminology used is from the Bureau of the Census. Understanding the Bureau's terminology is important to ensure appropriate use of the data. The index contains brief descriptions of some terms and notes the location of fuller descriptions for each type of information.

Each entry lists all the reports where a particular subject occurs. A searcher must still select a specific report, then go to the Table Finding Guide or Table of Contents within that report to identify the needed tables. For help in this process, read the tips listed below and use the information summarized in the table on page 13 entitled "1990 Census Print Reports."

Tips To Follow When Choosing Which Report to Use

1. Whenever possible, use 100% data

2. Use CPH-3, CPH-4 and CPH-6 only when you are working with the special geographies on which they report.

3. Use the detailed reports, CH-2 and CP-2, when they are the only source for the information you require.

Tips To Follow When Reading a Table

1. Always read the table heading to confirm you have the table you want.

2. Always read the row headers carefully to determine the universe of data being reported. For example, are the rows reporting "persons", "persons 16 and over", "occupied housing units", etc.

Information Included in the Index

Report Number

The report number, assigned by the Bureau of the Census, is the key piece of information being indexed. Knowing the number of the report that contains a particular subject-geography combination provides access to the Table of Contents, that appears within every report, and to the Table Finding Guide, that is included in most Census reports. Either of these features within a report points to specific data tables.

All reports included in this index are described in Part I, Section Two, "List of 1990 Census Print Reports." The report numbers used for indexing are shown in the left most column of the table.

For reports issued in geographic series, the first report number shown for each title is the reference used in the index for all the volumes issued in that geographic series. The summary volume(s) for each series cover the same subjects as the state reports, but at different geographic levels. These summary volumes have unique Table Finding Guides and are indexed separately using the specific report numbers assigned by the Bureau; they can be identified by a suffix to the report number beginning with a hyphen (e.g., -1, -1A, -1B, or -1C).

The subject report series, *CP-3* and *CH-3*, are based on subject rather than geography. Each subject report within a series deals with one topic and tabulates data for the entire United States only. See "Subject Reports" for a description of all printed reports in these series.

The supplementary report series (*CPH-S*, *CP-S*, and *CH-S*) contain reports that are United States summaries either for a type of geography or for a subject. See "Supplementary Reports" for a description of volumes in these series.

Subjects

The headings included in the index are the subjects as they are listed in the Table Finding Guides. Wording was changed only when it was necessary to establish consistency among slightly different terms used for subjects containing basically the same data. Cross-references have been added that serve as referrals to related topics (*see also*...) or as directives from a common phrase to the one used in the Table Finding Guide (*use* ...). Definitions for any subject used in a Table Finding Guide are given in Appendix B of each report where the subject occurs.

Geography

Each subject is indexed further by the major geographic levels at which data are reported, eg. county, Place, Tract, etc. These geographies appear in the Table Finding Guides usually as column headings. See "Abbreviations

and Codes Used in Indexing" for a brief explanation of these geographies. Fuller definitions for any geography used in a Table Finding Guide are given in Appendix A of each report where the geography occurs and in Chapter 6 of *Understanding the Census*.

Geographic Subheadings
There are situations where data for a particular subject-geography combination are reported in total and then further analyzed by some other geographic factor; eg. inside/outside MSA, urban/rural. When these added geographic factors occur, they are reported in the index as a subheading to the subject. Definitions for these added geographic factors used in a Table Finding Guide are given in Appendix A of each report where they occur.

Race and Hispanic Origin

Many Census tables analyze data by hispanic origin or by race and hispanic origin. In some instances, this information is conveyed in the wording of the subject heading used in the Table Finding Guide (as well as this Subject Index). More frequently, the Table Finding Guides indicate racial/hispanic breakdowns through the use of column headings or special symbols. These situations are handled in the Subject Index by adding special symbols adjacent to the report number. Either the * or the # is used depending on the level of detail contained in the report. See "Abbreviations and Codes Used in Indexing" for a brief explanation of these codes, and the footnotes of the applicable Table Finding Guides for fuller definitions.

Abbreviations and Symbols Used in Indexing

The Subject Index employs the following abbreviations and symbols to designate geographic and racial/hispanic coverage.

U. S.

A combination of the 50 states and the District of Columbia.

REGION

Census Regions consist of four groups of states: the West, Midwest, Northeast and South. This geography may also be indexed under REGION/DIV.

DIVISION

Census Divisions are sub groups of states within a region. This geography may also be indexed under REGION/DIV.

REGION/DIV

This abbreviation is used to index Regions and Divisions within a report series when the same level of detail is used for both these areas.

STATE

Each of the 50 states, plus the District of Columbia. Puerto Rico and the United States Virgin Islands are reported as the equivalent of a state in report series that are published by state, and as outlying areas in summary volumes.

COUNTY

The primary political division of most states. In some states they may be referred to as parishes, boroughs, or census counties.

SUBDIV

Every county in the United States is completely divided in County Subdivisions. These are either unincorporated political entities (called Minor Civil Divisions) or statistical constructs created by the Census Bureau (called Census County Divisions). This code is used when all County Subdivisions are included in a report.

SELECT SDV

This abbreviation is used to index County Subdivisions in the 12 states where they serve as general-purpose governments (Connecticut, Maine, Massachusetts, Michigan, Minnesota, New Hampshire, New Jersey, New York, Pennsylvania, Rhode Island, Vermont, and Wisconsin). In these reports they appear together with Places. In some reports, when only Places of a certain size are included, this is accommodated in the indexing for Places, but not in the indexing of the corresponding selected Subdivisions. For selected Subdivisions, the indexing for Places within the same report will reflect any variation in reporting detail that may pertain to the size of the community. (see PLC+10, etc.)

PLACE

All Incorporated Places (such as cities and villages), plus all Census Designated Places.

PLC 50+

Places of 50,000 population or greater.

PLC 10+

Places of 10,000 population or greater.

PLC 2.5-9

Places with population between 2,500 and 10,000.

PLC 1-2.5

Places with population between 1,000 and 2,500.

MSA

Metropolitan Statistical Areas, together with Primary and Consolidated MSAs. In most reports, the definitions used for MSAs were those established by the U.S. Office of Management and Budget on June 30, 1990. On June 30 1993, OMB established new definitions for MSAs. Report *CPH-S-1-1* is a special publication using the 1993 revised definition for reporting the 1990 Census data. The MSA abbreviation refers to both definitions.

URBANIZED

An Urbanized Area contains one or more Places together with a surrounding area that results in a population of at least 50,000.

NATIVE AM

American Indian and Alaska Native Areas may include tribal, political, territorial, or statistical areas defined for these populations.

OUTLYING

American Samoa, Guam, the Mariana Islands, and Palau. Use of the abbreviation "OUTLYING" covers all the geographic components defined within each of these jurisdictions. Puerto Rico, and Virgin Islands are reported as the equivalent of a state in report series that are published by state, and as outlying areas in summary volumes.

CONGRS DIS

Congressional Districts are the 435 districts represented in the U.S. House of Representatives for the 101st Congress.

TRACT

Tracts and Block Numbering Areas (BNA) are statistical subdivisions of counties.

*

Indicates the data are reported by race and hispanic origin to a level of detail that may include: black, white, native american, asian or pacific islander, hispanic origin, and white not of hispanic origin.

#

Indicates the data are reported by race and hispanic origin to a more detailed level than above for the asian or pacific islander and hispanic populations.

Subject Reports

A limited number of Subject Reports was issued for 1990, though additional Subject Reports were issued on CD-ROM. Each Subject Report focuses on national geography (the United States as a whole), though some also provide totals for large geographies, such as region/division, state, and/or metropolitan areas. Each Subject Report analyzes a list of subject characteristics as they relate to the main topic of the report. Below is a list of all printed 1990 Subject Reports published by the Census, together with descriptions of the subjects they address and their U.S. Superintendent of Documents number.

Housing Subject Reports

A single printed report was issued in this series for 1990. It provides detailed data for housing units located within Metropolitan territory in the United States. A second report, called *Residential Finance*, is actually not part of the Subject Report series, but is included here because it is similar in approach and coverage.

—Metropolitan Housing Characteristics

C3.224/4-2:990
Provides analysis of housing characteristics for the United

States and for the aggregated area contained within all Metropolitan Areas. The analysis contains a variety of cross tabulations between financial, structural, size, age, and ownership characteristics. More detailed geographic coverage can be found in the CD-ROM reports of the same title.

—Residential Finance

C3.224/13:1990 CH-4-1
This specialized report, mandated by federal law, is based on a sample survey conducted in 1991. It provides extraordinarily detailed information on mortgage financing for the nation as a whole, cross-tabulated by many characteristics. Unlike other housing reports, this volume tabulates data for the entire building, rather than individual housing units within the building.

Population Subject Reports

Seven printed reports were issued in this series for 1990. "Population Report" is a misnomer, since every report in the series except for *CP-3-4* contains both population and housing data for the specialized population groups being covered. The populations included in reports *CP-3-1*, *CP-3-2*, *CP-3-3*, and *CP-3-5* are each analyzed in the same way, with the exact same table formats for each.

—Foreign Born in the United States

C3.223/10:1990 CP-3-1
Gives detailed data based on the country of origin reported by foreign born. United States totals only.

-—Ancestry of the Population in the United States

C3.223/10:1990 CP-3-2
Gives data based on the country of ancestry reported by those not in the asian or pacific islander population, or in the hispanic population. (The latter groups are covered by separate Subject Reports, shown below.) United States totals only.

—Persons of Hispanic Origin in the United States

C3.223/10:1990 CP-3-3
Gives data based on the country of ancestry reported by those of hispanic origin. United States totals only.

—Education in the United States

C3.223/10:1990 CP-3-4

Gives data on educational attainment and school enroll-ment analyzed by age, sex, race, hispanic origin, and by earnings. This report does include state totals in parts of its analysis.

—Asian & Pacific Islanders in the United States

C3.223/10:1990 CP-3-5

Gives data based on the country of ancestry reported by those of asian or pacific islander origin. United States totals only.

—Characteristics of the Black Population

C3.223/10:1990 CP-3-6

Gives data, including cross tabulations among numerous characteristics, for the black population. Data are re-ported for the U.S., for states with 900,000 or more blacks, and for Metropolitan Areas with 400,000 or more blacks.

—Characteristics of American Indians by Tribe and Language

C3.223/10:1990 CP-3-7

Gives data based on tribal affiliation for native americans. For population characteristics, statistics are reported by state and by MSA in addition to the U.S. totals.

Supplementary Reports

Supplementary Reports present special compilations of Census data that either analyze responses for particular questions on the questionnaire or report on particular subgroups of the population. Below is a list of those reports printed for 1990, together with descriptions and U.S. Superintendent of Documents numbers for each.

Population Series

Two reports were issued in this series for 1990.

—Detailed Occupation and Other Characteristics from the EEO File for the United States

C3.223/12:1990 CP-S-1-1

A slim report containing four tables which summarize Equal Employment Opportunity data for the nation as a whole. Cross-tabulates detailed occupational data by sex, race, and hispanic origin. Also tabulates educational attainment of the civilian labor force by age, sex, race, and hispanic origin. More detailed geographic coverage can be found in the CD-ROM report.

—Detailed Ancestry Groups for States

C3.223/12:1990 CP-S-1-2

Shows the population size and geographic distribution of 215 ancestry groups--many more than can be found in the Subject Reports series.

Population and Housing Series

Two 1990 reports which provide both population and housing characteristics for special geographies.

—Metropolitan Areas as Defined by the Office of Management & Budget, June 30, 1993

C3.223/12:1990 CPH-S-1-1

Reports on the subjects listed in the original 1990 geographic report series but uses updated definitions for MSAs.

—Urbanized Areas of the United States and Puerto Rico

C3.223/12:1990 CPH-S-1-2

Reports population and housing counts, land area, and population density for Urbanized Areas and their geo-graphic components.

Part I
Section 2

List of 1990 Printed Reports

PRINTED 1990 CENSUS REPORTS

REPORT NO.	SUDOC STEM	REPORT TITLE	ISSUED	DATA
CPH-1 -1-1	C3.223/18:	Summary Population and Housing -US summary	-by state	100%
CPH-2 -2-1	C3.223/5:	Population and Housing Unit Counts 1990 & previous census -US summary	-by state	100%
CPH-3	C3.223/11:	Population and Housing Characteristics for Tracts/BNA's	-by MSA & non-MSA	100% & sample
CPH-4	C3.223/20:	Population and Housing Characteristics for Congressional Districts	-by state	100% & sample
CPH-5 -5-1	C3.223.23:	Summary Social, Economic, and Housing Characteristics -US summary	-by state	sample
CPH-6	C3.223/23: or C3.223/18:	Social, Economic, and Housing Characteristics	-by outlying area	100% & sample
CP-1 -1-1 -1-1A -1-1B -1-1C	C3.223/6: /6: /6-2: /6-3: /6-4:	General Population Characteristics - US summary - Native Areas - MSA's - Urbanized Areas	-by state	100%
CP-2 -2-1 -2-1A -2-1B -2-1C	C3.223/7: /7: /7-2: /7-3: /7-4:	Social & Economic Characteristics - US summary - Native Areas - MSA's - Urbanized Areas	-by state	sample
CP-3	C3.223/10:	Population Subject Reports	-by subject	sample
CH-1 -1-1 -1-1A -1-1B -1-1C	C3.224/3: /3: /3-2: /3-3: /3-4:	General Housing Characteristics - US summary - Native Areas - MSA's - Urbanized Areas	-by state	100%
CH-2 -2-1 -2-1A -2-1B -2-1C	C3.224/3: /3: /3-5: /3-6: /3-7:	Detailed Housing Characteristics - US summary - Native Areas - MSA's - Urbanized Areas	-by state	sample
CH-3	C3.224/4-2:	Housing Subject Reports	-by subject	sample
CH-4	C3.224/13:1990	Residential Finance	-by subject	sample
CPH-S, CP-S, & CH-S	C3.223/12:	Supplementary Reports	-US summaries	100% & sample

Part I
Section 3

Composite Index to Table Finding Guides:
A Subject Locator for Printed Reports of the 1990 Census

Composite Index to Table Finding Guides: A Subject Locator for Printed Reports of the 1990 Census

ABILITY TO SPEAK ENGLISH...
      see also..   : ANCESTRY: DETAILED CHARACTERISTICS...
                       : ASIANS AND PACIFIC ISLANDERS: DETAILED CHARACTERISTICS...
                       : FOREIGN BORN: DETAILED CHARACTERISTICS...
                       : HISPANIC ORIGIN: DETAILED CHARACTERISTICS...
                       : LANGUAGE SPOKEN AT HOME
                       : POPULATION CHARACTERISTICS OF AMERICAN INDIANS BY TRIBE

ABILITY TO SPEAK ENGLISH BY AGE, IN HOUSEHOLDS

U.S.	: CP-2-1#; CP-2-1B; CP-2-1C
REGION/DIV	: CP-2-1
STATE	: CP-2#
COUNTY	: CP-2#
SELECT SDV	: CP-2#
PLC 10+	: CP-2#
PLC 2.5-9	: CP-2#
MSA	: CP-2-1B#
URBANIZED	: CP-2-1C#
NATIVE AM	: CP-2; CP-2-1A*

—IN CENTRAL CITY/NOT IN CENTRAL CITY

MSA	: CP-2-1B

—IN CENTRAL PLACE/URBAN FRINGE

URBANIZED	: CP-2-1C

—INDIVIDUAL CENTRAL CITY

MSA	: CP-2-1B

—INDIVIDUAL CENTRAL PLACE

URBANIZED	: CP-2-1C

—INSIDE/OUTSIDE MSA
    U.S.   : CP-2-1*; CP-2-1B
    STATE   : CP-2*
—RURAL OR RURAL FARM
    COUNTY   : CP-2
—URBAN, RURAL & SIZE OF PLACE
    U.S.   : CP-2-1*; CP-2-1C
—URBAN, RURAL, SIZE OF PLACE, FARM
    STATE   : CP-2*

ABILITY TO SPEAK ENGLISH FOR PERSONS 60 YEARS AND OLDER
    NATIVE AM : CP-2-1A*

AGE
    see also..   : POPULATION CHARACTERISTICS OF AMERICAN INDIANS BY TRIBE

    U.S.   : CP-2-1#; CP-2-1B; CP-2-1C; CPH-1-1
    REGION/DIV : CP-2-1; CPH-1-1
    STATE   : CP-2#; CPH-1; CPH-1-1
    COUNTY   : CP-2*; CPH-1; CPH-3*; CPH-4
    SUBDIV   : CPH-1
    SELECT SDV : CP-2*; CPH-4
    PLACE   : CPH-1
    PLC 10+   : CP-2*; CPH-3*; CPH-4
    PLC 2.5-9 : CP-2
    MSA   : CP-2-1B*; CPH-1-1; CPH-3*
    URBANIZED : CP-2-1C*; CPH-1-1
    NATIVE AM : CP-2; CP-2-1A*; CPH-1; CPH-1-1; CPH-4
    OUTLYING : CPH-6
    CONGRS DIS : CPH-4*
    TRACT   : CPH-3*
—IN CENTRAL CITY/NOT IN CENTRAL CITY
    MSA   : CP-2-1B
—IN CENTRAL PLACE/URBAN FRINGE
    URBANIZED : CP-2-1C
—INDIVIDUAL CENTRAL CITY
    MSA   : CP-2-1B
—INDIVIDUAL CENTRAL PLACE
    URBANIZED : CP-2-1C
—INSIDE/OUTSIDE MSA
    U.S.   : CP-2-1*; CP-2-1B
    STATE   : CP-2*
—RURAL OR RURAL FARM
    COUNTY   : CP-2
—URBAN, RURAL & SIZE OF PLACE
    U.S.   : CP-2-1*; CP-2-1C
—URBAN, RURAL, SIZE OF PLACE, FARM
    STATE   : CP-2*

AGE (MEDIAN)
    use .....   : POPULATION GENERAL SUMMARY CHARACTERISTICS

AGE GROUP 50 OR OLDER BY SELECTED CHARACTERISTICS (BLACKS)
    use .....   : CHARACTERISTICS OF THE BLACK POPULATION
AGE GROUPS: ALL PERSONS & FEMALES
    use .....   : AGE
AGE GROUPS (NOT CROSSED BY SEX)
    PLC 1-2.5   : CP-1
AGE GROUPS (NOT CROSSED BY SEX) (PERCENT)
    use .....   : POPULATION: GENERAL SUMMARY CHARACTERISTICS
AGE GROUPS BY SEX
    see also..   : ANCESTRY: DETAILED CHARACTERISTICS...
                   : ASIANS AND PACIFIC ISLANDERS: DETAILED CHARACTERISTICS...
                   : FOREIGN BORN: DETAILED CHARACTERISTICS...
                   : HISPANIC ORIGIN: DETAILED CHARACTERISTICS...

    U.S.   : CP-1-1B; CP-1-1C
    MSA   : CP-1-1B#; CPH-S-1-1
    URBANIZED : CP-1-1C#
    NATIVE AM   : CP-1-1A*
  —IN CENTRAL CITY/NOT IN CENTRAL CITY
    U.S.   : CPH-S-1-1
    REGION/DIV : CPH-S-1-1
    STATE   : CPH-S-1-1
    MSA   : CP-1-1B; CPH-S-1-1
  —IN CENTRAL PLACE/URBAN FRINGE
    URBANIZED : CP-1-1C
  —INSIDE/OUTSIDE MSA
    U.S.   : CP-1-1B; CPH-S-1-1
    REGION/DIV : CPH-S-1-1
    STATE   : CPH-S-1-1
  —POPULATION SIZE CLASS OF MSA
    U.S.   : CP-1-1B
  —POPULATION SIZE CLASS OF URBANIZED AREA
    U.S.   : CP-1-1C
  —URBAN & RURAL & SIZE OF PLACE
    U.S.   : CP-1-1C
AGE GROUPS BY SEX (NO SINGLE YEAR DATA)
  —INSIDE/OUTSIDE MSA
    U.S.   : CP-1-1*
    REGION   : CP-1-1*
    STATE   : CP-1*
  —RURAL AREAS
    COUNTY   : CP-1
  —URBAN & RURAL & SIZE OF PLACE
    U.S.   : CP-1-1*
    REGION   : CP-1-1*
    STATE   : CP-1*
AGE GROUPS BY SEX FOR HOUSEHOLD POPULATION ONLY
    STATE   : CP-1

```
          COUNTY        : CP-1
          SELECT SDV    : CP-1
          PLC 10+       : CP-1
          PLC 2.5-9     : CP-1
          PLC 1-2.5     : CP-1
AGE GROUPS BY SEX WITH SINGLE YEARS THROUGH 21 YEARS
          U.S.          : CP-1-1#
          REGION        : CP-1-1#
          DIVISION      : CP-1-1*
          STATE         : CP-1#; CP-1-1*
          COUNTY        : CP-1#
          SELECT SDV    : CP-1#
          PLC 10+       : CP-1#
          PLC 2.5-9     : CP-1#
          NATIVE AM     : CP-1
   —FOR URBAN & RURAL & SIZE OF PLACE
          U.S.          : CP-1-1
          REGION        : CP-1-1
          STATE         : CP-1
   —INSIDE/OUTSIDE MSA
          U.S.          : CP-1-1
          REGION        : CP-1-1
          STATE         : CP-1
AGE GROUPS BY SEX WITH SINGLE YEARS THROUGH 89 YEARS
          U.S.          : CP-1-1*
          REGION        : CP-1-1*
          STATE         : CP-1*
AGE OF HOUSEHOLDER
          see also..    : HOUSEHOLDER 65 YEARS AND OVER

          U.S.          : CH-1-1#; CH-1-1B; CH-1-1C; CP-1-1#
          REGION        : CH-1-1#; CP-1-1#
          DIVISION      : CH-1-1*; CP-1-1*
          STATE         : CH-1#; CH-1-1*; CP-1#; CP-1-1*
          COUNTY        : CH-1#; CP-1#
          SELECT SDV    : CH-1#; CP-1#
          PLC 10+       : CH-1#; CP-1#
          PLC 2.5-9     : CH-1#; CP-1#
          MSA           : CH-1-1B#
          URBANIZED     : CH-1-1C#
          NATIVE AM     : CH-1-1A*; CP-1
          CONGRS DIS    : CPH
   —IN CENTRAL CITY/NOT IN CENTRAL CITY
          MSA           : CH-1-1B
   —IN CENTRAL PLACE/URBAN FRINGE
          URBANIZED     : CH-1-1C
   —INSIDE/OUTSIDE MSA
          U.S.          : CH-1-1*; CH-1-1B; CP-1-1*
```

```
        REGION/DIV  : CPH-S-1-1
        STATE       : CP-2; CPH-S-1-1
 —URBAN, RURAL & SIZE OF PLACE
        U.S.        : CP-2-1; CP-2-1C
 —URBAN, RURAL, SIZE OF PLACE, FARM
        STATE       : CP-2
ANCESTRY: DETAILED CHARACTERISTICS BY COUNTRY OF ORIGIN
        U.S.        : CP-3-2 FOR THOSE NOT HISPANIC OR ASIAN/PACIFIC
                    : CP-3-3 FOR THOSE OF HISPANIC ORIGIN
                    : CP-3-5 FOR ASIANS AND PACIFIC ISLANDERS
APPORTIONMENT
        U.S.        : CPH-2-1
        REGION/DIV  : CPH-2-1
        STATE       : CPH-2-1
AREA, LAND
        use .....   : LAND AREA
AREA, WATER
        use .....   : WATER AREA
ASIANS AND PACIFIC ISLANDERS: DETAILED CHARACTERISTICS BY RACIAL GROUP
        U.S.        : CP-3-5
BEDROOMS
        see also..  : CHARACTERISTICS OF THE BLACK POPULATION
                    : HOUSING CHARACTERISTICS OF AMERICAN INDIANS BY TRIBE

        U.S.        : CH-2-1#; CH-2-1B; CH-2-1C*; CPH-5-1
        REGION/DIV  : CPH-5-1
        REGION      : CH-2-1#
        DIVISION    : CH-2-1*
        STATE       : CH-2#; CH-2-1*; CPH-5; CPH-5-1
        COUNTY      : CH-2#; CPH-3*; CPH-4; CPH-5
        SUBDIV      : CPH-5
        SELECT SDV  : CH-2#; CPH-4
        PLACE       : CPH-5
        PLC 10+     : CH-2#; CPH-3*; CPH-4
        MSA         : CH-2-1B#; CPH-3*; CPH-5-1; CPH-S-1-1
        URBANIZED   : CH-2-1C#; CPH-5-1
        NATIVE AM   : CH-2-1A; CH-2-1A; CH-2-1A
        OUTLYING    : CPH-6
        CONGRS DIS  : CPH-4
        TRACT       : CPH-
 IN CENTRAL CITY/NOT IN CENTRAL CITY
        U.S.        : CPH-S-1-1
        REGION/DIV  : CPH-S-1-1
        STATE       : CPH-S-1-1
        MSA         : CH-2-1B; CPH-S-1-1
 —IN CENTRAL PLACE/URBAN FRINGE
        URBANIZED   : CH-2-1C*
 —INSIDE/OUTSIDE MSA
```

```
         SELECT SDV   : CH-1
         PLC 10+      : CH-1
         PLC 2.5-9    : CH-1
         MSA          : CH-1-1B
         URBANIZED    : CH-1-1C
    —IN CENTRAL CITY/NOT IN CENTRAL CITY
         MSA          : CH-1-1B
    —IN CENTRAL PLACE/URBAN FRINGE
         URBANIZED    : CH-1-1C
    —INSIDE/OUTSIDE MSA
         U.S.         : CH-1-1; CH-1-1B
         REGION       : CH-1-1
         STATE        : CH-1
    —POPULATION SIZE CLASS OF MSA
         U.S.         : CH-1-1B
    —POPULATION SIZE CLASS OF URBANIZED AREA
         U.S.         : CH-1-1C
    —URBAN & RURAL & SIZE OF PLACE
         U.S.         : CH-1-1; CH-1-1C
         REGION       : CH-1-1
         STATE        : CH-1
CARPOOLING
         use .....    : MEANS OF TRANSPORTATION TO WORK
CENTER OF POPULATION
         use .....    : POPULATION CENTER, 1790-1990
CHARACTERISTICS OF THE BLACK POPULATION
         see also..   : RACE
                      : Subjects with report number flagged by * or #


         U.S.         : CP-3-6
CITIZENSHIP
         see also..   : NATIVITY
                      : PLACE OF BIRTH


         OUTLYING     : CPH-6
         CONGRS DIS   : CPH-4
CLASS OF WORKER
         see also..   : ANCESTRY: DETAILED CHARACTERISTICS...
                      : ASIANS AND PACIFIC ISLANDERS: DETAILED CHARACTERISTICS...
                      : FOREIGN BORN: DETAILED CHARACTERISTICS...
                      : HISPANIC ORIGIN: DETAILED CHARACTERISTICS...


         U.S.         : CP-2-1#; CP-2-1B; CP-2-1C
         REGION/DIV   : CP-2-1
         STATE        : CP-2#
         COUNTY       : CP-2#; CPH-3*
         SELECT SDV   : CP-2#
         PLC 10+      : CP-2#; CPH-3
```

```
      PLC 2.5-9      : CP-2#
      MSA            : CP-2-1B#; CPH-3; CPH-S-1-1
      URBANIZED      : CP-2-1C#
      NATIVE AM      : CP-2; CP-2-1Λ*
      OUTLYING       : CPH-6
      CONGRS DIS     : CPH-4
      TRACT          : CPH-3
   —IN CENTRAL CITY/NOT IN CENTRAL CITY
      U.S.           : CPH-S-1-1
      REGION/DIV     : CPH-S-1-1
      STATE          : CPH-S-1-1
      MSA            : CP-2-1B; CPH-S-1-1
   —IN CENTRAL PLACE/URBAN FRINGE
      URBANIZED      : CP-2-1C
   —INDIVIDUAL CENTRAL CITY
      MSA            : CP-2-1B
   —INDIVIDUAL CENTRAL PLACE
      URBANIZED      : CP-2-1C
   —INSIDE/OUTSIDE MSA
      U.S.           : CP-2-1*; CP-2-1B; CPH-S-1-1
      REGION/DIV     : CPH-S-1-1
      STATE          : CP-2*; CPH-S-1-1
   —RURAL OR RURAL FARM
      COUNTY         : CP-2
   —URBAN, RURAL & SIZE OF PLACE
      U.S.           : CP-2-1*; CP-2-1C
   —URBAN, RURAL, SIZE OF PLACE, FARM
      STATE          : CP-2*
COMMUTING CHARACTERISTICS
   use .....         : JOURNEY TO WORK
CONDOMINIUM (PERCENT)
   use .....         : HOUSING: DETAILED SUMMARY CHARACTERISTICS
CONDOMINIUM CHARACTERISTICS BY MORTGAGE CHARACTERISTICS
      U.S.           : CH-4-1
      REGION         : CH-4-1
CONDOMINIUM STATUS
      U.S.           : CH-2-1; CH-2-1B; CH-2-1C; CPH-5-1
      REGION/DIV     : CPH-5-1
      REGION         : CH-2-1
      STATE          : CH-2; CPH-5; CPH-5-1
      COUNTY         : CH-2; CPH-3; CPH-4; CPH-5
      SUBDIV         : CPH-5
      SELECT SDV     : CH-2; CPH-4
      PLACE          : CPH-5
      PLC 10+        : CH-2; CPH-3; CPH-4
      MSA            : CH-2-1B; CPH-3; CPH-5-1; CPH-S-1-1
      URBANIZED      : CH-2-1C; CPH-5-1
      CONGRS DIS     : CPH-4
```

```
      TRACT          : CPH-3
—IN CENTRAL CITY/NOT IN CENTRAL CITY
      U.S.           : CPH-S-1-1
      REGION/DIV  : CPH-S-1-1
      STATE          : CPH-S-1-1
      MSA            : CH-2-1B; CPH-S-1
—IN CENTRAL PLACE/URBAN FRINGE
      URBANIZED   : CH-2-1C
—INSIDE/OUTSIDE MSA
      U.S.           : CH-2-1; CH-2-1B; CPH-S-1-1
      REGION/DIV  : CPH-S-1-1
      STATE          : CH-2; CPH-S-1-1
—URBAN & RURAL & SIZE OF PLACE
      U.S.           : CH-2-1; CH-2-1C
—URBAN, RURAL, SIZE OF PLACE, FARM
      STATE          : CH-2
CONDOMINIUM UNITS
—INSIDE/OUTSIDE MSA
      REGION      : CH-2-1
—URBAN & RURAL & SIZE OF PLACE
      REGION      : CH-2-1
```

CONDOMINIUM UNITS BY HOUSEHOLD COMPOSITION BY AGE OF HOUSEHOLDER FOR OWNER/RENTER

```
      use .....      : METROPOLITAN HOUSING CHARACTERISTICS
```

CONDOMINIUM UNITS BY STRUCTURAL & FINANCIAL HOUSING CHARACTERISTICS

```
      use .....      : METROPOLITAN HOUSING CHARACTERISTICS
```

CONGRESSIONAL APPORTIONMENT

```
      use .....      : APPORTIONMENT
```

CONSTRUCTION TYPE

```
      use .....      : TYPE OF CONSTRUCTION
```

CONTRACT RENT

```
      U.S.           : CH-1-1#; CH-1-1B*; CH-1-1C*; CPH-1-1
      REGION/DIV  : CPH-1-1
      REGION      : CH-1-1#
      DIVISION    : CH-1-1*
      STATE          : CH-1#; CH-1-1*; CPH-1; CPH-1-1
      COUNTY      : CH-1#; CPH-1; CPH-3*; CPH-4
      SUBDIV      : CH-1; CPH-1
      SELECT SDV  : CH-1#; CPH-4
      PLACE          : CPH-1
      PLC 50+        : CH-1-1
      PLC 10+        : CH-1#; CPH-3*; CPH-4
      PLC 2.5-9      : CH-1#
      PLC 1-2.5      : CH-1*
      MSA            : CH-1-1; CH-1-1B#; CPH-1-1; CPH-3*
      URBANIZED   : CH-1-1; CH-1-1C#; CPH-1-1
      NATIVE AM   : CH-1; CH-1-1; CH-1-1A*; CPH-1; CPH-1-1; CPH-4
      OUTLYING    : CPH-6
```

CONGRS DIS : CPH-4
TRACT : CPH-3*
—IN CENTRAL CITY/NOT IN CENTRAL CITY
MSA : CH-1-1B*
—IN CENTRAL PLACE/URBAN FRINGE
URBANIZED : CH-1-1C*
—INDIVIDUAL CENTRAL CITY
MSA : CH-1-1B
—INDIVIDUAL CENTRAL PLACE
URBANIZED : CH-1-1C
—INSIDE/OUTSIDE MSA
U.S. : CH-1-1*; CH-1-1B*
REGION : CH-1-1*
STATE : CH-1*
—POPULATION SIZE CLASS OF MSA
U.S. : CH-1-1B*
—POPULATION SIZE CLASS OF URBANIZED AREA
U.S. : CH-1-1C*
—URBAN & RURAL & SIZE OF PLACE
U.S. : CH-1-1*; CH-1-1C*
REGION : CH-1-1*
STATE : CH-1*
CONTRACT RENT (MEDIAN)
use ..... : HOUSING: GENERAL SUMMARY CHARACTERISTICS
CONTRACT RENT BY EDUCATIONAL ATTAINMENT (BLACKS)
use ..... : CHARACTERISTICS OF THE BLACK POPULATION
CONTRACT RENT BY HOUSEHOLD TYPE (BLACKS)
use ..... : CHARACTERISTICS OF THE BLACK POPULATION

CONTRACT RENT BY YEAR HOUSEHOLDER MOVED INTO UNIT
use ..... : METROPOLITAN HOUSING CHARACTERISTICS
COOKING FACILITIES
OUTLYING : CPH-6
COST OF HOUSING, OWNER OCCUPIED
use ..... : MORTGAGE STATUS AND SELECTED MONTHLY OWNER COSTS
COST OF HOUSING, RENTER OCCUPIED
use ..... : GROSS RENT
COUNTIES
use ..... : NUMBER OF COUNTIES
COUNTY SUBDIVISIONS
use ..... : NUMBER OF COUNTY SUBDIVISIONS AND TYPE OF SUBDIVISION
DENSITY OF HOUSING UNITS
use ..... : HOUSING UNIT DENSITY
DENSITY OF POPULATION
use ..... : POPULATION DENSITY
DISABILITY
see also.. : ANCESTRY: DETAILED CHARACTERISTICS...
: ASIANS AND PACIFIC ISLANDERS: DETAILED CHARACTERISTICS...

: FOREIGN BORN: DETAILED CHARACTERISTICS...
: HISPANIC ORIGIN: DETAILED CHARACTERISTICS...

U.S.	: CP-2-1#; CP-2-1B; CP-2-1C; CPH-5-1
REGION/DIV	: CP-2-1; CPH-5-1
STATE	: CP-2#; CPH-5; CPH-5-1
COUNTY	: CP-2*; CPH-3*; CPH-4; CPH-5
SUBDIV	: CPH-5
SELECT SDV	: CP-2*; CPH-4
PLACE	: CPH-5
PLC 10+	: CP-2*; CPH-3*; CPH-4
PLC 2.5-9	: CP-2
MSA	: CP-2-1B*; CPH-3*; CPH-5-1; CPH-S-1-1
URBANIZED	: CP-2-1C*; CPH-5-1
NATIVE AM	: CP-2; CP-2-1A*
OUTLYING	: CPH-6
CONGRS DIS	: CPH-4
TRACT	: CPH-3*

—IN CENTRAL CITY/NOT IN CENTRAL CITY
U.S.	: CPH-S-1-1
REGION/DIV	: CPH-S-1-1
STATE	: CPH-S-1-1
MSA	: CP-2-1B; CPH-S-1-1

—IN CENTRAL PLACE/URBAN FRINGE
URBANIZED	: CP-2-1C

—INDIVIDUAL CENTRAL CITY
MSA	: CP-2-1B

—INDIVIDUAL CENTRAL PLACE
URBANIZED	: CP-2-1C

—INSIDE/OUTSIDE MSA
U.S.	: CP-2-1*; CP-2-1B; CPH-S-1-1
REGION/DIV	: CPH-S-1-1
STATE	: CP-2*; CPH-S-1-1

—RURAL OR RURAL FARM
COUNTY	: CP-2

—URBAN, RURAL & SIZE OF PLACE
U.S.	: CP-2-1*; CP-2-1C

—URBAN, RURAL, SIZE OF PLACE, FARM
STATE	: CP-2*

DISABILITY BY AGE & SEX (BLACKS)
use	: CHARACTERISTICS OF THE BLACK POPULATION

DISABILITY BY TYPE OF GROUP QUARTERS (BLACKS)
U.S.	: CP-3-6
STATE	: CP-3-6 FOR STATES WITH MORE THAN 900,000 BLACKS
MSA	: CP-3-6 FOR AREAS WITH MORE THAN 400,000 BLACKS

DOWN PAYMENTS (HOUSING)
U.S.	: CH-4-1
REGION	: CH-4-1

DURATION OF VACANCY
    see also..   : VACANCY CHARACTERISTICS

    U.S.   : CH-1-1; CH-1-1B; CH-1-1C
    REGION   : CH-1-1
    STATE   : CH-1
    COUNTY   : CH-1
    SELECT SDV : CH-1
    PLC 10+   : CH-1
    PLC 2.5-9   : CH-1
    MSA   : CH-1-1B
    URBANIZED : CH-1-1C
    OUTLYING   : CPH-6
 —IN CENTRAL CITY/NOT IN CENTRAL CITY
    MSA   : CH-1-1B
 —IN CENTRAL PLACE/URBAN FRINGE
    URBANIZED : CH-1-1C
 —INSIDE/OUTSIDE MSA
    U.S.   : CH-1-1; CH-1-1B
    REGION   : CH-1-1
    STATE   : CH-1
 —POPULATION SIZE CLASS OF MSA
    U.S.   : CH-1-1B
 —POPULATION SIZE CLASS OF URBANIZED AREA
    U.S.   : CH-1-1C
 —URBAN & RURAL & SIZE OF PLACE
    U.S.   : CH-1-1; CH-1-1C
    REGION   : CH-1-1
    STATE   : CH-1
EARNINGS IN 1989 BY AGE & SEX, BY OCCUPATION, OR BY WORK STATUS (BLACKS)
    use .....   : CHARACTERISTICS OF THE BLACK POPULATION
EARNINGS IN 1989 BY EDUCATIONAL ATTAINMENT
    see also..   : INCOME IN 1989
                : CHARACTERISTICS OF THE BLACK POPULATION

    U.S.   : CP-3-4*
    STATE   : CP-3-4*
EDUCATIONAL ATTAINMENT
    see also..   : ANCESTRY: DETAILED CHARACTERISTICS...
                : ASIANS AND PACIFIC ISLANDERS: DETAILED CHARACTERISTICS...
                : FOREIGN BORN: DETAILED CHARACTERISTICS...
                : HISPANIC ORIGIN: DETAILED CHARACTERISTICS...
                : LABOR FORCE STATUS & EDUCATIONAL ATTAINMENT
                : POPULATION CHARACTERISTICS OF AMERICAN INDIANS BY TRIBE

    U.S.   : CP-2-1#; CP-2-1B; CP-2-1C; CPH-5-1
    REGION/DIV : CP-2-1; CPH-5-1
    STATE   : CP-2#; CPH-5; CPH-5-1

```
      COUNTY        : CP-2#; CPH-3*; CPH-4; CPH-5
      SUBDIV        : CPH-5
      SELECT SDV    : CP-2#; CPH-4
      PLACE         : CPH-5
      PLC 10+       : CP-2#; CPH-3*; CPH-4
      PLC 2.5-9     : CP-2#
      MSA           : CP-2-1B*; CPH-3*; CPH-5-1; CPH-S-1-1
      URBANIZED     : CP-2-1C#; CPH-5-1
      NATIVE AM     : CP-2; CP-2-1A*; CPH-4; CPH-5; CPH-5-1
      OUTLYING      : CPH-6
      CONGRS DIS    : CPH-4*
      TRACT         : CPH-3*
  —IN CENTRAL CITY/NOT IN CENTRAL CITY
      U.S.          : CPH-S-1-1
      REGION/DIV    : CPH-S-1-1
      STATE         : CPH-S-1-1
      MSA           : CP-2-1B; CPH-S-1-1
  —IN CENTRAL PLACE/URBAN FRINGE
      URBANIZED     : CP-2-1C
  —INDIVIDUAL CENTRAL CITY
      MSA           : CP-2-1B
  —INDIVIDUAL CENTRAL PLACE
      URBANIZED     : CP-2-1C
  —INSIDE/OUTSIDE MSA
      U.S.          : CP-2-1*; CP-2-1B; CPH-S-1-1
      REGION/DIV    : CPH-S-1-1
      STATE         : CP-2*; CPH-S-1-1
  —RURAL OR RURAL FARM
      COUNTY        : CP-2
  —URBAN, RURAL & SIZE OF PLACE
      U.S.          : CP-2-1*; CP-2-1C
  —URBAN, RURAL, SIZE OF PLACE, FARM
      STATE         : CP-2*
EDUCATIONAL ATTAINMENT (PERCENT)
      use .....     : POPULATION: DETAILED SUMMARY CHARACTERISTICS
EDUCATIONAL ATTAINMENT BY AGE
      STATE         : CP-3-4*
EDUCATIONAL ATTAINMENT BY AGE GROUPS FOR THE CIVILIAN LABOR FORCE
      U.S.          : CP-S-1-1*
EDUCATIONAL ATTAINMENT BY AGE, SEX
      U.S.          : CP-3-4*; CP-3-6
      STATE         : CP-3-4
                    : CP-3-6 FOR STATES WITH MORE THAN 900,000 BLACKS
      MSA           : CP-3-6 FOR AREAS WITH MORE THAN 400,000 BLACKS
EDUCATIONAL ATTAINMENT BY FAMILY TYPE & PRESENCE & AGE OF OWN CHILDREN
(BLACKS)
      use .....     : CHARACTERISTICS OF THE BLACK POPULATION
EDUCATIONAL ATTAINMENT BY OCCUPATION (BLACKS)
```

use .....   : CHARACTERISTICS OF THE BLACK POPULATION
EDUCATIONAL ATTAINMENT BY SEX FOR THE CIVILIAN LABOR FORCE
    U.S.   : CP-S-1-1*
EDUCATIONAL ATTAINMENT BY STRUCTURAL & FINANCIAL HOUSING CHARACTERISTICS
    use .....   : METROPOLITAN HOUSING CHARACTERISTICS
EDUCATIONAL ATTAINMENT FOR PERSONS 60 YEARS AND OLDER
    U.S.   : CP-2-1#; CP-2-1B; CP-2-1C
    REGION/DIV : CP-2-1
    STATE   : CP-2#
    COUNTY   : CP-2*
    SELECT SDV : CP-2*
    PLC 10+   : CP-2*
    PLC 2.5-9   : CP-2
    MSA   : CP-2-1B*
    URBANIZED   : CP-2-1C*
    NATIVE AM   : CP-2; CP-2-1A*
  —IN CENTRAL CITY/NOT IN CENTRAL CITY
    MSA   : CP-2-1B
  —IN CENTRAL PLACE/URBAN FRINGE
    URBANIZED   : CP-2-1C
  —INDIVIDUAL CENTRAL CITY
    MSA   : CP-2-1B
  —INDIVIDUAL CENTRAL PLACE
    URBANIZED   : CP-2-1C
  —INSIDE/OUTSIDE MSA
    U.S.   : CP-2-1*; CP-2-1B
    STATE   : CP-2*
  —URBAN, RURAL & SIZE OF PLACE
    U.S.   : CP-2-1*; CP-2-1C
  —URBAN, RURAL, SIZE OF PLACE, FARM
    STATE   : CP-2*
ELECTRIC POWER
    OUTLYING   : CPH-6
EMPLOYMENT STATUS
    use .....   : LABOR FORCE STATUS
ETHNIC ORIGIN
    use .....   : ANCESTRY
ETHNIC ORIGIN OR RACE
    OUTLYING   : CPH-6
FAMILIES AND FAMILY CHARACTERISTICS
    see also..   : CHARACTERISTICS OF THE BLACK POPULATION

    U.S.   : CPH-1-1
    REGION/DIV : CPH-1-1
    STATE   : CPH-1; CPH-1-1
    COUNTY   : CPH-1
    SUBDIV   : CPH-1
    PLACE   : CPH-1

```
    MSA           : CPH-1-1
    URBANIZED     : CPH-1-1
    NATIVE AM     : CPH-1; CPH-1-1
FAMILY INCOME
    use .....      : INCOME IN 1989
FAMILY TYPE AND PRESENCE OF OWN CHILDREN
    see also..     : ANCESTRY: DETAILED CHARACTERISTICS...
                   : ASIANS AND PACIFIC ISLANDERS: DETAILED CHARACTERISTICS...
                   : CHARACTERISTICS OF THE BLACK POPULATION
                   : FOREIGN BORN: DETAILED CHARACTERISTICS...
                   : HISPANIC ORIGIN: DETAILED CHARACTERISTICS...
                   : METROPOLITAN HOUSING CHARACTERISTICS
                   : POPULATION CHARACTERISTICS OF AMERICAN INDIANS BY TRIBE

    U.S.          : CP-1-1#; CP-1-1B; CP-1-1C; CP-2-1#; CP-2-1B; CP-2-1C; CPH-5-1
    REGION/DIV    : CP-2-1; CPH-5-1
    REGION        : CP-1-1#
    DIVISION      : CP-1-1*
    STATE         : CP-1#; CP-1-1*; CP-2#; CPH-5; CPH-5-1
    COUNTY        : CP-1#; CP-2#; CPH-3*; CPH-4; CPH-5
    SUBDIV        : CPH-5
    SELECT SDV    : CP-1#; CP-2#; CPH-4
    PLACE         : CPH-5
    PLC 10+       : CP-1#; CP-2#; CPH-3*; CPH-4
    PLC 2.5-9     : CP-1#; CP-2#
    PLC 1-2.5     : CP-1
    MSA           : CP-1-1B#; CP-2-1B*; CPH-3*; CPH-5-1; CPH-S-1-1
    URBANIZED     : CP-1-1C#; CP-2-1C#; CPH-5-1
    NATIVE AM     : CP-1; CP-1-1A*; CP-2; CP-2-1A*
    OUTLYING      : CPH-6
    CONGRS DIS    : CPH-4*
    TRACT         : CPH-3*
 —IN CENTRAL CITY/NOT IN CENTRAL CITY
    U.S.          : CPH-S-1-1
    REGION/DIV    : CPH-S-1-1
    STATE         : CPH-S-1-1
    MSA           : CP-1-1B; CP-2-1B; CPH-S-1-1
 —IN CENTRAL PLACE/URBAN FRINGE
    URBANIZED     : CP-1-1C; CP-2-1C
 —INDIVIDUAL CENTRAL CITY
    MSA           : CP-2-1B
 —INDIVIDUAL CENTRAL PLACE
    URBANIZED     : CP-2-1C
 —INSIDE/OUTSIDE MSA
    U.S.          : CP-1-1*; CP-1-1B; CP-2-1*; CP-2-1B; CPH-S-1-1
    REGION/DIV    : CPH-S-1-1
    REGION        : CP-1-1*
    STATE         : CP-1*; CP-2*; CPH-S-1-1
```

—POPULATION SIZE CLASS OF MSA
    U.S.   : CP-1-1B
—POPULATION SIZE CLASS OF URBANIZED AREA
    U.S.   : CP-1-1C
—RURAL AREAS
    COUNTY   : CP-1
—RURAL OR RURAL FARM
    COUNTY   : CP-2
—URBAN & RURAL & SIZE OF PLACE
    U.S.   : CP-1-1*; CP-1-1C; CP-2-1*; CP-2-1C
    REGION   : CP-1-1*
    STATE   : CP-1*
URBAN, RURAL, SIZE OF PLACE, FARM
    STATE   : CP-2*
FERTILITY
    see also..   : ANCESTRY: DETAILED CHARACTERISTICS...
               : ASIANS AND PACIFIC ISLANDERS: DETAILED CHARACTERISTICS...
               : FOREIGN BORN: DETAILED CHARACTERISTICS...
               : HISPANIC ORIGIN: DETAILED CHARACTERISTICS...
               : POPULATION CHARACTERISTICS OF AMERICAN INDIANS BY TRIBE

    U.S.   : CP-2-1#; CP-2-1B; CP-2-1C
    REGION/DIV : CP-2-1
    STATE   : CP-2#
    COUNTY   : CP-2#; CPH-3*
    SELECT SDV : CP-2#
    PLC 10+   : CP-2#; CPH-3*
    PLC 2.5-9 : CP-2#
    MSA   : CP-2-1B#; CPH-3*; CPH-S-1-1
    URBANIZED : CP-2-1C#
    NATIVE AM : CP-2; CP-2-1A*
    OUTLYING   : CPH-6
    CONGRS DIS : CPH-4
    TRACT   : CPH-3*
—IN CENTRAL CITY/NOT IN CENTRAL CITY
    U.S.   : CPH-S-1-1
    REGION/DIV : CPH-S-1-1
    STATE   : CPH-S-1-1
    MSA   : CP-2-1B; CPH-S-1-1
—IN CENTRAL PLACE/URBAN FRINGE
    URBANIZED : CP-2-1C
—INDIVIDUAL CENTRAL CITY
    MSA   : CP-2-1B
—INDIVIDUAL CENTRAL PLACE
    URBANIZED : CP-2-1C
—INSIDE/OUTSIDE MSA
    U.S.   : CP-2-1*; CP-2-1B; CPH-S-1-1
    REGION/DIV : CPH-S-1-1

```
        STATE          : CP-2*; CPH-S-1-1
        MSA            : CPH-S-1-1
—RURAL OR RURAL FARM
        COUNTY         : CP-2
—URBAN, RURAL & SIZE OF PLACE
        U.S.           : CP-2-1*; CP-2-1C
—URBAN, RURAL, SIZE OF PLACE, FARM
        STATE          : CP-2*
FERTILITY (PERCENT)
        use .....      : POPULATION: DETAILED SUMMARY CHARACTERISTICS
FERTILITY BY CHARACTERISTICS OF MOTHER
        use .....      : CHARACTERISTICS OF THE BLACK POPULATION
FINANCING
        U.S.           : CH-4-1
        REGION         : CH-4-1
FOREIGN BORN: DETAILED CHARACTERISTICS BY PLACE OF BIRTH
        see also..     : BIRTH PLACE OF THE FOREIGN BORN

        U.S.           : CP-3-1
GAY COUPLES
        use .....      : UNMARRIED PARTNER HOUSEHOLDS
GROSS RENT
        see also..     : ANCESTRY: DETAILED CHARACTERISTICS...
                       : ASIANS AND PACIFIC ISLANDERS: DETAILED CHARACTERISTICS...
                       : FOREIGN BORN: DETAILED CHARACTERISTICS...
                       : HISPANIC ORIGIN: DETAILED CHARACTERISTICS...
                       : HOUSING CHARACTERISTICS OF AMERICAN INDIANS BY TRIBE

        U.S.           : CH-2-1#; CH-2-1B; CH-2-1C; CPH-5-1
        REGION/DIV     : CPH-5-1
        REGION         : CH-2-1#
        DIVISION       : CH-2-1*
        STATE          : CH-2#; CH-2-1*; CPH-5; CPH-5-1
        COUNTY         : CH-2#; CPH-3*; CPH-4; CPH-5
        SUBDIV         : CPH-5
        SELECT SDV     : CH-2#; CPH-4
        PLACE          : CPH-5
        PLC 10+        : CH-2#; CPH-3*; CPH-4
        PLC 2.5-9      : CH-2#
        MSA            : CH-2-1B#; CPH-3*; CPH-5-1; CPH-S-1-1
        URBANIZED      : CH-2-1C#; CPH-5-1
        NATIVE AM      : CH-2; CH-2-1A; CPH-4; CPH-5; CPH-5-1
        OUTLYING       : CPH-6
        CONGRS DIS     : CPH-4; CPH-4*
        TRACT          : CPH-3*
—IN CENTRAL CITY/NOT IN CENTRAL CITY
        U.S.           : CPH-S-1-1
        REGION/DIV     : CPH-S-1-1
```

```
        REGION/DIV   : CPH-1-1; CPH-S-1-1
        STATE        : CPH-1; CPH-1-1; CPH-S-1-1
        COUNTY       : CPH-1; CPH-4
        SUBDIV       : CPH-1
        SELECT SDV   : CPH-4
        PLACE        : CPH-1
        PLC 10+      : CPH-4
        MSA          : CPH-1-1; CPH-S-1-1
        URBANIZED    : CPH-1-1
        NATIVE AM    : CP-1-1A*
        CONGRS DIS   : CPH-4
    —IN CENTRAL CITY/NOT IN CENTRAL CITY
        U.S.         : CPH-S-1-1
        REGION/DIV   : CPH-S-1-1
        STATE        : CPH-S-1-1
        MSA          : CPH-S-1-1
    —INSIDE/OUTSIDE MSA
        U.S.         : CPH-S-1-1
        REGION/DIV   : CPH-S-1-1
        STATE        : CPH-S-1-1
GROUP QUARTERS (10 TYPES)
        U.S.         : CP-1-1#; CP-1-1B; CP-1-1C
        REGION       : CP-1-1#
        DIVISION     : CP-1-1*
        STATE        : CP-1#; CP-1-1*
        COUNTY       : CP-1#
        SELECT SDV   : CP-1#
        PLC 10+      : CP-1#
        PLC 2.5-9    : CP-1#
        MSA          : CP-1-1B#
        URBANIZED    : CP-1-1C#
        NATIVE AM    : CP-1
    —IN CENTRAL CITY/NOT IN CENTRAL CITY
        MSA          : CP-1-1B
    —IN CENTRAL PLACE/URBAN FRINGE
        URBANIZED    : CP-1-1C
    —INSIDE/OUTSIDE MSA
        U.S.         : CP-1-1*; CP-1-1B
        REGION       : CP-1-1*
        STATE        : CP-1*
    —POPULATION SIZE CLASS OF MSA
        U.S.         : CP-1-1B
    —POPULATION SIZE CLASS OF URBANIZED AREA
        U.S.         : CP-1-1C
    —RURAL AREAS
        COUNTY       : CP-1
    —URBAN & RURAL & SIZE OF PLACE
        U.S.         : CP-1-1*; CP-1-1C
```

HOURS WORKED PER WEEK IN 1989
     U.S.   : CPH-5-1
     REGION/DIV : CPH-5-1
     STATE   : CPH-5; CPH-5-1
     COUNTY   : CPH-4; CPH-5
     SUBDIV   : CPH-5
     SELECT SDV : CPH-4
     PLACE   : CPH-5
     PLC 10+   : CPH-4
     MSA   : CPH-5-1
     URBANIZED : CPH-5-1
     CONGRS DIS : CPH-4
HOUSE HEATING FUEL
     see also..   : CHARACTERISTICS OF THE BLACK POPULATION
                   : HOUSING CHARACTERISTICS OF AMERICAN INDIANS BY TRIBE

     U.S.   : CH-2-1#; CH-2-1B; CH-2-1C; CPH-5-1
     REGION/DIV : CPH-5-1
     REGION   : CH-2-1#
     DIVISION   : CH-2-1*
     STATE   : CH-2#; CH-2-1*; CPH-5; CPH-5-1
     COUNTY   : CH-2#; CPH-3*; CPH-4; CPH-5
     SUBDIV   : CPH-5
     SELECT SDV : CH-2#; CPH-4
     PLACE   : CPH-5
     PLC 10+   : CH-2#; CPH-3*; CPH-4
     PLC 2.5-9   : CH-2#
     MSA   : CH-2-1B#; CPH-3*; CPH-5-1
     URBANIZED : CH-2-1C#; CPH-5-1
     NATIVE AM   : CH-2; CH-2-1A
     CONGRS DIS : CPH-4
     TRACT   : CPH-3*
 —IN CENTRAL CITY/NOT IN CENTRAL CITY
     MSA   : CH-2-1B
 —IN CENTRAL PLACE/URBAN FRINGE
     URBANIZED : CH-2-1C
 —INSIDE/OUTSIDE MSA
     U.S.   : CH-2-1*; CH-2-1B
     REGION   : CH-2-1*
     STATE   : CH-2*
 —RURAL & RURAL FARM
     COUNTY   : CH-2
 —URBAN & RURAL & SIZE OF PLACE
     U.S.   : CH-2-1*; CH-2-1C
     REGION   : CH-2-1*
 —URBAN, RURAL, SIZE OF PLACE, FARM
     STATE   : CH-2*

HOUSE HEATING FUEL BY STRUCTURAL & FINANCIAL HOUSING CHARACTERISTICS
    use ..... : METROPOLITAN HOUSING CHARACTERISTICS
HOUSEHOLD COMPOSITION
    use ..... : HOUSEHOLD TYPE AND RELATIONSHIP
HOUSEHOLD INCOME IN 1989
    see also.. : INCOME IN 1989

    U.S. : CH-2-1#; CH-2-1B; CH-2-1C
    REGION : CH-2-1#
    DIVISION : CH-2-1*
    STATE : CH-2#; CH-2-1*
    COUNTY : CH-2#; CPH-3*
    SELECT SDV : CH-2#
    PLC 10+ : CH-2#; CPH-3*
    PLC 2.5-9 : CH-2#
    MSA : CH-2-1B#; CPH-3*
    URBANIZED : CH-2-1C#
    NATIVE AM : CH-2; CH-2-1A
    OUTLYING : CPH-6
    CONGRS DIS : CPH-4
    TRACT : CPH-3*
—IN CENTRAL CITY/NOT IN CENTRAL CITY
    MSA : CH-2-1B
—IN CENTRAL PLACE/URBAN FRINGE
    URBANIZED : CH-2-1C
—INSIDE/OUTSIDE MSA
    U.S. : CH-2-1*; CH-2-1B
    REGION : CH-2-1*
    STATE : CH-2*
—RURAL & RURAL FARM
    COUNTY : CH-2
—URBAN & RURAL & SIZE OF PLACE
    U.S. : CH-2-1*; CH-2-1C
    REGION : CH-2-1*
—URBAN, RURAL, SIZE OF PLACE, FARM
    STATE : CH-2*
HOUSEHOLD INCOME IN 1989 BY AGE OF HOUSEHOLDER
    MSA : CPH-S-1-1
—IN CENTRAL CITY/NOT IN CENTRAL CITY
    U.S. : CPH-S-1-1
    REGION/DIV : CPH-S-1-1
    STATE : CPH-S-1-1
    MSA : CPH-S-1-1
—INSIDE/OUTSIDE MSA
    U.S. : CPH-S-1-1
    REGION/DIV : CPH-S-1-1
    STATE : CPH-S-1-1

HOUSEHOLD INCOME IN 1989 BY HOUSEHOLD COMPOSITION BY AGE OF HOUSEHOLDER FOR OWNER/RENTER
     use .....   : METROPOLITAN HOUSING CHARACTERISTICS
HOUSEHOLD INCOME IN 1989 BY STRUCTURAL & FINANCIAL HOUSING CHARACTERISTICS
     use .....   : METROPOLITAN HOUSING CHARACTERISTICS
HOUSEHOLD POPULATION BY AGE AND SEX
     U.S.   : CP-1-1*
     REGION   : CP-1-1*
     STATE   : CP-1*
HOUSEHOLD TYPE AND RELATIONSHIP
     see also..   : ANCESTRY: DETAILED CHARACTERISTICS...
                  : ASIANS AND PACIFIC ISLANDERS: DETAILED CHARACTERISTICS...
                  : FOREIGN BORN: DETAILED CHARACTERISTICS...
                  : HISPANIC ORIGIN: DETAILED CHARACTERISTICS...
                  : LIVING ARRANGEMENTS, SELECTED
                  : METROPOLITAN HOUSING CHARACTERISTICS
                  : POPULATION CHARACTERISTICS OF AMERICAN INDIANS BY TRIBE
                    RELATIONSHIP TO HOUSEHOLDER

     U.S.   : CP-2-1#; CP-2-1B; CP-2-1C
     REGION/DIV : CP-2-1
     STATE   : CP-2#
     COUNTY   : CP-2*; CPH-3*; CPH-4
     SELECT SDV : CP-2*; CPH-4
     PLC 10+   : CP-2*; CPH-3*; CPH-4
     PLC 2.5-9   : CP-2
     MSA   : CP-2-1B*; CPH-3*; CPH-S-1-1
     URBANIZED   : CP-2-1C*
     NATIVE AM   : CP-2; CP-2-1A*; CPH-4
     OUTLYING   : CPH-6
     CONGRS DIS : CPH-4
     TRACT   : CPH-3*
  —IN CENTRAL CITY/NOT IN CENTRAL CITY
     U.S.   : CPH-S-1-1
     REGION/DIV : CPH-S-1-1
     STATE   : CPH-S-1-1
     MSA   : CP-2-1B; CPH-S-1-1
  —IN CENTRAL PLACE/URBAN FRINGE
     URBANIZED   : CP-2-1C
  —INDIVIDUAL CENTRAL CITY
     MSA   : CP-2-1B
  —INDIVIDUAL CENTRAL PLACE
     URBANIZED   : CP-2-1C
  —INSIDE/OUTSIDE MSA
     U.S.   : CP-2-1*; CP-2-1B; CPH-S-1-1
     REGION/DIV : CPH-S-1-1
     STATE   : CP-2*; CPH-S-1-1
  —RURAL OR RURAL FARM
     COUNTY   : CP-2

—URBAN, RURAL & SIZE OF PLACE
U.S. : CP-2-1*; CP-2-1C
—URBAN, RURAL, SIZE OF PLACE, FARM
STATE : CP-2*
HOUSEHOLD TYPE AND RELATIONSHIP BY SELECTED CHARACTERISTICS (BLACKS)
U.S. : CP-3-6
STATE : CP-3-6 FOR STATES WITH MORE THAN 900,000 BLACKS
MSA : CP-3-6 FOR AREAS WITH MORE THAN 400,000 BLACKS
HOUSEHOLDER 65 YEARS AND OVER
see also.. : AGE OF HOUSEHOLDER

U.S. : CH-1-1#; CH-1-1B*; CH-1-1C*; CH-2-1#; CH-2-1B; CH-2-1C
REGION : CH-1-1#; CH-2-1#
DIVISION : CH-1-1*; CH-2-1*
STATE : CH-1#; CH-1-1*; CH-2#; CH-2-1*
COUNTY : CH-1#; CH-2#
SUBDIV : CH-1
SELECT SDV : CH-1#; CH-2#
PLC 50+ : CH-1-1
PLC 10+ : CH-1#; CH-2#
PLC 2.5-9 : CH-1#
PLC 1-2.5 : CH-1*
MSA : CH-1-1; CH-1-1B#; CH-2-1B#
URBANIZED : CH-1-1; CH-1-1C#; CH-2-1C#
NATIVE AM : CH-1; CH-1-1A*; CH-2; CH-2-1A
OUTLYING : CPH-6
CONGRS DIS : CPH-4
—IN CENTRAL CITY/NOT IN CENTRAL CITY
MSA : CH-1-1B*; CH-2-1B
—IN CENTRAL PLACE/URBAN FRINGE
URBANIZED : CH-1-1C*; CH-2-1C
—INDIVIDUAL CENTRAL CITY
MSA : CH-1-1B
—INDIVIDUAL CENTRAL PLACE
URBANIZED : CH-1-1C
—INSIDE/OUTSIDE MSA
U.S. : CH-1-1*; CH-1-1B*; CH-2-1*; CH-2-1B
REGION : CH-1-1*; CH-2-1*
STATE : CH-1*; CH-2*
—POPULATION SIZE CLASS OF MSA
U.S. : CH-1-1B*
—POPULATION SIZE CLASS OF URBANIZED AREA
U.S. : CH-1-1C*
—RURAL & RURAL FARM
COUNTY : CH-2
—URBAN & RURAL & SIZE OF PLACE
U.S. : CH-1-1*; CH-1-1C*; CH-2-1*; CH-2-1C
REGION : CH-1-1*; CH-2-1*
STATE : CH-1*

—URBAN, RURAL, SIZE OF PLACE, FARM
    STATE   : CH-2*

HOUSEHOLDERS BY AGE
    U.S.   : CP-1-1B; CP-1-1C
    MSA   : CP-1-1B#
    URBANIZED : CP-1-1C#
    NATIVE AM : CP-1-1
— CENTRAL CITY/NOT IN CENTRAL CITY
    MSA   : CP-1-1B
—IN CENTRAL PLACE/URBAN FRINGE
    URBANIZED : CP-1-1C
—INSIDE/OUTSIDE MSA
    U.S.   : CP-1-1B
—POPULATION SIZE CLASS OF MSA
    U.S.   : CP-1-1B
—POPULATION SIZE CLASS OF URBANIZED AREA
    U.S.   : CP-1-1C
—URBAN & RURAL & SIZE OF PLACE
    U.S.   : CP-1-1C

HOUSEHOLDERS BY RACE AND HISPANIC ORIGIN
    U.S.   : CH-1-1#; CH-1-1A*; CH-1-1B#; CH-1-1C#; CH-2-1*; CH-2-1B*; CH-2-1C*
    REGION/DIV : CH-1-1A*
    REGION   : CH-1-1#; CH-2-1*
    DIVISION   : CH-1-1#; CH-2-1*
    STATE   : CH-1#; CH-1-1#; CH-1-1A*; CH-2#; CH-2-1*
    COUNTY   : CH-1#; CH-2#
    SELECT SDV : CH-1#; CH-2#
    PLC 50+   : CH-1-1#; CH-2-1*
    PLC 10+   : CH-1#; CH-2#
    PLC 2.5-9 : CH-1#; CH-2#
    PLC 1-2.5 : CH-1#
    MSA   : CH-1-1#; CH-1-1B#; CH-2-1*; CH-2-1B*
    URBANIZED : CH-1-1#; CH-1-1C#; CH-2-1*; CH-2-1C#
    NATIVE AM : CH-1-1A*
—IN CENTRAL CITY/NOT IN CENTRAL CITY
    MSA   : CH-1-1B#; CH-2-1B*
—IN CENTRAL PLACE/URBAN FRINGE
    URBANIZED : CH-1-1C#; CH-2-1C*
—INDIVIDUAL CENTRAL CITY
    MSA   : CH-1-1B#; CH-2-1B*
—INDIVIDUAL CENTRAL PLACE
    URBANIZED : CH-1-1C#; CH-2-1C*
—INSIDE/OUTSIDE MSA
    U.S.   : CH-1-1#; CH-1-1B#; CH-2-1*; CH-2-1B*
    REGION   : CH-1-1*; CH-2-1*
    STATE   : CH-1#; CH-2#
—POPULATION SIZE CLASS OF MSA
    U.S.   : CH-1-1B#

—POPULATION SIZE CLASS OF URBANIZED AREA
    U.S.   : CH-1-1C#
—RURAL & RURAL FARM
    COUNTY   : CH-2*
—URBAN & RURAL & SIZE OF PLACE
    U.S.   : CH-1-1#; CH-1-1C#; CH-2-1*; CH-2-1C*
    REGION   : CH-1-1*; CH-2-1*
    STATE   : CH-1#
—URBAN, RURAL, SIZE OF PLACE, FARM
    STATE   : CH-2#
HOUSEHOLDS AND HOUSEHOLD CHARACTERISTICS
    U.S.   : CPH-1-1
    REGION/DIV : CPH-1-1
    STATE   : CPH-1; CPH-1-1
    COUNTY   : CPH-1
    SUBDIV   : CPH-1
    PLACE   : CPH-1
    MSA   : CPH-1-1
    URBANIZED : CPH-1-1
    NATIVE AM : CPH-1; CPH-1-1
HOUSEHOLDS BY NUMBER OF STRUCTURES OCCUPIED
    OUTLYING : CPH-6
HOUSEHOLDS BY SIZE
    see also..   : ANCESTRY: DETAILED CHARACTERISTICS...
                : ASIANS AND PACIFIC ISLANDERS: DETAILED CHARACTERISTICS...
                : FOREIGN BORN: DETAILED CHARACTERISTICS...
                : HISPANIC ORIGIN: DETAILED CHARACTERISTICS...
                : POPULATION CHARACTERISTICS OF AMERICAN INDIANS BY TRIBE

    U.S.   : CP-1-1*; CP-1-1B; CP-1-1C
    REGION   : CP-1-1*
    STATE   : CP-1*
    COUNTY   : CP-1*
    SELECT SDV : CP-1*
    PLC 10+   : CP-1*
    MSA   : CP-1-1B*
    URBANIZED : CP-1-1C*
    NATIVE AM : CP-1-1A*
    OUTLYING : CPH-6
—IN CENTRAL CITY/NOT IN CENTRAL CITY
    MSA   : CP-1-1B
—IN CENTRAL PLACE/URBAN FRINGE
    URBANIZED : CP-1-1C
—INSIDE/OUTSIDE MSA
    U.S.   : CP-1-1; CP-1-1B
    REGION   : CP-1-1
    STATE   : CP-1
—POPULATION SIZE CLASS OF MSA
    U.S.   : CP-1-1B

—POPULATION SIZE CLASS OF URBANIZED AREA
    U.S.   : CP-1-1C
—URBAN & RURAL & SIZE OF PLACE
    U.S.   : CP-1-1; CP-1-1C
    REGION   : CP-1-1
    STATE   : CP-1
HOUSING CHARACTERISTICS OF AMERICAN INDIANS BY TRIBE
    see also..   : POPULATION CHARACTERISTICS OF AMERICAN INDIANS BY TRIBE
                 : POPULATION COUNTS OF AMERICAN INDIANS BY TRIBE

    U.S.   : CP-3-7
HOUSING CONSTRUCTION TYPE
    use .....   : TYPE OF CONSTRUCTION
HOUSING: DETAILED SUMMARY CHARACTERISTICS
    U.S.   : CH-2-1*; CH-2-1A; CH-2-1B*; CH-2-1C*
    REGION/DIV : CH-2-1A
    REGION   : CH-2-1*
    DIVISION   : CH-2-1*
    STATE   : CH-2*; CH-2-1*; CH-2-1A
    COUNTY   : CH-2*
    SELECT SDV : CH-1*; CH-2*
    PLC 50+   : CH-2-1
    PLC 10+   : CH-2*
    PLC 2.5-9   : CH-2*
    MSA   : CH-2-1; CH-2-1B*
    URBANIZED   : CH-2-1; CH-2-1C*
    NATIVE AM   : CH-2; CH-2-1; CH-2-1A
—IN CENTRAL CITY/NOT IN CENTRAL CITY
    MSA   : CH-2-1B*
—IN CENTRAL PLACE/URBAN FRINGE
    URBANIZED   : CH-2-1C*
—INDIVIDUAL CENTRAL CITY
    MSA   : CH-2-1B
—INDIVIDUAL CENTRAL PLACE
    URBANIZED   : CH-2-1C
—INSIDE/OUTSIDE MSA
    U.S.   : CH-2-1*; CH-2-1B*
    REGION   : CH-2-1*
    STATE   : CH-1
—URBAN & RURAL & SIZE OF PLACE
    U.S.   : CH-2-1*; CH-2-1C*
    REGION   : CH-2-1*
—URBAN, RURAL, SIZE OF PLACE, FARM
    STATE   : CH-2*
HOUSING: GENERAL SUMMARY CHARACTERISTICS
    U.S.   : CH-1-1*; CH-1-1B*; CH-1-1C*
    REGION   : CH-1-1*
    DIVISION   : CH-1-1*
    STATE   : CH-1*; CH-1-1*

```
        COUNTY     : CH-1*
        SUBDIV     : CH-1
        PLC 50+    : CH-1-1
        PLC 10+    : CH-1*
        PLC 2.5-9  : CH-1*
        PLC 1-2.5  : CH-1*
        MSA        : CH-1-1; CH-1-1B*
        URBANIZED  : CH-1-1; CH-1-1C*
        NATIVE AM  : CH-1; CH-1-1; CH-1-1A*
        OUTLYING   : CPH-6
—IN CENTRAL CITY/NOT IN CENTRAL CITY
        MSA        : CH-1-1B*
—IN CENTRAL PLACE/URBAN FRINGE
        URBANIZED  : CH-1-1C*
—INDIVIDUAL CENTRAL CITY
        MSA        : CH-1-1B
—INDIVIDUAL CENTRAL PLACE
        URBANIZED  : CH-1-1C
—INSIDE/OUTSIDE MSA
        U.S.       : CH-1-1*; CH-1-1B*
        REGION     : CH-1-1*
        STATE      : CH-1*
—POPULATION SIZE CLASS OF MSA
        U.S.       : CH-1-1B*
—POPULATION SIZE CLASS OF URBANIZED AREA
        U.S.       : CH-1-1C*
—URBAN & RURAL & SIZE OF PLACE
        U.S.       : CH-1-1*; CH-1-1C*
        REGION     : CH-1-1*
        STATE      : CH-1*
HOUSING UNIT AGE
    use .....      : YEAR STRUCTURE WAS BUILT
HOUSING UNIT COUNTS
    see also..     : HOUSING: DETAILED SUMMARY CHARACTERISTICS
                   : HOUSING: GENERAL SUMMARY CHARACTERISTICS

        U.S.       : CPH-2-1; CPH-S-1-1; CPH-S-1-2
        REGION/DIV : CPH-S-1-1
        STATE      : CPH-2-1
        COUNTY     : CPH-2-1
        MSA        : CPH-S-1-1
        URBANIZED  : CPH-2-1; CPH-S-1-2
        OUTLYING   : CPH-2-1
—CENTRAL PLACE/URBAN FRINGE
        U.S.       : CPH-S-1-2
        URBANIZED  : CPH-2-1; CPH-S-1-2
—CENTRAL PLACE/URBAN FRINGE WITH COMPONENT PARTS
        URBANIZED  : CPH-S-1-2
```

—EXTENDED CITIES BY URBAN & RURAL
     STATE   : CPH-S-1-2
—IN CENTRAL CITY/NOT IN CENTRAL CITY
     U.S.   : CPH-S-1-1
     REGION/DIV : CPH-S-1-1
     MSA   : CPH-S-1-1
—INSIDE/OUTSIDE MSA
     U.S.   : CPH-2-1; CPH-S-1-1
     REGION/DIV : CPH-S-1-1
—INSIDE/OUTSIDE MSA BY SIZE OF PLACE
     U.S.   : CPH-2-1
     STATE   : CPH-2
—INSIDE/OUTSIDE MSA BY URBAN & RURAL & SIZE AND TYPE OF PLACE
     U.S.   : CPH-S-1-2
—INSIDE/OUTSIDE MSA BY URBAN & RURAL & SIZE OF PLACE
     U.S.   : CPH-2-1
     STATE   : CPH-2
—INSIDE/OUTSIDE URBANIZED AREA
     U.S.   : CPH-2-1
     REGION/DIV : CPH-2-1
     STATE   : CPH-2-1
—INSIDE/OUTSIDE URBANIZED AREA BY SIZE OF PLACE
     STATE   : CPH-2
—SIZE OF PLACE: POPULATION SIZE CLASS OF URBANIZED AREA
     U.S.   : CPH-2-1
     URBANIZED   : CPH-2; CPH-2-1
—URBAN & RURAL
     U.S.   : CPH-2-1; CPH-S-1-2
     REGION/DIV : CPH-2-1
     STATE   : CPH-2-1; CPH-S-1-2
     COUNTY   : CPH-2-1
—URBAN & RURAL & BY POPULATION SIZE CLASS OF MSA
     U.S.   : CPH-2-1
     MSA   : CPH-2; CPH-2-1
—URBAN & RURAL & BY SIZE OF PLACE
     U.S.   : CPH-2-1; CPH-2-1; CPH-S-1-2
     REGION/DIV : CPH-2-1
     STATE   : CPH-2; CPH-2-1
     COUNTY   : CPH-2
—URBAN BY INSIDE/OUTSIDE URBANIZED AREA
     U.S.   : CPH-S-1-2
     REGION/DIV : CPH-S-1-2
     STATE   : CPH-S-1-2
HOUSING UNIT COUNTS, 1990 & CHANGE FROM PREVIOUS CENSUSES
     STATE   : CPH-2-1
—URBAN AND RURAL
     COUNTY   : CPH-2
HOUSING UNIT COUNTS, 1990 & PREVIOUS CENSUSES
     U.S.   : CPH-2-1

```
        REGION/DIV  : CPH-2-1
        STATE       : CPH-2-1
        COUNTY      : CPH-2-1
        SUBDIV      : CPH-2
        SELECT SDV  : CPH-2-1
        PLACE       : CPH-2; CPH-2-1 FOR PLACES OF 2,500 OR MORE
        MSA         : CPH-2; CPH-2-1
        URBANIZED   : CPH-2
     —IN CENTRAL CITY
        MSA         : CPH-2-1
HOUSING UNIT COUNTS, 1990 & PREVIOUS CENSUSES WITH CHANGE
        U.S.        : CPH-2-1
        STATE       : CPH-2; CPH-S-1-1
        COUNTY      : CPH-2
     —IN CENTRAL CITY/NOT IN CENTRAL CITY
        STATE       : CPH-S-1-1
     —INSIDE/OUTSIDE MSA
        STATE       : CPH-S-1-1
     —URBAN & RURAL
        U.S.        : CPH-2-1
        REGION/DIV  : CPH-2-1
        STATE       : CPH-2; CPH-2-1
HOUSING UNIT COUNTS, CHANGE FROM PREVIOUS CENSUSES
        STATE       : CPH-2-1
        COUNTY      : CPH-2-1
HOUSING UNIT DENSITY
        U.S.        : CPH-2-1; CPH-S-1-2
        STATE       : CPH-2; CPH-2-1
        COUNTY      : CPH-2; CPH-2-1
        SUBDIV      : CPH-2
        SELECT SDV  : CPH-2-1
        PLACE       : CPH-2; CPH-2-1 FOR PLACES OF 2,500 OR MORE
        MSA         : CPH-2; CPH-2-1
        URBANIZED   : CPH-2; CPH-2-1; CPH-S-1-2
     —CENTRAL CITY
        MSA         : CPH-2-1
     —CENTRAL PLACE/URBAN FRINGE
        U.S.        : CPH-S-1-2
        URBANIZED   : CPH-2-1; CPH-S-1-2
     —CENTRAL PLACE/URBAN FRINGE WITH COMPONENT PARTS
        URBANIZED   : CPH-S-1-2
     —EXTENDED CITIES BY URBAN & RURAL
        STATE       : CPH-S-1-2
     —URBAN & RURAL
        U.S.        : CPH-S-1-2
        STATE       : CPH-S-1-2
HOUSING UNIT DENSITY, 1990 & PREVIOUS CENSUSES
        U.S.        : CPH-2-1
        REGION/DIV  : CPH-2-1
        STATE       : CPH-2-1
```

HOUSING UNIT DISTRIBUTION, 1990 & PREVIOUS CENSUSES
    REGION/DIV : CPH-2-1
HOUSING UNIT RANK
    COUNTY   : CPH-2-1
HOUSING UNIT RANK, 1990 & PREVIOUS CENSUSES WITH CHANGE
    REGION/DIV : CPH-2-1
    STATE   : CPH-2-1
  —URBAN & RURAL
    REGION/DIV : CPH-2-1
    STATE   : CPH-2-1
HOUSING UNITS RATES OF CHANGE
    U.S.   : CPH-2-1
    REGION/DIV : CPH-2-1
HOUSING VALUE
    use .....   : VALUE OF HOUSING UNIT
INCOME: FAMILY
    use .....   : INCOME IN 1989
INCOME: HOUSEHOLD
    use .....   : HOUSEHOLD INCOME IN 1989
INCOME: MEDIAN
    use .....   : INCOME IN 1989
INCOME: MEDIAN BY SELECTED CHARACTERISTICS
    use .....   : MEDIAN INCOME IN 1989 BY SELECTED CHARACTERISTICS
INCOME: PER CAPITA
    use .....   : INCOME IN 1989
INCOME IN 1989
    see also..   : ANCESTRY: DETAILED CHARACTERISTICS...
                  : ASIANS AND PACIFIC ISLANDERS: DETAILED CHARACTERISTICS...
                  : EARNINGS IN 1989 BY EDUCATIONAL ATTAINMENT
                  : FOREIGN BORN: DETAILED CHARACTERISTICS...
                  : HISPANIC ORIGIN: DETAILED CHARACTERISTICS...
                  : HOUSEHOLD INCOME IN 1989
                  : INCOME TYPE IN 1989
                  : MEDIAN INCOME IN 1989 BY SELECTED CHARACTERISTICS
                  : POPULATION CHARACTERISTICS OF AMERICAN INDIAN BY TRIBE

    U.S.   : CP-2-1#; CP-2-1B; CP-2-1C; CPH-5-1
    REGION/DIV : CP-2-1; CPH-5-1
    STATE   : CP-2#; CPH-5; CPH-5-1
    COUNTY   : CP-2#; CPH-3*; CPH-4; CPH-5
    SUBDIV   : CPH-5
    SELECT SDV : CP-2#; CPH-4
    PLACE   : CPH-5
    PLC 10+   : CP-2#; CPH-3*; CPH-4
    PLC 2.5-9   : CP-2#
    MSA   : CP-2-1B#; CPH-3*; CPH-5-1; CPH-S-1-1
    URBANIZED   : CP-2-1C#; CPH-5-1
    NATIVE AM   : CP-2; CP-2-1A*; CPH-4; CPH-5; CPH-5-1

—URBAN & RURAL & SIZE OF PLACE
    U.S.   : CH-2-1*; CH-2-1C
    REGION   : CH-2-1*
—URBAN, RURAL, SIZE OF PLACE, FARM
    STATE   : CH-2*
INCOME IN 1989 BY SELECTED FAMILY CHARACTERISTICS (BLACKS)
    U.S.   : CP-3-6
    STATE   : CP-3-6 FOR STATES WITH MORE THAN 900,000 BLACKS
    MSA   : CP-3-6 FOR AREAS WITH MORE THAN 400,000 BLACKS
INCOME IN 1989 BY SELECTED HOUSEHOLD CHARACTERISTICS (BLACKS)
    use .....   : CHARACTERISTICS OF THE BLACK POPULATION
INCOME IN 1989 BY SELECTED MONTHLY OWNER COSTS AS A % OF HOUSEHOLD INCOME
    U.S.   : CH-2-1#; CH-2-1B; CH-2-1C
    REGION   : CH-2-1#
    DIVISION   : CH-2-1*
    STATE   : CH-2#; CH-2-1*
    COUNTY   : CH-2#
    SELECT SDV : CH-2#
    PLC 10+   : CH-2#
    MSA   : CH-2-1B#; CPH-S-1-1
    URBANIZED : CH-2-1C#
    NATIVE AM : CH-2-1A
—IN CENTRAL CITY/NOT IN CENTRAL CITY
    U.S.   : CPH-S-1-1
    REGION/DIV : CPH-S-1-1
    STATE   : CPH-S-1-1
    MSA   : CH-2-1B; CPH-S-1-1
—IN CENTRAL PLACE/URBAN FRINGE
    URBANIZED : CH-2-1C
—INSIDE/OUTSIDE MSA
    U.S.   : CH-2-1*; CH-2-1B; CPH-S-1-1
    REGION/DIV : CPH-S-1-1
    REGION   : CH-2-1*
    STATE   : CH-2*; CPH-S-1-1
—URBAN & RURAL & SIZE OF PLACE
    U.S.   : CH-2-1*; CH-2-1C
    REGION   : CH-2-1*
—URBAN, RURAL, SIZE OF PLACE, FARM
    STATE   : CH-2*
INCOME IN 1989 FOR FAMILIES BY CONTRACT RENT, OR BY VALUE (BLACKS)
    U.S.   : CP-3-6
    STATE   : CP-3-6 FOR STATES WITH MORE THAN 900,000 BLACKS
    MSA   : CP-3-6 FOR AREAS WITH MORE THAN 400,000 BLACKS
INCOME IN 1989 FOR PERSONS 60 YEARS AND OLDER
    U.S.   : CP-2-1#; CP-2-1B; CP-2-1C
    REGION/DIV : CP-2-1
    STATE   : CP-2#
    COUNTY   : CP-2*
    SELECT SDV : CP-2*

```
      PLC 10+        : CP-2*
      PLC 2.5-9      : CP-2
      MSA            : CP-2-1B*
      URBANIZED   : CP-2-1C*
      NATIVE AM    : CP-2; CP-2-1A*
  —IN CENTRAL CITY/NOT IN CENTRAL CITY
      MSA            : CP-2-1B
  —IN CENTRAL PLACE/URBAN FRINGE
      URBANIZED   : CP-2-1C
  —INDIVIDUAL CENTRAL CITY
      MSA            : CP-2-1B
  —INDIVIDUAL CENTRAL PLACE
      URBANIZED   : CP-2-1C
  —INSIDE/OUTSIDE MSA
      U.S.             : CP-2-1*; CP-2-1B
      STATE          : CP-2*
  —URBAN, RURAL & SIZE OF PLACE
      U.S.             : CP-2-1*; CP-2-1C
  —URBAN, RURAL, SIZE OF PLACE, FARM
      STATE          : CP-2*
INCOME IN 1989 FOR PERSONS BY AGE & SEX, OR BY EDUCATIONAL ATTAINMENT (BLACKS)
      use .....        : CHARACTERISTICS OF THE BLACK POPULATION
INCOME LEVELS
      use .....        : INCOME IN 1989
INCOME OF OWNER BY MORTGAGE CHARACTERISTICS
      U.S.             : CH-4-1
      REGION       : CH-4-1
INCOME TYPE IN 1989
      see also..       : ANCESTRY: DETAILED CHARACTERISTICS...
                       : ASIANS AND PACIFIC ISLANDERS: DETAILED CHARACTERISTICS...
                       : FOREIGN BORN: DETAILED CHARACTERISTICS...
                       : HISPANIC ORIGIN: DETAILED CHARACTERISTICS...
                       : INCOME IN 1989

      U.S.             : CP-2-1#; CP-2-1B; CP-2-1C
      REGION/DIV   : CP-2-1
      STATE          : CP-2#
      COUNTY       : CP-2#
      SELECT SDV   : CP-2#
      PLC 10+        : CP-2#
      PLC 2.5-9      : CP-2#
      MSA            : CP-2-1B#
      URBANIZED   : CP-2-1C#
      NATIVE AM    : CP-2; CP-2-1A*
      OUTLYING    : CPH-6
  —IN CENTRAL CITY/NOT IN CENTRAL CITY
      MSA            : CP-2-1B
  —IN CENTRAL PLACE/URBAN FRINGE
      URBANIZED   : CP-2-1C
```

—INDIVIDUAL CENTRAL CITY
    MSA   : CP-2-1B
—INDIVIDUAL CENTRAL PLACE
    URBANIZED : CP-2-1C
—INSIDE/OUTSIDE MSA
    U.S.   : CP-2-1*; CP-2-1B
    STATE   : CP-2*
—RURAL OR RURAL FARM
    COUNTY   : CP-2
—URBAN, RURAL & SIZE OF PLACE
    U.S.   : CP-2-1*; CP-2-1C
—URBAN, RURAL, SIZE OF PLACE, FARM
    STATE   : CP-2*

INDUSTRY
    see also..   : ANCESTRY: DETAILED CHARACTERISTICS...
                 : ASIANS AND PACIFIC ISLANDERS: DETAILED CHARACTERISTICS...
                 : FOREIGN BORN: DETAILED CHARACTERISTICS...
                 : HISPANIC ORIGIN: DETAILED CHARACTERISTICS...

    U.S.   : CP-2-1#; CP-2-1B; CP-2-1C
    REGION/DIV : CP-2-1
    STATE   : CP-2#
    COUNTY   : CP-2#; CPH-3
    SELECT SDV : CP-2#
    PLC 10+   : CP-2#; CPH-3
    PLC 2.5-9 : CP-2#
    MSA   : CP-2-1B#; CPH-3; CPH-S-1-1
    URBANIZED : CP-2-1C#
    NATIVE AM : CP-2; CP-2-1A*
    OUTLYING : CPH-6
    CONGRS DIS : CPH-4
    TRACT   : CPH-3
—IN CENTRAL CITY/NOT IN CENTRAL CITY
    U.S.   : CPH-S-1-1
    REGION/DIV : CPH-S-1-1
    STATE   : CPH-S-1-1
    MSA   : CP-2-1B; CPH-S-1-1
—IN CENTRAL PLACE/URBAN FRINGE
    URBANIZED : CP-2-1C
—INDIVIDUAL CENTRAL CITY
    MSA   : CP-2-1B
—INDIVIDUAL CENTRAL PLACE
    URBANIZED : CP-2-1C
—INSIDE/OUTSIDE MSA
    U.S.   : CP-2-1*; CP-2-1B; CPH-S-1-1
    REGION/DIV : CPH-S-1-1
    STATE   : CP-2*; CPH-S-1-1
—RURAL OR RURAL FARM
    COUNTY   : CP-2

—URBAN, RURAL & SIZE OF PLACE
    U.S.   : CP-2-1*; CP-2-1C
—URBAN, RURAL, SIZE OF PLACE, FARM
    STATE   : CP-2*
INDUSTRY BY EARNINGS AND WORK STATUS IN 1989 (BLACKS)
    use .....   : CHARACTERISTICS OF THE BLACK POPULATION
INSTITUTIONALIZED PERSONS AND OTHERS IN GROUP QUARTERS...
    see also..   : GROUP QUARTERS
INSTITUTIONALIZED PERSONS AND OTHERS IN GROUP QUARTERS BY AGE AND SEX
    U.S.   : CP-1-1*
    REGION   : CP-1-1*
    STATE   : CP-1*
INSTITUTIONALIZED PERSONS AND OTHERS IN GROUP QUARTERS FOR SELECTED AGE GROUPS
    U.S.   : CP-1-1#; CP-1-1B; CP-1-1C
    REGION   : CP-1-1#
    DIVISION : CP-1-1*
    STATE   : CP-1#; CP-1-1*
    COUNTY   : CP-1#
    SELECT SDV : CP-1#
    PLC 10+   : CP-1#
    PLC 2.5-9 : CP-1#
    MSA   : CP-1-1B#
    URBANIZED : CP-1-1C#
    NATIVE AM : CP-1
—IN CENTRAL CITY/NOT IN CENTRAL CITY
    MSA   : CP-1-1B
—IN CENTRAL PLACE/URBAN FRINGE
    URBANIZED : CP-1-1C
—INSIDE/OUTSIDE MSA
    U.S.   : CP-1-1*; CP-1-1B
    REGION   : CP-1-1*
    STATE   : CP-1*
—POPULATION SIZE CLASS OF MSA
    U.S.   : CP-1-1B
—POPULATION SIZE CLASS OF URBANIZED AREA
    U.S.   : CP-1-1C
—RURAL AREAS
    COUNTY   : CP-1
—URBAN & RURAL & SIZE OF PLACE
    U.S.   : CP-1-1*; CP-1-1C
    REGION   : CP-1-1*
    STATE   : CP-1*
JOURNEY TO WORK
    see also..   : MEANS OF TRANSPORTATION TO WORK

    U.S.   : CP-2-1#; CP-2-1B; CP-2-1C
    REGION/DIV : CP-2-1
    STATE   : CP-2#

```
        COUNTY        : CP-2*; CPH-3*
        SELECT SDV    : CP-2*
        PLC 10+       : CP-2*; CPH-3*
        PLC 2.5-9     : CP-2
        MSA           : CP-2-1B*; CPH-3*
        URBANIZED     : CP-2-1C*
        NATIVE AM     : CP-2; CP-2-1A*
        OUTLYING      : CPH-6
        TRACT         : CPH-3*
  —IN CENTRAL CITY/NOT IN CENTRAL CITY
        MSA           : CP-2-1B
  —IN CENTRAL PLACE/URBAN FRINGE
        URBANIZED     : CP-2-1C
  —INDIVIDUAL CENTRAL CITY
        MSA           : CP-2-1B
  —INDIVIDUAL CENTRAL PLACE
        URBANIZED     : CP-2-1C
  —INSIDE/OUTSIDE MSA
        U.S.          : CP-2-1*; CP-2-1B
        STATE         : CP-2*
  —RURAL OR RURAL FARM
        COUNTY        : CP-2
  —URBAN, RURAL & SIZE OF PLACE
        U.S.          : CP-2-1*; CP-2-1C
  —URBAN, RURAL, SIZE OF PLACE, FARM
        STATE         : CP-2*
KITCHEN FACILITIES
        see also..    : ANCESTRY: DETAILED CHARACTERISTICS...
                      : ASIANS AND PACIFIC ISLANDERS: DETAILED CHARACTERISTICS...
                      : CHARACTERISTICS OF THE BLACK POPULATION
                      : FOREIGN BORN: DETAILED CHARACTERISTICS...
                      : HISPANIC ORIGIN: DETAILED CHARACTERISTICS...
                      : HOUSING CHARACTERISTICS OF AMERICAN INDIANS BY TRIBE

        U.S.          : CH-2-1#; CH-2-1B; CH-2-1C; CPH-5-1
        REGION/DIV    : CPH-5-1
        REGION        : CH-2-1#
        DIVISION      : CH-2-1*
        STATE         : CH-2#; CH-2-1*; CPH-5; CPH-5-1
        COUNTY        : CH-2#; CPH-3*; CPH-4; CPH-5
        SUBDIV        : CPH-5
        SELECT SDV    : CH-2#; CPH-4
        PLACE         : CPH-5
        PLC 10+       : CH-2#; CPH-3*; CPH-4
        MSA           : CH-2-1B#; CPH-3*; CPH-5-1; CPH-S-1-1
        URBANIZED     : CH-2-1C#; CPH-5-1
        NATIVE AM     : CH-2-1A
        OUTLYING      : CPH-6
```

```
        CONGRS DIS  : CPH-4
        TRACT       : CPH-3*
—IN CENTRAL CITY/NOT IN CENTRAL CITY
        U.S.         : CPH-S-1-1
        REGION/DIV  : CPH-S-1-1
        STATE       : CPH-S-1-1
        MSA          : CH-2-1B; CPH-S-1-1
—IN CENTRAL PLACE/URBAN FRINGE
        URBANIZED   : CH-2-1C
—INSIDE/OUTSIDE MSA
        U.S.         : CH-2-1*; CH-2-1B; CPH-S-1-1
        REGION/DIV  : CPH-S-1-1
        REGION       : CH-2-1*
        STATE        : CH-2*; CPH-S-1-1
—RURAL & RURAL FARM
        COUNTY      : CH-2
—URBAN & RURAL & SIZE OF PLACE
        U.S.         : CH-2-1*; CH-2-1C
        REGION       : CH-2-1*
—URBAN, RURAL, SIZE OF PLACE, FARM
        STATE        : CH-2*
```

KITCHEN FACILITIES BY HOUSEHOLD COMPOSITION BY AGE OF HOUSEHOLDER FOR OWNER/RENTER

```
        use .....     : METROPOLITAN HOUSING CHARACTERISTICS
```

KITCHEN FACILITIES BY STRUCTURAL & FINANCIAL HOUSING CHARACTERISTICS

```
        use .....     : METROPOLITAN HOUSING CHARACTERISTICS
```

LABOR FORCE STATUS

```
        see also..    : ANCESTRY: DETAILED CHARACTERISTICS...
                      : ASIANS AND PACIFIC ISLANDERS: DETAILED CHARACTERISTICS...
                      : FOREIGN BORN: DETAILED CHARACTERISTICS...
                      : HISPANIC ORIGIN: DETAILED CHARACTERISTICS...
                      : HOURS WORKED PER WEEK IN 1989
                      : LAST OCCUPATION OF EXPERIENCED UNEMPLOYED
                      : WEEKS WORKED IN 1989
                      : WORK STATUS IN 1989

        U.S.          : CP-2-1#; CP-2-1B; CP-2-1C; CP-3-6; CPH-5-1
        REGION/DIV   : CP-2-1; CPH-5-1
        STATE         : CP-2#
                      : CP-3-6 FOR STATES WITH MORE THAN 900,000 BLACKS
                      : CPH-5; CPH-5-1
        COUNTY       : CP-2#; CPH-3*; CPH-4; CPH-5
        SUBDIV        : CPH-5
        SELECT SDV   : CP-2#; CPH-4
        PLACE         : CPH-5
        PLC 10+       : CP-2#; CPH-3*; CPH-4
        PLC 2.5-9     : CP-2#
        MSA           : CP-2-1B#
```

```
                  : CP-3-6 FOR AREAS WITH MORE THAN 400,000 BLACKS
U.S.              : CPH-3*; CPH-5-1; CPH-S-1-1
URBANIZED         : CP-2-1C#; CPH-5-1
NATIVE AM         : CP-2; CP-2-1A*; CPH-4; CPH-5; CPH-5-1
OUTLYING          : CPH-6
CONGRS DIS        : CPH-4*
TRACT             : CPH-3*
```
—IN CENTRAL CITY/NOT IN CENTRAL CITY
```
U.S.              : CPH-S-1-1
REGION/DIV        : CPH-S-1-1
STATE             : CPH-S-1-1
MSA               : CP-2-1B; CPH-S-1-1
```
—IN CENTRAL PLACE/URBAN FRINGE
```
URBANIZED         : CP-2-1C
```
—INDIVIDUAL CENTRAL CITY
```
MSA               : CP-2-1B
```
—INDIVIDUAL CENTRAL PLACE
```
URBANIZED         : CP-2-1C
```
—INSIDE/OUTSIDE MSA
```
U.S.              : CP-2-1*; CP-2-1B; CPH-S-1-1
REGION/DIV        : CPH-S-1-1
STATE             : CP-2*; CPH-S-1-1
```
—RURAL OR RURAL FARM
```
COUNTY            : CP-2
```
—URBAN, RURAL & SIZE OF PLACE
```
U.S.              : CP-2-1*; CP-2-1C
```
—URBAN, RURAL, SIZE OF PLACE, FARM
```
STATE             : CP-2*
```
LABOR FORCE STATUS & EDUCATIONAL ENROLLMENT/ATTAINMENT
```
see also..        : EDUCATIONAL ATTAINMENT

U.S.              : CPH-5-1
REGION/DIV        : CPH-5-1
STATE             : CPH-5; CPH-5-1
COUNTY            : CPH-5
SUBDIV            : CPH-5
PLACE             : CPH-5
MSA               : CPH-5-1
URBANIZED         : CPH-5-1
NATIVE AM         : CPH-5; CPH-5-1
CONGRS DIS        : CPH-4*
```
LABOR FORCE STATUS AND SCHOOL ENROLLMENT
```
see also..        : SCHOOL ENROLLMENT AND TYPE OF SCHOOL
                  : POPULATION CHARACTERISTICS OF AMERICAN INDIANS BY TRIBE

U.S.              : CP-2-1#; CP-2-1B; CP-2-1C
REGION/DIV        : CP-2-1
STATE             : CP-2#
COUNTY            : CP-2*
```

```
     SELECT SDV   : CP-2*
     PLC 10+      : CP-2*
     PLC 2.5-9    : CP-2
     MSA          : CP-2-1B*
     URBANIZED    : CP-2-1C*
     NATIVE AM    : CP-2; CP-2-1A*
  —IN CENTRAL CITY/NOT IN CENTRAL CITY
     MSA             : CP-2-1B
  —IN CENTRAL PLACE/URBAN FRINGE
     URBANIZED    : CP-2-1C
  —INDIVIDUAL CENTRAL CITY
     MSA             : CP-2-1B
  —INDIVIDUAL CENTRAL PLACE
     URBANIZED    : CP-2-1C
  —INSIDE/OUTSIDE MSA
     U.S.            : CP-2-1*; CP-2-1B
     STATE           : CP-2*
  —RURAL OR RURAL FARM
     COUNTY          : CP-2
  —URBAN, RURAL & SIZE OF PLACE
     U.S.            : CP-2-1*; CP-2-1C
  —URBAN, RURAL, SIZE OF PLACE, FARM
     STATE           : CP-2*
LABOR FORCE STATUS BY AGE & BY PRESENCE OF OWN CHILDREN
     U.S.            : CP-2-1#; CP-2-1B; CP-2-1C
     REGION/DIV   : CP-2-1
     STATE        : CP-2#
     COUNTY       : CP-2#
     SELECT SDV   : CP-2#
     PLC 10+      : CP-2#
     PLC 2.5-9    : CP-2#
     MSA          : CP-2-1B#
     URBANIZED    : CP-2-1C#
     NATIVE AM    : CP-2; CP-2-1A*
  —IN CENTRAL CITY/NOT IN CENTRAL CITY
     MSA             : CP-2-1B
  —IN CENTRAL PLACE/URBAN FRINGE
     URBANIZED    : CP-2-1C
  —INDIVIDUAL CENTRAL CITY
     MSA             : CP-2-1B
  —INDIVIDUAL CENTRAL PLACE
     URBANIZED    : CP-2-1C
  —INSIDE/OUTSIDE MSA
     U.S.            : CP-2-1*; CP-2-1B
     STATE           : CP-2*
  —RURAL OR RURAL FARM
     COUNTY          : CP-2
  —URBAN, RURAL & SIZE OF PLACE
     U.S.            : CP-2-1*; CP-2-1C
```

—URBAN, RURAL, SIZE OF PLACE, FARM
    STATE   : CP-2*
LABOR FORCE STATUS BY YEAR STRUCTURE BUILT
    use .....   : METROPOLITAN HOUSING CHARACTERISTICS
LABOR FORCE STATUS OF FAMILY MEMBERS
    see also..   : POPULATION CHARACTERISTICS OF AMERICAN INDIANS BY TRIBE

    U.S.   : CP-2-1#; CP-2-1B; CP-2-1C
    REGION/DIV : CP-2-1
    STATE   : CP-2#
    COUNTY   : CP-2*
    SELECT SDV : CP-2*
    PLC 10+   : CP-2*
    PLC 2.5-9 : CP-2
    MSA   : CP-2-1B*
    URBANIZED : CP-2-1C*
    NATIVE AM : CP-2
    OUTLYING   : CPH-6
—IN CENTRAL CITY/NOT IN CENTRAL CITY
    MSA   : CP-2-1B
—IN CENTRAL PLACE/URBAN FRINGE
    URBANIZED : CP-2-1C
—INDIVIDUAL CENTRAL CITY
    MSA   : CP-2-1B
—INDIVIDUAL CENTRAL PLACE
    URBANIZED : CP-2-1C
—INSIDE/OUTSIDE MSA
    U.S.   : CP-2-1*; CP-2-1B
    STATE   : CP-2*
—URBAN, RURAL & SIZE OF PLACE
    U.S.   : CP-2-1*; CP-2-1C
—URBAN, RURAL, SIZE, OF PLACE, FARM
    STATE   : CP-2*
LAND AREA
    U.S.   : CPH-1-1; CPH-2-1; CPH-S-1-1; CPH-S-1-2
    REGION/DIV : CPH-1-1; CPH-2-1; CPH-S-1-1
    STATE   : CPH-1; CPH-1-1; CPH-2; CPH-2-1; CPH-S-1-1
    COUNTY   : CPH-1; CPH-2; CPH-2-1; CPH-3; CPH-4
    SUBDIV   : CPH-1; CPH-2
    SELECT SDV : CPH-2-1; CPH-4
    PLACE   : CPH-1; CPH-2; CPH-2-1 FOR PLACES OF 2,500 OR MORE
    PLC 10+   : CPH-3; CPH-4
    MSA   : CPH-1-1; CPH-2; CPH-2-1; CPH-3; CPH-S-1-1
    URBANIZED : CPH-1-1; CPH-2; CPH-2-1; CPH-S-1-2
    NATIVE AM : CPH-1; CPH-1-1; CPH-4
    OUTLYING   : CPH-2-1
    CONGRS DIS : CPH-4
    TRACT   : CPH-3

—CENTRAL PLACE/URBAN FRINGE
    U.S.   : CPH-S-1-2
    URBANIZED : CPH-2-1; CPH-S-1-2
—CENTRAL PLACE/URBAN FRINGE WITH COMPONENT PARTS
    URBANIZED : CPH-S-1-2
—EXTENDED CITIES BY URBAN & RURAL
    STATE   : CPH-S-1-2
—IN CENTRAL CITY
    MSA   : CPH-2-1
—IN CENTRAL CITY/NOT IN CENTRAL CITY
    U.S.   : CPH-S-1-1
    REGION/DIV : CPH-S-1-1
    STATE   : CPH-S-1-1
    MSA   : CPH-S-1-1
—INSIDE/OUTSIDE MSA
    U.S.   : CPH-S-1-1
    REGION/DIV : CPH-S-1-1
    STATE   : CPH-S-1-1
—INSIDE/OUTSIDE MSA BY SIZE OF PLACE
    U.S.   : CPH-2-1
    STATE   : CPH-2
—INSIDE/OUTSIDE MSA BY URBAN & RURAL & BY SIZE & TYPE OF PLACE
    U.S.   : CPH-S-1-2
—INSIDE/OUTSIDE MSA BY URBAN & RURAL & SIZE OF PLACE
    U.S.   : CPH-2-1
    STATE   : CPH-2
—INSIDE/OUTSIDE URBANIZED AREA
    U.S.   : CPH-2-1
    REGION/DIV : CPH-2-1
    STATE   : CPH-2-1
—INSIDE/OUTSIDE URBANIZED AREA BY SIZE OF PLACE
    STATE   : CPH-2
—SIZE OF PLACE: POPULATION SIZE CLASS OF URBANIZED AREA
    U.S.   : CPH-2-1
    URBANIZED : CPH-2; CPH-2-1
—URBAN & RURAL
    U.S.   : CPH-2-1; CPH-S-1-2
    REGION/DIV : CPH-2-1
    STATE   : CPH-2; CPH-2-1; CPH-S-1-2
    COUNTY   : CPH-2; CPH-2-1
—URBAN & RURAL & BY SIZE OF PLACE
    U.S.   : CPH-2-1; CPH-S-1-2
    STATE   : CPH-2
    COUNTY   : CPH-2
—URBAN & RURAL BY POPULATION SIZE CLASS OF MSA
    U.S.   : CPH-2-1
    MSA   : CPH-2; CPH-2-1

—URBAN BY INSIDE/OUTSIDE URBANIZED AREA
     U.S.   : CPH-S-1-2
     REGION/DIV   : CPH-S-1-2
     STATE   : CPH-S-1-2
LANGUAGE SPOKEN AT HOME...
     see also..   : ABILITY TO SPEAK ENGLISH
LANGUAGE SPOKEN AT HOME (DETAILED LIST)
     see also..   : POPULATION CHARACTERISTICS OF AMERICAN INDIANS BY TRIBE

     U.S.   : CP-2-1; CP-2-1B; CP-2-1C
     REGION/DIV   : CP-2-1
     STATE   : CP-2
     COUNTY   : CP-2
     SELECT SDV   : CP-2
     PLC 10+   : CP-2
     MSA   : CP-2-1B
     URBANIZED   : CP-2-1C
—IN CENTRAL CITY/NOT IN CENTRAL CITY
     MSA   : CP-2-1B
—IN CENTRAL PLACE/URBAN FRINGE
     URBANIZED   : CP-2-1C
—INDIVIDUAL CENTRAL CITY
     MSA   : CP-2-1B
—INDIVIDUAL CENTRAL PLACE
     URBANIZED   : CP-2-1C
—INSIDE/OUTSIDE MSA
     U.S.   : CP-2-1; CP-2-1B
     STATE   : CP-2
—URBAN, RURAL & SIZE OF PLACE
     U.S.   : CP-2-1; CP-2-1C
—URBAN, RURAL, SIZE OF PLACE, FARM
     STATE   : CP-2
LANGUAGE SPOKEN AT HOME AND ABILITY TO SPEAK ENGLISH
     see also..   : ABILITY TO SPEAK ENGLISH

     U.S.   : CP-2-1; CP-2-1B; CP-2-1C; CPH-5-1
     REGION/DIV   : CP-2-1; CPH-5-1
     STATE   : CP-2; CPH-5; CPH-5-1
     COUNTY   : CP-2; CPH-3*; CPH-4; CPH-5
     SUBDIV   : CPH-5
     SELECT SDV   : CP-2; CPH-4
     PLACE   : CPH-5
     PLC 10+   : CP-2; CPH-3*; CPH-4
     PLC 2.5-9   : CP-2
     MSA   : CP-2-1B; CPH-3*; CPH-5-1; CPH-S-1-1
     URBANIZED   : CP-2-1C; CPH-5-1
     OUTLYING   : CPH-6
     CONGRS DIS   : CPH-4
     TRACT   : CPH-3*

—IN CENTRAL CITY/NOT IN CENTRAL CITY
    U.S.   : CPH-S-1-1
    REGION/DIV : CPH-S-1-1
    STATE   : CPH-S-1-1
    MSA   : CP-2-1B; CPH-S-1-1
—IN CENTRAL PLACE/URBAN FRINGE
    URBANIZED : CP-2-1C
—INDIVIDUAL CENTRAL CITY
    MSA   : CP-2-1B
—INDIVIDUAL CENTRAL PLACE
    URBANIZED : CP-2-1C
—INSIDE/OUTSIDE MSA
    U.S.   : CP-2-1; CP-2-1B; CPH-S-1-1
    REGION/DIV : CPH-S-1-1
    STATE   : CP-2; CPH-S-1-1
—URBAN, RURAL & SIZE OF PLACE
    U.S.   : CP-2-1; CP-2-1C
—URBAN, RURAL, SIZE OF PLACE, FARM
    STATE   : CP-2
LAST OCCUPATION OF EXPERIENCED UNEMPLOYED
    see also..   : LABOR FORCE STATUS

    U.S.   : CP-2-1*; CP-2-1B; CP-2-1C
    REGION/DIV : CP-2-1
    STATE   : CP-2*
    COUNTY   : CP-2
    SELECT SDV : CP-2
    PLC 10+   : CP-2
    MSA   : CP-2-1B
    URBANIZED : CP-2-1C
—IN CENTRAL CITY/NOT IN CENTRAL CITY
    MSA   : CP-2-1B
—IN CENTRAL PLACE/URBAN FRINGE
    URBANIZED : CP-2-1C
—INDIVIDUAL CENTRAL CITY
    MSA   : CP-2-1B
—INDIVIDUAL CENTRAL PLACE
    URBANIZED : CP-2-1C
—INSIDE/OUTSIDE MSA
    U.S.   : CP-2-1; CP-2-1B
    STATE   : CP-2
—URBAN, RURAL & SIZE OF PLACE
    U.S.   : CP-2-1; CP-2-1C
—URBAN, RURAL, SIZE OF PLACE, FARM
    STATE   : CP-2
LENGTH OF SERVICE
    OUTLYING : CPH-6

LITERACY
  see also..   : EDUCATIONAL ATTAINMENT

  OUTLYING : CPH-6
LIVING ARRANGEMENTS FOR PERSONS 60 YEARS AND OLDER
  U.S.   : CP-2-1#; CP-2-1B; CP-2-1C
  REGION/DIV : CP-2-1
  STATE   : CP-2#
  COUNTY : CP-2*
  SELECT SDV : CP-2*
  PLC 10+ : CP-2*
  PLC 2.5-9 : CP-2
  MSA   : CP-2-1B*
  URBANIZED : CP-2-1C*
  NATIVE AM : CP-2; CP-2-1A*
 —IN CENTRAL CITY/NOT IN CENTRAL CITY
  MSA   : CP-2-1B
 —IN CENTRAL PLACE/URBAN FRINGE
  URBANIZED : CP-2-1C
 —INDIVIDUAL CENTRAL CITY
  MSA   : CP-2-1B
 —INDIVIDUAL CENTRAL PLACE
  URBANIZED : CP-2-1C
 —INSIDE/OUTSIDE MSA
  U.S.   : CP-2-1*; CP-2-1B
  STATE   : CP-2*
 —URBAN, RURAL & SIZE OF PLACE
  U.S.   : CP-2-1*; CP-2-1C
 —URBAN, RURAL, SIZE OF PLACE, FARM
  STATE   : CP-2*
LIVING ARRANGEMENTS, SELECTED
  see also..   : ANCESTRY: DETAILED CHARACTERISTICS
         : ASIANS AND PACIFIC ISLANDERS: DETAILED CHARACTERISTICS...
         : FOREIGN BORN: DETAILED CHARACTERISTICS...
         : HISPANIC ORIGIN: DETAILED CHARACTERISTICS...
         : HOUSEHOLD TYPE AND RELATIONSHIP
         : POPULATION CHARACTERISTICS OF AMERICAN INDIANS BY TRIBE

  U.S.   : CP-2-1#; CP-2-1B; CP-2-1C
  REGION/DIV : CP-2-1
  STATE   : CP-2#
  COUNTY : CP-2*
  SELECT SDV : CP-2*
  PLC 10+ : CP-2*
  PLC 2.5-9 : CP-2
  MSA   : CP-2-1B*
  URBANIZED : CP-2-1C*
  NATIVE AM : CP-2; CP-2-1A*

—IN CENTRAL CITY/NOT IN CENTRAL CITY
    MSA   : CP-2-1B
—IN CENTRAL PLACE/URBAN FRINGE
    URBANIZED   : CP-2-1C
—INDIVIDUAL CENTRAL CITY
    MSA   : CP-2-1B
—INDIVIDUAL CENTRAL PLACE
    URBANIZED   : CP-2-1C
—INSIDE/OUTSIDE MSA
    U.S.   : CP-2-1*; CP-2-1B
    STATE   : CP-2*
—URBAN, RURAL & SIZE OF PLACE
    U.S.   : CP-2-1*; CP-2-1C
—URBAN, RURAL, SIZE OF PLACE, FARM
    STATE   : CP-2*
MALES PER 100 FEMALES
    use .....   : POPULATION: GENERAL SUMMARY CHARACTERISTICS
MARITAL STATUS BY HOUSEHOLD INCOME IN 1989
    use .....   : METROPOLITAN HOUSING CHARACTERISTICS
MARITAL STATUS BY SELECTED CHARACTERISTICS (BLACKS)
    U.S.   : CP-3-6
    STATE   : CP-3-6 FOR STATES WITH MORE THAN 900,000 BLACKS
    MSA   : CP-3-6 FOR AREAS WITH MORE THAN 400,000 BLACKS
MARITAL STATUS BY SEX
    see also..   : ANCESTRY: DETAILED CHARACTERISTICS...
                   : ASIANS AND PACIFIC ISLANDERS: DETAILED CHARACTERISTICS...
                   : FOREIGN BORN: DETAILED CHARACTERISTICS...
                   : HISPANIC ORIGIN: DETAILED CHARACTERISTICS...
                   : POPULATION CHARACTERISTICS OF AMERICAN INDIANS BY TRIBE

    U.S.   : CP-1-1#
    REGION   : CP-1-1#
    DIVISION   : CP-1-1*
    STATE   : CP-1#; CP-1-1*
    COUNTY   : CP-1#; CPH-3*
    SELECT SDV : CP-1#
    PLC 10+   : CP-1#; CPH-3*
    PLC 2.5-9   : CP-1#
    MSA   : CP-1-1B#; CPH-3*; CPH-S-1-1
    URBANIZED : CP-1-1C#
    NATIVE AM   : CP-1; CP-1-1A*
    OUTLYING   : CPH-6
    CONGRS DIS : CPH-4
    TRACT   : CPH-3*
—IN CENTRAL CITY/NOT IN CENTRAL CITY
    U.S.   : CPH-S-1-1
    REGION/DIV : CPH-S-1-1
    STATE   : CPH-S-1-1
    MSA   : CPH-S-1-1

—INSIDE/OUTSIDE MSA
    U.S. : CP-1-1*; CPH-S-1-1
    REGION/DIV : CPH-S-1-1
    REGION : CP-1-1*
    STATE : CP-1*; CPH-S-1-1
—RURAL AREAS
    COUNTY : CP-1
—URBAN & RURAL & SIZE OF PLACE
    U.S. : CP-1-1*
    REGION : CP-1-1*
    STATE : CP-1*

MARITAL STATUS BY SEX BY AGE
    U.S. : CP-1-1*
    REGION : CP-1-1*
    STATE : CP-1*

MARITAL STATUS BY SEX WITH AGE FOR NOW MARRIED, EXCEPT SEPARATED
    U.S. : CP-1-1*; CP-1-1B; CP-1-1C
    REGION : CP-1-1*
    STATE : CP-1*
    COUNTY : CP-1*
    SELECT SDV : CP-1*
    PLC 10+ : CP-1*
    MSA : CP-1-1B*
    URBANIZED : CP-1-1C*
—IN CENTRAL CITY/NOT IN CENTRAL CITY
    MSA : CP-1-1B
—IN CENTRAL PLACE/URBAN FRINGE
    URBANIZED : CP-1-1C
—INSIDE/OUTSIDE MSA
    U.S. : CP-1-1; CP-1-1B
    REGION : CP-1-1
    STATE : CP-1
—POPULATION SIZE CLASS OF MSA
    U.S. : CP-1-1B
—POPULATION SIZE CLASS OF URBANIZED AREA
    U.S. : CP-1-1C
—URBAN & RURAL & SIZE OF PLACE
    U.S. : CP-1-1; CP-1-1C
    REGION : CP-1-1
    STATE : CP-1

MEALS INCLUDED IN RENT
    U.S. : CH-1-1#; CH-1-1B*; CH-1-1C*; CPH-1-1
    REGION/DIV : CPH-1-1
    REGION : CH-1-1#
    DIVISION : CH-1-1*
    STATE : CH-1#; CH-1-1*; CPH-1; CPH-1-1
    COUNTY : CH-1#; CPH-1; CPH-3*; CPH-4
    SUBDIV : CH-1; CPH-1
    SELECT SDV : CH-1#; CPH-4

```
        PLACE           : CPH-1
        PLC 50+         : CH-1-1
        PLC 10+         : CH-1#; CPH-3*; CPH-4
        PLC 2.5-9       : CH-1*
        PLC 1-2.5       : CH-1*
        MSA             : CH-1-1; CH-1-1B#; CPH-1-1; CPH-3*
        URBANIZED       : CH-1-1; CH-1-1C#; CPH-1-1
        NATIVE AM       : CH-1-1A*
        CONGRS DIS      : CPH-4
        TRACT           : CPH-3*
    —IN CENTRAL CITY/NOT IN CENTRAL CITY
        MSA             : CH-1-1B*
    —IN CENTRAL PLACE/URBAN FRINGE
        URBANIZED       : CH-1-1C*
    —INDIVIDUAL CENTRAL CITY
        MSA             : CH-1-1B
    —INDIVIDUAL CENTRAL PLACE
        URBANIZED       : CH-1-1C
    —INSIDE/OUTSIDE MSA
        U.S.            : CH-1-1*; CH-1-1B*
        REGION          : CH-1-1*
        STATE           : CH-1*
    —POPULATION SIZE CLASS OF MSA
        U.S.            : CH-1-1B*
    —POPULATION SIZE CLASS OF URBANIZED AREA
        U.S.            : CH-1-1C*
    —URBAN & RURAL & SIZE OF PLACE
        U.S.            : CH-1-1*; CH-1-1C*
        REGION          : CH-1-1*
        STATE           : CH-1*
MEALS INCLUDED IN RENT (PERCENT)
    use .....           : HOUSING: GENERAL SUMMARY CHARACTERISTICS
MEALS INCLUDED IN RENT BY AGE OF HOUSEHOLDER
    U.S.                : CP-3-6
    STATE               : CP-3-6 FOR STATES WITH MORE THAN 900,000 BLACKS
    MSA                 : CP-3-6 FOR AREAS WITH MORE THAN 400,000 BLACKS
MEALS INCLUDED IN RENT BY STRUCTURAL & FINANCIAL HOUSING CHARACTERISTICS
    use .....           : METROPOLITAN HOUSING CHARACTERISTICS
MEANS OF TRANSPORTATION TO WORK
    see also..          : JOURNEY TO WORK

    U.S.                : CP-2-1#; CP-2-1B; CP-2-1C; CPH-5-1
    REGION/DIV          : CP-2-1; CPH-5-1
    STATE               : CP-2#; CPH-5; CPH-5; CPH-5-1
    COUNTY              : CP-2*; CPH-3*; CPH-4; CPH-5
    SUBDIV              : CPH-5
    SELECT SDV          : CP-2*; CPH-4
    PLACE               : CPH-5
    PLC 10+             : CP-2*; CPH-3*; CPH-4
```

```
      PLC 2.5-9        : CP-2
      MSA              : CP-2-1B*; CPH-3*; CPH-5-1; CPH-S-1-1
      URBANIZED    : CP-2-1C*; CPH-5-1
      NATIVE AM    : CP-2; CP-2-1A*
      OUTLYING     : CPH-6
      CONGRS DIS   : CPH-4
      TRACT            : CPH-3*
   —IN CENTRAL CITY/NOT IN CENTRAL CITY
      U.S.                : CPH-S-1-1
      REGION/DIV   : CPH-S-1-1
      STATE            : CPH-S-1-1
      MSA              : CP-2-1B; CPH-S-1-1
   —IN CENTRAL PLACE/URBAN FRINGE
      URBANIZED    : CP-2-1C
   —INDIVIDUAL CENTRAL CITY
      MSA              : CP-2-1B
   —INDIVIDUAL CENTRAL PLACE
      URBANIZED    : CP-2-1C
   —INSIDE/OUTSIDE MSA
      U.S.                : CP-2-1*; CP-2-1B; CPH-S-1-1
      REGION/DIV   : CPH-S-1-1
      STATE            : CP-2*; CPH-S-1-1
   —RURAL OR RURAL FARM
      COUNTY       : CP-2
   —URBAN, RURAL & SIZE OF PLACE
      U.S.                : CP-2-1*; CP-2-1C
   —URBAN, RURAL, SIZE OF PLACE, FARM
      STATE            : CP-2*
```

MEANS OF TRANSPORTATION TO WORK BY TRAVEL TIME TO WORK
```
      STATE            : CP-3-6 FOR STATES WITH MORE THAN 900,000 BLACKS
```
MEANS OF TRANSPORTATION TO WORK BY YEAR HOUSEHOLDER MOVED INTO UNIT
```
      use .....          : METROPOLITAN HOUSING CHARACTERISTICS
```
MEDIAN INCOME IN 1989
```
      use .....          : INCOME IN 1989
```
MEDIAN INCOME IN 1989 BY SELECTED CHARACTERISTICS

```
      U.S.                : CP-2-1#; CP-2-1B; CP-2-1C
      REGION/DIV   : CP-2-1
      STATE            : CP-2#
      COUNTY       : CP-2#
      SELECT SDV   : CP-2#
      PLC 10+          : CP-2#
      PLC 2.5-9        : CP-2#
      MSA              : CP-2-1B#
      URBANIZED    : CP-2-1C#
      NATIVE AM    : CP-2; CP-2-1A*
   —IN CENTRAL CITY/NOT IN CENTRAL CITY
      MSA              : CP-2-1B
```

—IN CENTRAL PLACE/URBAN FRINGE
    URBANIZED : CP-2-1C
—INDIVIDUAL CENTRAL CITY
    MSA   : CP-2-1B
—INDIVIDUAL CENTRAL PLACE
    URBANIZED : CP-2-1C
—INSIDE/OUTSIDE MSA
    U.S.   : CP-2-1*; CP-2-1B
    STATE   : CP-2*
—RURAL OR RURAL FARM
    COUNTY   : CP-2
—URBAN, RURAL & SIZE OF PLACE
    U.S.   : CP-2-1*; CP-2-1C
—URBAN, RURAL, SIZE OF PLACE, FARM
    STATE   : CP-2*
METROPOLITAN HOUSING CHARACTERISTICS
    U.S.   : CH-3-1*
 —IN CENTRAL CITY/NOT IN CENTRAL CITY
    U.S.   : CH-3-1
 —INSIDE MSA
    U.S.   : CH-3-1
MILITARY BENEFITS
    OUTLYING   : CPH-6
MILITARY DEPENDENCY
    OUTLYING   : CPH-6
MILITARY SERVICE
    use .....   : PERIOD OF MILITARY SERVICE
MOBILE HOME CHARACTERISTICS BY MORTGAGE CHARACTERISTICS
    U.S.   : CH-4-1
    REGION   : CH-4-1
MOBILE HOMES
    U.S.   : CH-2-1; CH-2-1B; CH-2-1C
    REGION   : CH-2-1
    STATE   : CH-2
    COUNTY   : CH-2
    SELECT SDV : CH-2
    PLC 10+   : CH-2
    MSA   : CH-2-1B; CPH-S-1-1
    URBANIZED : CH-2-1C
 —IN CENTRAL CITY/NOT IN CENTRAL CITY
    U.S.   : CPH-S-1-1
    REGION/DIV : CPH-S-1-1
    STATE   : CPH-S-1-1
    MSA   : CH-2-1B; CPH-S-1-1
 —IN CENTRAL PLACE/URBAN FRINGE
    URBANIZED : CH-2-1C
 —INSIDE/OUTSIDE MSA
    U.S.   : CH-2-1; CH-2-1B; CPH-S-1-1
    REGION/DIV : CPH-S-1-1

```
        REGION        : CH-2-1
        STATE         : CH-2; CPH-S-1-1
  —URBAN & RURAL & SIZE OF PLACE
        U.S.          : CH-2-1; CH-2-1C
        REGION        : CH-2-1
  —URBAN, RURAL, SIZE OF PLACE, FARM
        STATE         : CH-2
MOBILITY
        use .....     : RESIDENCE IN 1985
MONTHLY OWNER COSTS
        use .....     : MORTGAGE STATUS AND SELECTED MONTHLY OWNER COSTS
MONTHLY OWNER COSTS AS A % OF HOUSEHOLD INCOME
        see also..    : MORTGAGE STATUS & SELECTED MONTHLY OWNER COSTS AS A % OF
HOUSEHOLD INCOME

        U.S.          : CH-3-1*
  —IN CENTRAL CITY/NOT IN CENTRAL CITY
        U.S.          : CH-3-1
  —INSIDE MSA
        U.S.          : CH-3-1
MONTHLY OWNER COSTS AS A % OF HOUSEHOLD INCOME BY HOUSEHOLD COMPOSITION
BY AGE OF HOUSEHOLDER FOR OWNER/RENTER
        use .....     : METROPOLITAN HOUSING CHARACTERISTICS
MONTHLY OWNER COSTS AS A % OF HOUSEHOLD INCOME BY STRUCTURAL & FINANCIAL
HOUSING CHARACTERISTICS
        use .....     : METROPOLITAN HOUSING CHARACTERISTICS
MORTGAGE CHARACTERISTICS
        U.S.          : CH-4-1
        REGION        : CH-4-1
MORTGAGE STATUS AND SELECTED MONTHLY OWNER COSTS
        see also..    : ANCESTRY: DETAILED CHARACTERISTICS...
                      : ASIANS AND PACIFIC ISLANDERS: DETAILED CHARACTERISTICS...
                      : FOREIGN BORN: DETAILED CHARACTERISTICS...
                      : HISPANIC ORIGIN: DETAILED CHARACTERISTICS...
                      : HOUSING CHARACTERISTICS OF AMERICAN INDIANS BY TRIBE
                      : SECOND MORTGAGE OR HOME EQUITY LOAN

        U.S.          :  CH-2-1#; CH-2-1B; CH-2-1C; CPH-5-1
        REGION/DIV    :  CPH-5-1
        REGION        : CH-2-1#
        DIVISION      : CH-2-1*
        STATE         : CH-2#; CH-2-1*; CPH-5; CPH-5-1
        COUNTY        : CH-2#; CPH-3*; CPH-4; CPH-5
        SUBDIV        : CPH-5
        SELECT SDV    : CH-2#; CPH-4
        PLACE         : CPH-5
        PLC 10+       : CH-2#; CPH-3*; CPH-4
        PLC 2.5-9     : CH-2#
        MSA           : CH-2-1B#; CPH-3*; CPH-5-1; CPH-S-1-1
```

```
        URBANIZED    : CH-2-1C#; CPH-5-1
        NATIVE AM    : CH-2; CH-2-1A; CPH-4; CPH-5; CPH-5-1
        OUTLYING     : CPH-6
        CONGRS DIS   : CPH-4; CPH-4*
        TRACT        : CPH-3*
   —IN CENTRAL CITY/NOT IN CENTRAL CITY
        U.S.         : CPH-S-1-1
        REGION/DIV   : CPH-S-1-1
        STATE        : CPH-S-1-1
        MSA          : CH-2-1B; CPH-S-1-1
   —IN CENTRAL PLACE/URBAN FRINGE
        URBANIZED    : CH-2-1C
   —INSIDE/OUTSIDE MSA
        U.S.         : CH-2-1*; CH-2-1B; CPH-S-1-1
        REGION/DIV   : CPH-S-1-1
        REGION       : CH-2-1*
        STATE        : CH-2*; CPH-S-1-1
   —RURAL & RURAL FARM
        COUNTY       : CH-2
   —URBAN & RURAL & SIZE OF PLACE
        U.S.         : CH-2-1*; CH-2-1C
        REGION       : CH-2-1*
   —URBAN, RURAL, SIZE OF PLACE, FARM
        STATE        : CH-2*
MORTGAGE STATUS AND SELECTED MONTHLY OWNER COSTS (MEDIAN)
        use .....        : HOUSING: DETAILED SUMMARY CHARACTERISTICS
MORTGAGE STATUS AND SELECTED MONTHLY OWNER COSTS AS A % OF HOUSEHOLD
INCOME
        see also..       : MONTHLY OWNER COSTS AS A % OF HOUSEHOLD INCOME

        U.S.         : CH-2-1; CH-2-1B; CH-2-1C
        REGION       : CH-2-1
        STATE        : CH-2
        COUNTY       : CH-2
        SELECT SDV   : CH-2
        PLC 10+      : CH-2
        PLC 2.5-9    : CH-2#
        MSA          : CH-2-1B; CPH-S-1-1
        URBANIZED    : CH-2-1C
        NATIVE AM    : CH-2
        OUTLYING     : CPH-6
   —IN CENTRAL CITY/NOT IN CENTRAL CITY
        U.S.         : CPH-S-1-1
        REGION/DIV   : CPH-S-1-1
        STATE        : CPH-S-1-1
        MSA          : CH-2-1B; CPH-S-1-1
   —IN CENTRAL PLACE/URBAN FRINGE
        URBANIZED    : CH-2-1C
```

—INSIDE/OUTSIDE MSA
    U.S.   : CH-2-1; CH-2-1B; CPH-S-1-1
    REGION/DIV : CPH-S-1-1
    REGION   : CH-2-1
    STATE   : CH-2; CPH-S-1-1
—RURAL & RURAL FARM
    COUNTY   : CH-2
—URBAN & RURAL & SIZE OF PLACE
    U.S.   : CH-2-1; CH-2-1C
    REGION   : CH-2-1
—URBAN, RURAL, SIZE OF PLACE, FARM
    STATE   : CH-2

MORTGAGE STATUS AND SELECTED MONTHLY OWNER COSTS AS A % OF HOUSEHOLD INCOME BY AGE OF HOUSEHOLDER (BLACKS)
    U.S.   : CP-3-6
    STATE   : CP-3-6 FOR STATES WITH MORE THAN 900,000 BLACKS
    MSA   : CP-3-6 FOR AREAS WITH MORE THAN 400,000 BLACKS

MORTGAGE STATUS AND SELECTED MONTHLY OWNER COSTS BY HOUSEHOLD COMPOSITION BY AGE OF HOUSEHOLDER FOR OWNER/RENTER
    use .....   : METROPOLITAN HOUSING CHARACTERISTICS

MORTGAGE STATUS AND SELECTED MONTHLY OWNER COSTS BY STRUCTURAL & FINANCIAL HOUSING CHARACTERISTICS
    use .....   : METROPOLITAN HOUSING CHARACTERISTICS

NATIVE AMERICANS AS A RACIAL GROUP
    use .....   : SUBJECTS WITH REPORT #'s FLAGGED BY * FOR RACE

NATIVE AMERICANS BY TRIBE, HOUSING CHARACTERISTICS
    use .....   : HOUSING CHARACTERISTICS OF AMERICAN INDIANS BY TRIBE

NATIVE AMERICANS BY TRIBE, POPULATION CHARACTERISTICS
    use .....   : POPULATION CHARACTERISTICS OF AMERICAN INDIANS BY TRIBE

NATIVE AMERICANS BY TRIBE, POPULATION COUNTS
    use .....   : POPULATION COUNTS OF AMERICAN INDIANS BY TRIBE

NATIVE AMERICANS ON INDIAN LANDS
    use .....   : Subjects with "Native American" geography as a subheading

NATIVITY
    see also..   : CITIZENSHIP
                   : PLACE OF BIRTH

    U.S.   : CP-2-1; CP-2-1B; CP-2-1C; CPH-5-1
    REGION/DIV : CP-2-1; CPH-5-1
    STATE   : CP-2; CPH-5-1
    COUNTY   : CP-2; CPH-4; CPH-5
    SUBDIV   : CPH-5
    SELECT SDV : CP-2; CPH-4
    PLACE   : CPH-5
    PLC 10+   : CP-2; CPH-4
    PLC 2.5-9   : CP-2
    MSA   : CP-2-1B; CPH-5-1
    URBANIZED : CP-2-1C; CPH-5-1
    CONGRS DIS : CPH-4

—IN CENTRAL CITY/NOT IN CENTRAL CITY
    MSA   : CP-2-1B
—IN CENTRAL PLACE/URBAN FRINGE
    URBANIZED : CP-2-1C
—INDIVIDUAL CENTRAL CITY
    MSA   : CP-2-1B
—INDIVIDUAL CENTRAL PLACE
    URBANIZED : CP-2-1C
—INSIDE/OUTSIDE MSA
    U.S.   : CP-2-1; CP-2-1B
    STATE   : CP-2
—URBAN, RURAL & SIZE OF PLACE
    U.S.   : CP-2-1; CP-2-1C
—URBAN, RURAL, SIZE OF PLACE, FARM
    STATE   : CP-2
NONRELATIVES PRESENT BY SIZE OF HOUSEHOLD
    use .....   : HOUSEHOLD TYPE AND RELATIONSHIP
NUMBER OF CENSUS TRACTS AND BLOCK NUMBERING AREAS
    U.S.   : CPH-2-1
    STATE   : CPH-2-1
    COUNTY   : CPH-2-1
  —INSIDE/OUTSIDE MSA
    U.S.   : CPH-2-1
NUMBER OF COUNTIES ANALYZED BY SELECTED CHARACTERISTICS
    U.S.   : CPH-2-1
    REGION/DIV : CPH-2-1
    STATE   : CPH-2-1
NUMBER OF COUNTY SUBDIVISIONS AND TYPES OF SUBDIVISIONS
    U.S.   : CPH-2-1
    REGION/DIV : CPH-2-1
    STATE   : CPH-2-1
NUMBER OF PLACES
    STATE   : CPH-2
  —INSIDE/OUTSIDE MSA BY SIZE OF PLACE
    U.S.   : CPH-2-1
    STATE   : CPH-2
  —INSIDE/OUTSIDE MSA BY URBAN & RURAL & SIZE OF PLACE
    U.S.   : CPH-2-1
    STATE   : CPH-2
  —URBAN & RURAL & BY SIZE OF PLACE
    STATE   : CPH-2
  —URBAN AND RURAL
    STATE   : CPH-2
NUMBER OF PLACES AND TYPES OF PLACES
    U.S.   : CPH-2-1
    REGION/DIV : CPH-2-1
    STATE   : CPH-2-1
  —INSIDE/OUTSIDE MSA BY URBAN & RURAL BY SIZE
    U.S.   : CPH-S-1-2

NUMBER OF PLACES, 1990 & PREVIOUS CENSUSES
    U.S.   : CPH-S-1-2
  —URBAN & RURAL & BY SIZE OF PLACE
    U.S.   : CPH-2-1; CPH-S-1-2
OCCUPATION
    see also..   : ANCESTRY: DETAILED CHARACTERISTICS...
                   : ASIANS AND PACIFIC ISLANDERS: DETAILED CHARACTERISTICS...
                   : FOREIGN BORN: DETAILED CHARACTERISTICS...
                   : HISPANIC ORIGIN: DETAILED CHARACTERISTICS...
                   : LAST OCCUPATION OF THE EXPERIENCED UNEMPLOYED
                   : POPULATION CHARACTERISTICS OF AMERICAN INDIANS BY TRIBE

    U.S.   : CP-2-1#; CP-2-1B; CP-2-1C
    REGION/DIV : CP-2-1
    STATE   : CP-2#
    COUNTY   : CP-2#; CPH-3*
    SELECT SDV : CP-2#
    PLC 10+   : CP-2#; CPH-3*
    PLC 2.5-9 : CP-2#
    MSA   : CP-2-1B#; CPH-3*; CPH-S-1-1
    URBANIZED : CP-2-1C#
    NATIVE AM : CP-2; CP-2-1A*
    OUTLYING : CPH-6
    CONGRS DIS : CPH-4
    TRACT   : CPH-3*
  —IN CENTRAL CITY/NOT IN CENTRAL CITY
    U.S.   : CPH-S-1-1
    REGION/DIV : CPH-S-1-1
    STATE   : CPH-S-1-1
    MSA   : CP-2-1B; CPH-S-1-1
  —IN CENTRAL PLACE/URBAN FRINGE
    URBANIZED : CP-2-1C
  —INDIVIDUAL CENTRAL CITY
    MSA   : CP-2-1B
  —INDIVIDUAL CENTRAL PLACE
    URBANIZED : CP-2-1C
  —INSIDE/OUTSIDE MSA
    U.S.   : CP-2-1*; CP-2-1B; CPH-S-1-1
    REGION/DIV : CPH-S-1-1
    STATE   : CP-2*; CPH-S-1-1
  —RURAL OR RURAL FARM
    COUNTY   : CP-2
  —URBAN, RURAL & SIZE OF PLACE
    U.S.   : CP-2-1*; CP-2-1C
  —URBAN, RURAL, SIZE OF PLACE, FARM
    STATE   : CP-2*
OCCUPATION BY SELECTED WORK CHARACTERISTICS (BLACKS)
    use .....   : CHARACTERISTICS OF THE BLACK POPULATION

OCCUPATION, DETAILS FOR THE CIVILIAN LABOR FORCE
    U.S.   : CP-S-1-1*
OWNER COSTS
    use .....   : MORTGAGE STATUS AND SELECTED MONTHLY OWNER COSTS
OWNERSHIP OF HOME BY MORTGAGE CHARACTERISTICS
    U.S.   : CH-4-1*
    REGION   : CH-4-1*
OWNERSHIP OF HOUSING UNIT
    use .....   : TENURE
PACIFIC ISLANDERS: DETAILED CHARACTERISTICS BY RACIAL GROUP
    use .....   : ASIANS AND PACIFIC ISLANDERS: DETAILED CHARACTERISTICS BY
RACIAL GROUP
PER CAPITA INCOME
    use .....   : INCOME IN 1989
PERIOD OF MILITARY SERVICE
    see also..   : VETERAN STATUS

    U.S.   : CP-2-1#; CP-2-1B; CP-2-1C
    REGION/DIV : CP-2-1
    STATE   : CP-2#
    COUNTY   : CP-2*
    SELECT SDV : CP-2*
    PLC 10+   : CP-2*
    PLC 2.5-9   : CP-2
    MSA   : CP-2-1B*
    URBANIZED   : CP-2-1C*
    NATIVE AM   : CP-2
    OUTLYING   : CPH-6
    CONGRS DIS : CPH-4
  —IN CENTRAL CITY/NOT IN CENTRAL CITY
    MSA   : CP-2-1B
  —IN CENTRAL PLACE/URBAN FRINGE
    URBANIZED   : CP-2-1C
  —INDIVIDUAL CENTRAL CITY
    MSA   : CP-2-1B
  —INDIVIDUAL CENTRAL PLACE
    URBANIZED   : CP-2-1C
  —INSIDE/OUTSIDE MSA
    U.S.   : CP-2-1*; CP-2-1B
    STATE   : CP-2*
  —URBAN, RURAL & SIZE OF PLACE
    U.S.   : CP-2-1*; CP-2-1C
  —URBAN, RURAL, SIZE OF PLACE, FARM
    STATE   : CP-2*
PERIOD OF MILITARY SERVICE FOR PERSON 60 YEARS AND OLDER
    NATIVE AM   : CP-2-1A*

PERSONS IN UNIT
      see also..   : CHARACTERISTICS OF THE BLACK POPULATION
                : HOUSING CHARACTERISTICS OF AMERICAN INDIANS BY TRIBE

      U.S.   : CH-1-1#; CH-1-1B*; CH-1-1C*
      REGION   : CH-1-1#
      DIVISION   : CH-1-1*
      STATE   : CH-1#; CH-1-1*
      COUNTY   : CH-1#; CPH-3*; CPH-4
      SUBDIV   : CH-1
      SELECT SDV : CH-1#; CPH-4
      PLC 50+   : CH-1-1
      PLC 10+   : CH-1#; CPH-3*; CPH-4
      PLC 2.5-9   : CH-1#
      PLC 1-2.5   : CH-1*
      MSA   : CH-1-1; CH-1-1B#; CPH-3*
      URBANIZED : CH-1-1; CH-1-1C#
      NATIVE AM : CH-1; CH-1-1; CH-1-1A*
      OUTLYING   : CPH-6
      CONGRS DIS : CPH-4
      TRACT   : CPH-3*
    —IN CENTRAL CITY/NOT IN CENTRAL CITY
      MSA   : CH-1-1B*
    —IN CENTRAL PLACE/URBAN FRINGE
      URBANIZED : CH-1-1C*
    —INDIVIDUAL CENTRAL CITY
      MSA   : CH-1-1B
    —INDIVIDUAL CENTRAL PLACE
      URBANIZED : CH-1-1C
    —INSIDE/OUTSIDE MSA
      U.S.   : CH-1-1*; CH-1-1B*
      REGION   : CH-1-1*
      STATE   : CH-1*
    —POPULATION SIZE CLASS OF MSA
      U.S.   : CH-1-1B*
    —POPULATION SIZE CLASS OF URBANIZED AREA
      U.S.   : CH-1-1C*
    —URBAN & RURAL & SIZE OF PLACE
      U.S.   : CH-1-1*; CH-1-1C*
      REGION   : CH-1-1*
      STATE   : CH-1*
PERSONS IN UNIT BY HOUSEHOLD COMPOSITION BY AGE OF HOUSEHOLDER FOR OWNER/
RENTER
      use .....   : METROPOLITAN HOUSING CHARACTERISTICS
PERSONS IN UNIT BY STRUCTURAL & FINANCIAL HOUSING CHARACTERISTICS
      use .....   : METROPOLITAN HOUSING CHARACTERISTICS
PERSONS PER OCCUPIED UNIT
      U.S.   : CPH-1-1
      REGION/DIV : CPH-1-1

```
    STATE         : CPH-1; CPH-1-1
    COUNTY        : CPH-1
    SUBDIV        : CPH-1
    PLACE         : CPH-1
    MSA           : CPH-1-1; CPH-S-1-1
    URBANIZED     : CPH-1-1
    OUTLYING      : CPH-6
 —IN CENTRAL CITY/NOT IN CENTRAL CITY
    U.S.          : CPH-S-1-1
    REGION/DIV    : CPH-S-1-1
    STATE         : CPH-S-1-1
    MSA           : CPH-S-1-1
 —INSIDE/OUTSIDE MSA
    U.S.          : CPH-S-1-1
    REGION/DIV    : CPH-S-1-1
    STATE         : CPH-S-1-1
PERSONS PER OCCUPIED UNIT (MEDIAN)
    use .....      : HOUSING: GENERAL SUMMARY CHARACTERISTICS
PERSONS PER ROOM
    see also..     : CHARACTERISTICS OF THE BLACK POPULATION
                   : HOUSING CHARACTERISTICS OF AMERICAN INDIANS BY TRIBE

    U.S.          : CH-1-1#; CH-1-1B*; CH-1-1C*; CPH-1-1
    REGION/DIV    : CPH-1-1
    REGION        : CH-1-1#
    DIVISION      : CH-1-1*
    STATE         : CH-1#; CH-1-1*; CPH-1; CPH-1-1
    COUNTY        : CH-1#; CPH-1; CPH-3*; CPH-4
    SUBDIV        : CH-1; CPH-1
    SELECT SDV    : CH-1#; CPH-4
    PLACE         : CPH-1
    PLC 50+       : CH-1-1
    PLC 10+       : CH-1#; CPH-3*; CPH-4
    PLC 2.5-9     : CH-1#
    PLC 1-2.5     : CH-1*
    MSA           : CH-1-1; CH-1-1B#; CPH-1-1; CPH-3*
    URBANIZED     : CH-1-1; CH-1-1C#; CPH-1-1
    NATIVE AM     : CH-1; CH-1-1; CH-1-1A*
    OUTLYING      : CPH-6
    CONGRS DIS    : CPH-4
    TRACT         : CPH-3*
 —IN CENTRAL CITY/NOT IN CENTRAL CITY
    MSA           : CH-1-1B*
 —IN CENTRAL PLACE/URBAN FRINGE
    URBANIZED     : CH-1-1C*
 —INDIVIDUAL CENTRAL CITY
    MSA           : CH-1-1B
 —INDIVIDUAL CENTRAL PLACE
    URBANIZED     : CH-1-1C
```

—INSIDE/OUTSIDE MSA
    U.S.   : CH-1-1*; CH-1-1B*
    REGION   : CH-1-1*
    STATE   : CH-1*
—POPULATION SIZE CLASS OF MSA
    U.S.   : CH-1-1B*
—POPULATION SIZE CLASS OF URBANIZED AREA
    U.S.   : CH-1-1C*
—URBAN & RURAL & SIZE OF PLACE
    U.S.   : CH-1-1*; CH-1-1C*
    REGION   : CH-1-1*
    STATE   : CH-1*
PERSONS PER ROOM (MEAN)
    use .....   : HOUSING: GENERAL SUMMARY CHARACTERISTICS
PERSONS PER ROOM BY HOUSEHOLD COMPOSITION BY AGE OF HOUSEHOLDER FOR OWNER/
RENTER
    use .....   : METROPOLITAN HOUSING CHARACTERISTICS
PERSONS PER ROOM BY STRUCTURAL & FINANCIAL HOUSING CHARACTERISTICS
    use .....   : METROPOLITAN HOUSING CHARACTERISTICS
PLACE OF BIRTH
    see also..   : BIRTH PLACE
                     : CITIZENSHIP
                     : FOREIGN BORN
                     : NATIVITY

    U.S.   : CP-2-1#; CP-2-1B; CP-2-1C; CPH-5-1
    REGION/DIV : CP-2-1; CPH-5-1
    STATE   : CP-2#; CPH-5; CPH-5-1
    COUNTY   : CP-2#; CPH-3*; CPH-4; CPH-5
    SUBDIV   : CPH-5
    SELECT SDV : CP-2#; CPH-4
    PLACE   : CPH-5
    PLC 10+   : CP-2#; CPH-3*; CPH-4
    PLC 2.5-9 : CP-2#
    MSA   : CP-2-1B#; CPH-3*; CPH-5-1; CPH-S-1-1
    URBANIZED : CP-2-1C#; CPH-5-1
    NATIVE AM : CP-2
    OUTLYING   : CPH-6
    CONGRS DIS : CPH-4
    TRACT   : CPH-3*
—IN CENTRAL CITY/NOT IN CENTRAL CITY
    U.S.   : CPH-S-1-1
    REGION/DIV : CPH-S-1-1
    STATE   : CPH-S-1-1
    MSA   : CP-2-1B; CPH-S-1-1
—IN CENTRAL PLACE/URBAN FRINGE
    URBANIZED : CP-2-1C
—INDIVIDUAL CENTRAL CITY
    MSA   : CP-2-1B

—INDIVIDUAL CENTRAL PLACE
    URBANIZED   : CP-2-1C
—INSIDE/OUTSIDE MSA
    U.S.   : CP-2-1*; CP-2-1B; CPH-S-1-1
    REGION/DIV : CPH-S-1-1
    STATE   : CP-2*; CPH-S-1-1
—RURAL OR RURAL FARM
    COUNTY   : CP-2
—URBAN, RURAL & SIZE OF PLACE
    U.S.   : CP-2-1*; CP-2-1C
—URBAN, RURAL, SIZE OF PLACE, FARM
    STATE   : CP-2*
PLACE OF BIRTH (PERCENT)
    use .....   : POPULATION: DETAILED SUMMARY CHARACTERISTICS
PLACE OF BIRTH OF PARENTS
    OUTLYING : CPH-6
PLACE OF WORK
    U.S.   : CP-2-1#; CP-2-1B
    REGION/DIV : CP-2-1
    STATE   : CP-2#
    COUNTY   : CP-2*; CPH-3*
    SELECT SDV : CP-2*
    PLC 10+   : CP-2*; CPH-3*
    PLC 2.5-9 : CP-2
    MSA   : CP-2-1B*; CPH-3*
    NATIVE AM : CP-2; CP-2-1A*; CP-2-1A*
    TRACT   : CPH-3*
—IN CENTRAL CITY/NOT IN CENTRAL CITY
    MSA   : CP-2-1B
—INDIVIDUAL CENTRAL CITY
    MSA   : CP-2-1B
—INSIDE/OUTSIDE MSA
    U.S.   : CP-2-1B
—RURAL OR RURAL FARM
    COUNTY   : CP-2
—URBAN, RURAL & SIZE OF PLACE
    U.S.   : CP-2-1
PLACE OF WORK BY TRAVEL TIME TO WORK (BLACKS)
    STATE   : CP-3-6 FOR STATES WITH MORE THAN 900,000 BLACKS
PLACES
    use .....   : NUMBER OF PLACES
PLUMBING FACILITIES
    see also..   : CHARACTERISTICS OF THE BLACK POPULATION
                 : HOUSING CHARACTERISTICS OF AMERICAN INDIANS BY TRIBE

    U.S.   : CH-2-1#; CH-2-1B; CH-2-1C; CPH-5-1
    REGION/DIV : CPH-5-1
    REGION   : CH-2-1#
    DIVISION   : CH-2-1*

```
      STATE         : CH-2#; CH-2-1*; CPH-5; CPH-5-1
      COUNTY        : CH-2#; CPH-3*; CPH-4; CPH-5
      SUBDIV        : CPH-5
      SELECT SDV    : CH-2#; CPH-4
      PLACE         : CPH-5
      PLC 10+       : CH-2#; CPH-3*; CPH-4
      PLC 2.5-9     : CH-2#
      MSA           : CH-2-1B#; CPH-3*; CPH-5-1; CPH-S-1-1
      URBANIZED     : CH-2-1C#; CPH-5-1
      NATIVE AM     : CH-2; CPH-4; CPH-5; CPH-5-1
      OUTLYING      : CPH-6
      CONGRS DIS    : CPH-4; CPH-4
      TRACT         : CPH-3*
  —IN CENTRAL CITY/NOT IN CENTRAL CITY
      U.S.          : CPH-S-1-1
      REGION/DIV    : CPH-S-1-1
      STATE         : CPH-S-1-1
      MSA           : CH-2-1B; CPH-S-1-1
  —IN CENTRAL PLACE/URBAN FRINGE
      URBANIZED     : CH-2-1C
  —INSIDE/OUTSIDE MSA
      U.S.          : CH-2-1*; CH-2-1B; CPH-S-1-1
      REGION/DIV    : CPH-S-1-1
      REGION        : CH-2-1*
      STATE         : CH-2*; CPH-S-1-1
  —RURAL & RURAL FARM
      COUNTY        : CH-2
  —URBAN & RURAL & SIZE OF PLACE
      U.S.          : CH-2-1*; CH-2-1C
      REGION        : CH-2-1*
  —URBAN, RURAL, SIZE OF PLACE, FARM
      STATE         : CH-2*
PLUMBING FACILITIES (PERCENT)
      use .....     : HOUSING: DETAILED SUMMARY CHARACTERISTICS
PLUMBING FACILITIES BY HOUSEHOLD COMPOSITION BY AGE OF HOUSEHOLDER FOR
OWNER/RENTER
      use .....     : METROPOLITAN HOUSING CHARACTERISTICS
PLUMBING FACILITIES BY PERSONS PER ROOM
      see also..    : ANCESTRY: DETAILED CHARACTERISTICS...
                    : ASIANS AND PACIFIC ISLANDERS: DETAILED CHARACTERISTICS...
                    : FOREIGN BORN: DETAILED CHARACTERISTICS...
                    : HISPANIC ORIGIN: DETAILED CHARACTERISTICS...

      MSA           : CPH-S-1-1
      NATIVE AM     : CH-2-1A
  —IN CENTRAL CITY/NOT IN CENTRAL CITY
      U.S.          : CPH-S-1-1
      REGION/DIV    : CPH-S-1-1
      STATE         : CPH-S-1-1
      MSA           : CPH-S-1-1
```

—INSIDE/OUTSIDE MSA
    U.S.   : CPH-S-1-1
    REGION/DIV : CPH-S-1-1
    STATE   : CPH-S-1-1
PLUMBING FACILITIES BY PERSONS PER ROOM BY STRUCTURAL & FINANCIAL HOUSING CHARACTERISTICS
    use .....   : METROPOLITAN HOUSING CHARACTERISTICS
PLUMBING FACILITIES BY STRUCTURAL & FINANCIAL HOUSING CHARACTERISTICS
    use .....   : METROPOLITAN HOUSING CHARACTERISTICS
POPULATION CENTER, 1790-1990
    U.S.   : CPH-2-1
POPULATION CHARACTERISTICS OF AMERICAN INDIANS BY TRIBE
    see also..   : HOUSING CHARACTERISTICS OF AMERICAN INDIANS BY TRIBE
               : POPULATION COUNTS OF AMERICAN INDIANS BY TRIBE

    U.S.   : CP-3-7
    STATE   : CP-3-7
    MSA   : CP-3-7
POPULATION COUNTS
    see also..   : HOUSING: DETAILED SUMMARY CHARACTERISTICS
               : HOUSING: GENERAL SUMMARY CHARACTERISTICS
               : POPULATION: DETAILED SUMMARY CHARACTERISTICS
               : POPULATION: GENERAL SUMMARY CHARACTERISTICS

    U.S.   : CPH-2-1; CPH-S-1-1#; CPH-S-1-2
    REGION/DIV : CPH-S-1-1#
    STATE   : CPH-2-1
    COUNTY   : CPH-2-1
    MSA   : CPH-S-1-1#
    URBANIZED : CPH-2-1; CPH-S-1-2
    OUTLYING : CPH-2-1
—CENTRAL PLACE/URBAN FRINGE
    U.S.   : CPH-S-1-2
    URBANIZED : CPH-2-1; CPH-S-1-2
—CENTRAL PLACE/URBAN FRINGE WITH COMPONENT PARTS
    URBANIZED : CPH-S-1-2
—EXTENDED CITIES BY URBAN & RURAL
    STATE   : CPH-S-1-2
—IN CENTRAL CITY/NOT IN CENTRAL CITY
    U.S.   : CPH-S-1-1#
    REGION/DIV : CPH-S-1-1#
    STATE   : CPH-S-1-1
    MSA   : CPH-S-1-1#
—IN CENTRAL CITY/NOT IN CENTRAL CITY BY URBAN & RURAL & FARM
    MSA   : CPH-S-1-1
—INSIDE/OUTSIDE MSA
    U.S.   : CPH-2-1; CPH-S-1-1#
    REGION/DIV : CPH-S-1-1#
    STATE   : CPH-S-1-1

—INSIDE/OUTSIDE MSA BY SIZE OF PLACE
    U.S.   : CPH-2-1
    STATE   : CPH-2
—INSIDE/OUTSIDE MSA BY URBAN & RURAL & FARM
    U.S.   : CPH-S-1-1
    REGION/DIV : CPH-S-1-1
    STATE   : CPH-S-1-1
—INSIDE/OUTSIDE MSA BY URBAN & RURAL & SIZE OF PLACE
    U.S.   : CPH-2-1
    STATE   : CPH-2
—INSIDE/OUTSIDE MSA BY URBAN & RURAL BY SIZE & TYPE OF PLACE
    U.S.   : CPH-S-1-2
—INSIDE/OUTSIDE URBANIZED AREA
    U.S.   : CPH-2-1
    REGION/DIV : CPH-2-1
    STATE   : CPH-2-1
—INSIDE/OUTSIDE URBANIZED AREA BY SIZE OF PLACE
    STATE   : CPH-2
—SIZE OF PLACE: POPULATION SIZE CLASS OF URBANIZED AREA
    U.S.   : CPH-2-1
    URBANIZED : CPH-2; CPH-2-1
—URBAN & RURAL
    U.S.   : CPH-2-1; CPH-S-1-2
    REGION/DIV : CPH-2-1
    STATE   : CPH-2-1; CPH-2-1; CPH-S-1-2
    COUNTY   : CPH-2-1
—URBAN & RURAL & BY SIZE OF PLACE
    U.S.   : CPH-2-1
    REGION/DIV : CPH-2-1
    STATE   : CPH-2-1
    COUNTY   : CPH-2
—URBAN & RURAL BY POPULATION SIZE CLASS OF MSA
    U.S.   : CPH-2-1
    MSA   : CPH-2; CPH-2-1
—URBAN BY INSIDE/OUTSIDE URBANIZED AREA
    U.S.   : CPH-S-1-2
    REGION/DIV : CPH-S-1-2
    STATE   : CPH-S-1-2
—URBAN, RURAL, AND FARM
    COUNTY   : CPH-3
    PLC 10+   : CPH-3
    MSA   : CPH-3; CPH-S-1-1
    CONGRS DIS : CPH-4
    TRACT   : CPH-3
POPULATION COUNTS BY RACE AND HISPANIC ORIGIN
    U.S.   : CP-1-1#; CP-1-1A*; CP-1-1B#; CP-1-1C#; CP-2-1*; CP-2-1A; CP-2-1B#; CP-2-1C#
    REGION/DIV : CP-1-1A*; CP-2-1*; CP-2-1A
    REGION   : CP-1-1#

```
        DIVISION       : CP-1-1#
        STATE          : CP-1#; CP-1-1#; CP-1-1A*; CP-2#; CP-2-1A
        COUNTY         : CP-1#; CP-2*
        SUBDIV         : CP-1*
        SELECT SDV     : CP-1#; CP-2*
        PLC 50+        : CP-1-1#; CP-2-1#
        PLC 10+        : CP-1#; CP-2*
        PLC 2.5-9      : CP-1#; CP-2*
        PLC 1-2.5      : CP-1#
        MSA            : CP-1-1#; CP-1-1B#; CP-2-1#; CP-2-1B#
        URBANIZED      : CP-1-1#; CP-1-1C#; CP-2-1#; CP-2-1C#
        NATIVE AM      : CP-1; CP-1-1*; CP-1-1A*; CP-2-1A*
—IN CENTRAL CITY/NOT IN CENTRAL CITY
        MSA            : CP-1-1B#
—IN CENTRAL PLACE/URBAN FRINGE
        URBANIZED      : CP-1-1C#
—INDIVIDUAL CENTRAL CITY
        MSA            : CP-1-1B#
—INDIVIDUAL CENTRAL PLACE
        URBANIZED      : CP-1-1C#
—INSIDE/OUTSIDE MSA
        U.S.           : CP-1-1#; CP-1-1B#; CP-2-1*; CP-2-1B#
        REGION         : CP-1-1#
        STATE          : CP-1#; CP-2*
—POPULATION SIZE CLASS OF MSA
        U.S.           : CP-1-1B#
—POPULATION SIZE CLASS OF URBANIZED AREA
        U.S.           : CP-1-1C#
—RURAL & RURAL FARM
        COUNTY         : CP-2*
—RURAL AREAS
        COUNTY         : CP-1#
—URBAN & RURAL & SIZE OF PLACE
        U.S.           : CP-1-1#; CP-1-1C#; CP-2-1*; CP-2-1C#
        REGION         : CP-1-1#
        STATE          : CP-1#
—URBAN, RURAL, SIZE OF PLACE, FARM
        STATE          : CP-2*
POPULATION COUNTS BY RACE AND HISPANIC ORIGIN FOR HOUSEHOLD POPULATION ONLY
        U.S.           : CPH-S-1-1
        REGION/DIV     : CPH-S-1-1
        STATE          : CP-1#; CPH-S-1-1
        COUNTY         : CP-1#
        SELECT SDV     : CP-1#
        PLC 10+        : CP-1#
        PLC 2.5-9      : CP-1#
        PLC 1-2.5      : CP-1#
        MSA            : CPH-S-1
```

—IN CENTRAL CITY/NOT IN CENTRAL CITY
    U.S.   : CPH-S-1-1
    REGION/DIV : CPH-S-1-1
    STATE   : CPH-S-1-1
    MSA   : CPH-S-1-1
—INSIDE/OUTSIDE MSA
    U.S.   : CPH-S-1-1
    REGION/DIV : CPH-S-1-1
    STATE   : CPH-S-1-1
POPULATION COUNTS OF AMERICAN INDIANS BY TRIBE
    see also..   : HOUSING CHARACTERISTICS OF AMERICAN INDIANS BY TRIBE
                         : POPULATION CHARACTERISTICS OF AMERICAN INDIANS BY TRIBE

    U.S.   : CP-3-7
    REGION/DIV : CP-3-7
    STATE   : CP-3-7
POPULATION COUNTS, 1990 & CHANGE FROM PREVIOUS CENSUSES
—URBAN AND RURAL
    COUNTY   : CPH-2
POPULATION COUNTS, 1990 & PREVIOUS CENSUSES
    U.S.   : CPH-2-1; CPH-S-1-2
    REGION/DIV : CPH-2-1
    STATE   : CPH-2-1
    COUNTY   : CPH-2-1
    SUBDIV   : CPH-2
    SELECT SDV : CPH-2-1
    PLACE   : CPH-2; CPH-2; CPH-2-1 FOR PLACES OF 2,500 OR MORE
                         : CPH-2-1 FOR PLACES OF 100,000 OR MORE
    MSA   : CPH-2; CPH-2-1
    URBANIZED   : CPH-2
—IN CENTRAL CITY
    MSA   : CPH-2-1
—URBAN & RURAL & BY SIZE OF PLACE
    U.S.   : CPH-2-1; CPH-S-1-2
    STATE   : CPH-2
POPULATION COUNTS, 1990 & PREVIOUS CENSUSES WITH CHANGE
    U.S.   : CPH-2-1
    STATE   : CPH-2; CPH-S-1-1#
    COUNTY   : CPH-2
—IN CENTRAL CITY/NOT IN CENTRAL CITY
    STATE   : CPH-S-1-1#
—INSIDE/OUTSIDE MSA
    STATE   : CPH-S-1-1#
—URBAN & RURAL
    U.S.   : CPH-2-1
    REGION/DIV : CPH-2-1
    STATE   : CPH-2; CPH-2-1

POPULATION COUNTS, CHANGE FROM PREVIOUS CENSUSES
     STATE   : CPH-2-1
     COUNTY   : CPH-2-1
POPULATION DENSITY
     U.S.   : CPH-1-1; CPH-2-1; CPH-S-1-2
     REGION/DIV : CPH-1-1
     STATE   : CPH-1; CPH-1-1; CPH-2; CPH-2-1
     COUNTY   : CPH-1; CPH-2; CPH-2-1; CPH-4
     SUBDIV   : CPH-1; CPH-2
     SELECT SDV : CPH-2-1; CPH-4
     PLACE   : CPH-1; CPH-2
     PLC 10+   : CPH-4
     MSA   : CPH-1-1; CPH-2; CPH-2-1
     URBANIZED : CPH-1-1; CPH-2; CPH-2-1; CPH-S-1-2
     CONGRS DIS : CPH-4
  —CENTRAL PLACE/URBAN FRINGE
     U.S.   : CPH-S-1-2
     URBANIZED : CPH-2-1; CPH-S-1-2
  —CENTRAL PLACE/URBAN FRINGE WITH COMPONENT PARTS
     URBANIZED : CPH-S-1-2
  —EXTENDED CITIES BY URBAN & RURAL
     STATE   : CPH-S-1-2
  —IN CENTRAL CITY
     MSA   : CPH-2-1
  —URBAN & RURAL
     U.S.   : CPH-S-1-2
     STATE   : CPH-S-1-2
POPULATION DENSITY, 1990 & PREVIOUS CENSUSES
     U.S.   : CPH-2-1
     REGION/DIV : CPH-2-1
     STATE   : CPH-2-1
POPULATION: DETAILED SUMMARY CHARACTERISTICS
     U.S.   : CP-2-1*; CP-2-1B*; CP-2-1C
     REGION/DIV : CP-2-1*
     STATE   : CP-2*
     COUNTY   : CP-2*
     SELECT SDV : CP-2*
     PLC 50+   : CP-2-1
     PLC 10+   : CP-2*
     PLC 2.5-9 : CP-2*
     MSA   : CP-2-1
     URBANIZED : CP-2-1
     NATIVE AM : CP-2; CP-2-1; CP-2-1A*
  —INSIDE/OUTSIDE MSA
     U.S.   : CP-2-1*; CP-2-1B*
     STATE   : CP-2*
  —URBAN, RURAL & SIZE OF PLACE
     U.S.   : CP-2-1*; CP-2-1C

—URBAN, RURAL, SIZE OF PLACE, FARM
  STATE   : CP-2*
POPULATION DISTRIBUTION, 1990 & PREVIOUS CENSUSES
  REGION/DIV : CPH-2-1
POPULATION: GENERAL SUMMARY CHARACTERISTICS
  see also..   : POPULATION CHARACTERISTICS OF AMERICAN INDIANS BY TRIBE

  U.S.   : CP-1-1*; CP-1-1B*; CP-1-1C*
  REGION   : CP-1-1*
  DIVISION : CP-1-1*
  STATE   : CP-1*; CP-1-1*
  COUNTY   : CP-1*
  SUBDIV   : CP-1
  SELECT SDV : CP-1*
  PLC 50+   : CP-1-1
  PLC 10+   : CP-1*
  PLC 2.5-9 : CP-1*
  PLC 1-2.5 : CP-1*
  MSA   : CP-1-1; CP-1-1B*
  URBANIZED : CP-1-1; CP-1-1C*
  NATIVE AM : CP-1; CP-1-1*; CP-1-1A*
  OUTLYING : CPH-6
—IN CENTRAL CITY/NOT IN CENTRAL CITY
  MSA   : CP-1-1B*
—IN CENTRAL PLACE/URBAN FRINGE
  URBANIZED : CP-1-1C*
—INDIVIDUAL CENTRAL CITY
  MSA   : CP-1-1B
—INDIVIDUAL CENTRAL PLACE
  URBANIZED : CP-1-1C
—INSIDE/OUTSIDE MSA
  U.S.   : CP-1-1*; CP-1-1B*
  REGION   : CP-1-1*
  STATE   : CP-1*
—POPULATION SIZE CLASS OF MSA
  U.S.   : CP-1-1B*
—POPULATION SIZE CLASS OF URBANIZED AREA
  U.S.   : CP-1-1C*
—URBAN & RURAL & SIZE OF PLACE
  U.S.   : CP-1-1*; CP-1-1C*
  REGION   : CP-1-1*
  STATE   : CP-1*
POPULATION RANK
  COUNTY   : CPH-2-1
  PLACE   : CPH-2 FOR PLACES 2,500 OR GREATER
        : CPH-2-1 FOR PLACES OF 100,000 OR MORE
  MSA   : CPH-2-1; CPH-S-1-1
  URBANIZED : CPH-2-1; CPH-S-1-2

POPULATION RANK, 1990 & PREVIOUS CENSUSES WITH CHANGE
    REGION/DIV : CPH-2-1
    STATE   : CPH-2-1
  —URBAN & RURAL
    REGION/DIV : CPH-2-1
    STATE   : CPH-2-1
POPULATION RATES OF CHANGE
    U.S.   : CPH-2-1
    REGION/DIV : CPH-2-1
POVERTY STATUS BY HOUSEHOLD COMPOSITION BY AGE OF HOUSEHOLDER FOR OWNER/
RENTER
    use .....   : METROPOLITAN HOUSING CHARACTERISTICS
POVERTY STATUS BY STRUCTURAL & FINANCIAL HOUSING CHARACTERISTICS
    use .....   : METROPOLITAN HOUSING CHARACTERISTICS
POVERTY STATUS IN 1989
    see also..   : ANCESTRY: DETAILED CHARACTERISTICS...
                   : ASIANS AND PACIFIC ISLANDERS: DETAILED CHARACTERISTICS...
                   : FOREIGN BORN: DETAILED CHARACTERISTICS...
                   : HISPANIC ORIGIN: DETAILED CHARACTERISTICS...
                   : POPULATION CHARACTERISTICS OF AMERICAN INDIANS BY TRIBE

    U.S.   : CH-2-1#; CH-2-1B; CH-2-1C; CP-2-1#; CP-2-1B; CP-2-1C; CPH-5-1
    REGION/DIV   : CP-2-1; CPH-5-1
    REGION   : CH-2-1#
    DIVISION   : CH-2-1*
    STATE   : CH-2#; CH-2-1*; CP-2#; CPH-5; CPH-5-1
    COUNTY   : CH-2#; CP-2#; CPH-3*; CPH-4; CPH-5
    SUBDIV   : CPH-5
    SELECT SDV   : CH-2#; CP-2#; CPH-4
    PLACE   : CPH-5
    PLC 10+   : CH-2#; CP-2#; CPH-3*; CPH-4
    PLC 2.5-9   : CH-2#; CP-2#
    MSA   : CH-2-1B#; CP-2-1B#; CPH-3*; CPH-5-1; CPH-S-1-1
    URBANIZED   : CH-2-1C#; CP-2-1C#; CPH-5-1
    NATIVE AM   : CH-2; CH-2-1A; CP-2; CP-2-1A*; CPH-4; CPH-5; CPH-5-1
    OUTLYING   : CPH-6
    CONGRS DIS   : CPH-4*
    TRACT   : CPH-3*
  —IN CENTRAL CITY/NOT IN CENTRAL CITY
    U.S.   : CPH-S-1-1
    REGION/DIV   : CPH-S-1-1
    STATE   : CPH-S-1-1
    MSA   : CH-2-1B; CP-2-1B; CPH-S-1-1
  —IN CENTRAL PLACE/URBAN FRINGE
    URBANIZED   : CH-2-1C; CP-2-1C
  —INDIVIDUAL CENTRAL CITY
    MSA   : CP-2-1B
  —INDIVIDUAL CENTRAL PLACE
    URBANIZED   : CP-2-1C

—INSIDE/OUTSIDE MSA
    U.S.   : CH-2-1*; CH-2-1B; CP-2-1*; CP-2-1B; CPH-S-1-1
    REGION/DIV : CPH-S-1-1
    REGION   : CH-2-1*
    STATE   : CH-2*; CP-2*; CPH-S-1-1
—RURAL & RURAL FARM
    COUNTY   : CH-2; CP-2
—URBAN & RURAL & SIZE OF PLACE
    U.S.   : CH-2-1*; CH-2-1C; CP-2-1*; CP-2-1C
    REGION   : CH-2-1*
—URBAN, RURAL, SIZE OF PLACE, FARM
    STATE   : CH-2*; CP-2*
POVERTY STATUS IN 1989 FOR FAMILIES BY SELECTED FAMILY CHARACTERISTICS (BLACKS)
    use .....   : CHARACTERISTICS OF THE BLACK POPULATION
POVERTY STATUS IN 1989 FOR PERSONS 60 YEARS AND OLDER
    U.S.   : CP-2-1#; CP-2-1B; CP-2-1C
    REGION/DIV : CP-2-1
    STATE   : CP-2#
    COUNTY   : CP-2*
    SELECT SDV : CP-2*
    PLC 10+   : CP-2*
    PLC 2.5-9   : CP-2
    MSA   : CP-2-1B*
    URBANIZED   : CP-2-1C*
    NATIVE AM   : CP-2; CP-2-1A*
—IN CENTRAL CITY/NOT IN CENTRAL CITY
    MSA   : CP-2-1B
—IN CENTRAL PLACE/URBAN FRINGE
    URBANIZED   : CP-2-1C
—INDIVIDUAL CENTRAL CITY
    MSA   : CP-2-1B
—INDIVIDUAL CENTRAL PLACE
    URBANIZED   : CP-2-1C
—INSIDE/OUTSIDE MSA
    U.S.   : CP-2-1*; CP-2-1B
    STATE   : CP-2*
—URBAN, RURAL & SIZE OF PLACE
    U.S.   : CP-2-1*; CP-2-1C
—URBAN, RURAL, SIZE OF PLACE, FARM
    STATE   : CP-2*
POVERTY STATUS IN 1989 FOR PERSONS BY SELECTED CHARACTERISTICS (BLACKS)
    U.S.   : CP-3-6
    STATE   : CP-3-6 FOR STATES WITH MORE THAN 900,000 BLACKS
    MSA   : CP-3-6 FOR AREAS WITH MORE THAN 400,000 BLACKS
POVERTY STATUS IN 1989, RATIO TO INCOME
    MSA   : CPH-S-1-1
—IN CENTRAL CITY/NOT IN CENTRAL CITY
    U.S.   : CPH-S-1-1
    REGION/DIV : CPH-S-1-1

RELATIONSHIP TO HOUSEHOLDER
    see also..   : HOUSEHOLD TYPE AND RELATIONSHIP

    U.S.   : CP-1-1#; CP-1-1B; CP-1-1C
    REGION   : CP-1-1#
    DIVISION   : CP-1-1*
    STATE   : CP-1#; CP-1-1*
    COUNTY   : CP-1#
    SELECT SDV : CP-1#
    PLC 10+   : CP-1#
    PLC 2.5-9   : CP-1#
    PLC 1-2.5   : CP-1
    MSA   : CP-1-1B#
    URBANIZED   : CP-1-1C#
    NATIVE AM   : CP-1; CP-1-1A*
 —IN CENTRAL CITY/NOT IN CENTRAL CITY
    MSA   : CP-1-1B
 —IN CENTRAL PLACE/URBAN FRINGE
    URBANIZED : CP-1-1C
 —INSIDE/OUTSIDE MSA
    U.S.   : CP-1-1*; CP-1-1B
    REGION   : CP-1-1*
    STATE   : CP-1*
 —POPULATION SIZE CLASS OF MSA
    U.S.   : CP-1-1B
 —POPULATION SIZE CLASS OF URBANIZED AREA
    U.S.   : CP-1-1C
 —RURAL AREAS
    COUNTY   : CP-1
 —URBAN & RURAL & SIZE OF PLACE
    U.S.   : CP-1-1*; CP-1-1C
    REGION   : CP-1-1*
    STATE   : CP-1*
RELATIONSHIP TO HOUSEHOLDER (PERCENT)
    use .....   : POPULATION: GENERAL SUMMARY CHARACTERISTICS
RELATIONSHIP TO HOUSEHOLDER BY AGE AND SEX
    U.S.   : CP-1-1*
    REGION   : CP-1-1*
    STATE   : CP-1*
RELATIONSHIP TO HOUSEHOLDER FOR SELECTED AGE GROUPS
    U.S.   : CP-1-1#; CP-1-1B; CP-1-1C
    REGION   : CP-1-1#
    DIVISION   : CP-1-1*
    STATE   : CP-1#; CP-1-1*
    COUNTY   : CP-1#
    SELECT SDV : CP-1#
    PLC 10+   : CP-1#
    PLC 2.5-9   : CP-1#

```
        MSA           : CP-1-1B#
        URBANIZED     : CP-1-1C#
        NATIVE AM     : CP-1; CP-1-1A*
—IN CENTRAL CITY/NOT IN CENTRAL CITY
        MSA           : CP-1-1B
—IN CENTRAL PLACE/URBAN FRINGE
        URBANIZED     : CP-1-1C
—INSIDE/OUTSIDE MSA
        U.S.          : CP-1-1*; CP-1-1B
        REGION        : CP-1-1*
        STATE         : CP-1*
—POPULATION SIZE CLASS OF MSA
        U.S.          : CP-1-1B
—POPULATION SIZE CLASS OF URBANIZED AREA
        U.S.          : CP-1-1C
—RURAL AREAS
        COUNTY        : CP-1
—URBAN & RURAL & SIZE OF PLACE
        U.S.          : CP-1-1*; CP-1-1C
        REGION        : CP-1-1*
        STATE         : CP-1*
RELOCATION
    use .....         : RESIDENCE IN 1985
RENT, CONTRACT
    use .....         : CONTRACT RENT
RENT, GROSS
    use .....         : GROSS RENT
RENTAL PROPERTY CHARACTERISTICS BY MORTGAGE CHARACTERISTICS
        U.S.          : CH-4-1
        REGION        : CH-4-1
RESIDENCE IN 1985
    see also..        : POPULATION CHARACTERISTICS OF AMERICAN INDIANS BY TRIBE
                      : YEAR HOUSEHOLDER MOVED INTO UNIT POPULATION

        U.S.          : CP-2-1#; CP-2-1B; CP-2-1C; CPH-5-1
        REGION/DIV    : CP-2-1; CPH-5-1
        STATE         : CP-2#; CPH-5; CPH-5-1
        COUNTY        : CP-2#; CPH-3*; CPH-4; CPH-5
        SUBDIV        : CPH-5
        SELECT SDV    : CP-2#; CPH-4
        PLACE         : CPH-5
        PLC 10+       : CP-2#; CPH-3*; CPH-4
        PLC 2.5-9     : CP-2#
        MSA           : CP-2-1B#; CPH-3*; CPH-5-1; CPH-S-1-1
        URBANIZED     : CP-2-1C#; CPH-5-1
        NATIVE AM     : CP-2
        OUTLYING      : CPH-6
        CONGRS DIS    : CPH-4
        TRACT         : CPH-3*
```

—IN CENTRAL CITY/NOT IN CENTRAL CITY
    U.S. : CPH-S-1-1
    REGION/DIV : CPH-S-1-1
    STATE : CPH-S-1-1
    MSA : CP-2-1B; CPH-S-1-1
—IN CENTRAL PLACE/URBAN FRINGE
    URBANIZED : CP-2-1C
—INDIVIDUAL CENTRAL CITY
    MSA : CP-2-1B
—INDIVIDUAL CENTRAL PLACE
    URBANIZED : CP-2-1C
—INSIDE/OUTSIDE MSA
    U.S. : CP-2-1*; CP-2-1B; CPH-S-1-1
    REGION/DIV : CPH-S-1-1
    STATE : CP-2*; CPH-S-1-1
—RURAL OR RURAL FARM
    COUNTY : CP-2
—URBAN, RURAL & SIZE OF PLACE
    U.S. : CP-2-1*; CP-2-1C
—URBAN, RURAL, SIZE OF PLACE, FARM
    STATE : CP-2*
RESIDENCE IN 1985 (PERCENT)
    use ..... : POPULATION: DETAILED SUMMARY CHARACTERISTICS
RESIDENCE IN 1985 FOR PERSONS 60 YEARS AND OLDER
    NATIVE AM : CP-2-1A*
ROOMS IN HOUSING UNIT
    see also.. : CHARACTERISTICS OF THE BLACK POPULATION
             : HOUSING CHARACTERISTICS OF AMERICAN INDIANS BY TRIBE

    U.S. : CH-1-1#; CH-1-1B*; CH-1-1C*; CPH-1-1
    REGION/DIV : CPH-1-1
    REGION : CH-1-1#
    DIVISION : CH-1-1*
    STATE : CH-1#; CH-1-1*; CPH-1; CPH-1-1
    COUNTY : CH-1#; CPH-1; CPH-3*; CPH-4
    SUBDIV : CH-1; CPH-1
    SELECT SDV : CH-1#; CPH-4
    PLACE : CPH-1
    PLC 50+ : CH-1-1
    PLC 10+ : CH-1#; CPH-3*; CPH-4
    PLC 2.5-9 : CH-1#
    PLC 1-2.5 : CH-1*
    MSA : CH-1-1; CH-1-1B#; CPH-1-1; CPH-3*; CPH-S-1-1
    URBANIZED : CH-1-1; CH-1-1C#; CPH-1-1
    NATIVE AM : CH-1; CH-1-1; CH-1-1A*
    OUTLYING : CPH-6
    CONGRS DIS : CPH-4
    TRACT : CPH-3*

—IN CENTRAL CITY/NOT IN CENTRAL CITY
    U.S.   : CPH-S-1-1
    REGION/DIV : CPH-S-1-1
    STATE   : CPH-S-1-1
    MSA   : CH-1-1B*; CPH-S-1-1
—IN CENTRAL PLACE/URBAN FRINGE
    URBANIZED : CH-1-1C*
—INDIVIDUAL CENTRAL CITY
    MSA   : CH-1-1B
—INDIVIDUAL CENTRAL PLACE
    URBANIZED : CH-1-1C
—INSIDE/OUTSIDE MSA
    U.S.   : CH-1-1*; CH-1-1B*; CPH-S-1-1
    REGION/DIV : CPH-S-1-1
    REGION   : CH-1-1*
    STATE   : CH-1*; CPH-S-1-1
—POPULATION SIZE CLASS OF MSA
    U.S.   : CH-1-1B*
—POPULATION SIZE CLASS OF URBANIZED AREA
    U.S.   : CH-1-1C*
—URBAN & RURAL & SIZE OF PLACE
    U.S.   : CH-1-1*; CH-1-1C*
    REGION   : CH-1-1*
    STATE   : CH-1*
ROOMS IN HOUSING UNIT (MEDIAN)
    use .....   : HOUSING: GENERAL SUMMARY CHARACTERISTICS
ROOMS IN HOUSING UNIT BY STRUCTURAL & FINANCIAL HOUSING CHARACTERISTICS
    use .....   : METROPOLITAN HOUSING CHARACTERISTICS
SCHOOL ENROLLMENT (PERCENT)
    use .....   : POPULATION: DETAILED SUMMARY CHARACTERISTICS
SCHOOL ENROLLMENT AND TYPE OF SCHOOL
    see also..   : ANCESTRY :DETAILED CHARACTERISTICS...
                : ASIANS AND PACIFIC ISLANDERS: DETAILED CHARACTERISTICS...
                : FOREIGN BORN :DETAILED CHARACTERISTICS...
                : HISPANIC ORIGIN: DETAILED CHARACTERISTICS...
                : LABOR FORCE STATUS AND SCHOOL ENROLLMENT
                : POPULATION CHARACTERISTICS OF AMERICAN INDIANS BY TRIBE

    U.S.   : CP-2-1#; CP-2-1B; CP-2-1C; CPH-5-1
    REGION/DIV : CP-2-1; CPH-5-1
    STATE   : CP-2#; CPH-5; CPH-5-1
    COUNTY   : CP-2#; CPH-3*; CPH-5
    SUBDIV   : CPH-5
    SELECT SDV : CP-2#; CPH-4
    PLACE   : CPH-5
    PLC 10+   : CP-2#; CPH-3*; CPH-4
    PLC 2.5-9 : CP-2#
    MSA   : CP-2-1B#; CPH-3*; CPH-5-1; CPH-S-1-1

```
        URBANIZED   : CP-2-1C#; CPH-5-1
        NATIVE AM   : CP-2; CP-2-1A*; CPH-4; CPH-5; CPH-5-1
        OUTLYING    : CPH-6
        CONGRS DIS  : CPH-4*
        TRACT       : CPH-3*
    —IN CENTRAL CITY/NOT IN CENTRAL CITY
        U.S.        : CPH-S-1-1
        REGION/DIV  : CPH-S-1-1
        STATE       : CPH-S-1-1
        MSA         : CP-2-1B; CPH-S-1-1
    —IN CENTRAL PLACE/URBAN FRINGE
        URBANIZED   : CP-2-1C
    —INDIVIDUAL CENTRAL CITY
        MSA         : CP-2-1B
    —INDIVIDUAL CENTRAL PLACE
        URBANIZED   : CP-2-1C
    —INSIDE/OUTSIDE MSA
        U.S.        : CP-2-1*; CP-2-1B; CPH-S-1-1
        REGION/DIV  : CPH-S-1-1
        STATE       : CP-2*; CPH-S-1-1
    —RURAL & RURAL FARM
        COUNTY      : CP-2
    —URBAN, RURAL & SIZE OF PLACE
        U.S.        : CP-2-1*; CP-2-1C
    —URBAN, RURAL, SIZE, OF PLACE, FARM
        STATE       : CP-2*
SCHOOL ENROLLMENT AND TYPE OF SCHOOL BY AGE
        STATE       : CP-3-4
SCHOOL ENROLLMENT AND TYPE OF SCHOOL BY AGE & SEX
        U.S.        : CP-3-4*
SCHOOL ENROLLMENT BY FAMILY TYPE AND EDUCATIONAL ATTAINMENT (BLACKS)
        U.S.        : CP-3-6
        STATE       : CP-3-6 FOR STATES WITH MORE THAN 900,000 BLACKS
        MSA         : CP-3-6 FOR AREAS WITH MORE THAN 400,000 BLACKS
SCHOOL ENROLLMENT BY WORK STATUS (BLACKS)
        U.S.        : CP-3-6
        STATE       : CP-3-6 FOR STATES WITH MORE THAN 900,000 BLACKS
        MSA         : CP-3-6 FOR AREAS WITH MORE THAN 400,000 BLACKS
SECOND MORTGAGE OR HOME EQUITY LOAN
        see also..  : MORTGAGE CHARACTERISTICS

        U.S.        : CH-2-1; CH-2-1B; CH-2-1C
        REGION      : CH-2-1
        STATE       : CH-2
        COUNTY      : CH-2
        SELECT SDV  : CH-2
        PLC 10+     : CH-2
        MSA         : CH-2-1B
        URBANIZED   : CH-2-1C
```

—IN CENTRAL CITY/NOT IN CENTRAL CITY
    MSA   : CH-2-1B
—IN CENTRAL PLACE/URBAN FRINGE
    URBANIZED   : CH-2-1C
—INSIDE/OUTSIDE MSA
    U.S.   : CH-2-1; CH-2-1B
    REGION   : CH-2-1
    STATE   : CH-2
—URBAN & RURAL & SIZE OF PLACE
    U.S.   : CH-2-1; CH-2-1C
    REGION   : CH-2-1
—URBAN, RURAL, SIZE OF PLACE, FARM
    STATE   : CH-2

SECOND MORTGAGE OR HOME EQUITY LOAN BY STRUCTURAL & FINANCIAL HOUSING
CHARACTERISTICS
    use .....   : METROPOLITAN HOUSING CHARACTERISTICS

SELECTED LIVING ARRANGEMENTS
    use .....   : LIVING ARRANGEMENTS, SELECTED

SELECTED MONTHLY OWNER COSTS
    use .....   : MORTGAGE STATUS & SELECTED MONTHLY OWNER COSTS

SEWAGE DISPOSAL
    see also..   : CHARACTERISTICS OF THE BLACK POPULATION
               : HOUSING CHARACTERISTICS OF AMERICAN INDIANS BY TRIBE

    U.S.   : CH-2-1#; CH-2-1B; CH-2-1C; CPH-5-1
    REGION/DIV : CPH-5-1
    REGION   : CH-2-1#
    DIVISION   : CH-2-1*
    STATE   : CH-2#; CH-2-1*; CPH-5; CPH-5-1
    COUNTY   : CH-2#; CPH-3*; CPH-4; CPH-5
    SUBDIV   : CPH-5
    SELECT SDV : CH-2#; CPH-4
    PLACE   : CPH-5
    PLC 10+   : CH-2#; CPH-3*; CPH-4
    PLC 2.5-9   : CH-2#
    MSA   : CH-2-1B#; CPH-3*; CPH-5-1; CPH-S-1-1
    URBANIZED   : CH-2-1C#; CPH-5-1
    NATIVE AM   : CH-2; CH-2-1A
    OUTLYING   : CPH-6
    CONGRS DIS : CPH-4
    TRACT   : CPH-3*
—IN CENTRAL CITY/NOT IN CENTRAL CITY
    U.S.   : CPH-S-1-1
    REGION/DIV : CPH-S-1-1
    STATE   : CPH-S-1-1
    MSA   : CH-2-1B; CPH-S-1-1
—IN CENTRAL PLACE/URBAN FRINGE
    URBANIZED   : CH-2-1C

—INSIDE/OUTSIDE MSA

U.S.	: CH-2-1*; CH-2-1B; CPH-S-1-1
REGION/DIV	: CPH-S-1-1
REGION	: CH-2-1*
STATE	: CH-2*; CPH-S-1-1

—RURAL & RURAL FARM

COUNTY	: CH-2

—URBAN & RURAL & SIZE OF PLACE

U.S.	: CH-2-1*; CH-2-1C
REGION	: CH-2-1*

—URBAN, RURAL, SIZE OF PLACE, FARM

STATE	: CH-2*

SEX

see also..	: POPULATION CHARACTERISTICS OF AMERICAN INDIANS BY TRIBE

U.S.	: CPH-1-1
REGION/DIV	: CPH-1-1
STATE	: CPH-1; CPH-1-1
COUNTY	: CPH-1; CPH-3*; CPH-4
SUBDIV	: CPH-1
SELECT SDV	: CPH-4
PLACE	: CPH-1
PLC 10+	: CPH-3*; CPH-4
MSA	: CPH-1-1; CPH-3*
URBANIZED	: CPH-1-1
NATIVE AM	: CPH-1; CPH-1-1; CPH-4
CONGRS DIS	: CPH-4*
TRACT	: CPH-3*

SEX OF OWNER BY MORTGAGE CHARACTERISTICS

U.S.	: CH-4-1
REGION	: CH-4-1

SOURCE OF WATER

see also..	: CHARACTERISTICS OF THE BLACK POPULATION
	: HOUSING CHARACTERISTICS OF AMERICAN INDIANS BY TRIBE

U.S.	: CH-2-1#; CH-2-1B; CH-2-1C; CPH-5-1
REGION/DIV	: CPH-5-1
REGION	: CH-2-1#
DIVISION	: CH-2-1*
STATE	: CH-2#; CH-2-1*; CPH-5; CPH-5-1
COUNTY	: CH-2#; CPH-3*; CPH-4; CPH-5
SUBDIV	: CPH-5
SELECT SDV	: CH-2#; CPH-4
PLACE	: CPH-5
PLC 10+	: CH-2#; CPH-3*; CPH-4
PLC 2.5-9	: CH-2#
MSA	: CH-2-1B#; CPH-3*; CPH-5-1; CPH-S-1-1
URBANIZED	: CH-2-1C#; CPH-5-1

```
     NATIVE AM    : CH-2; CH-2-1A
     OUTLYING    : CPH-6
     CONGRS DIS  : CPH-4
     TRACT       : CPH-3*
—IN CENTRAL CITY/NOT IN CENTRAL CITY
     U.S.           : CPH-S-1-1
     REGION/DIV  : CPH-S-1-1
     STATE       : CPH-S-1-1
     MSA           : CH-2-1B; CPH-S-1-1
—IN CENTRAL PLACE/URBAN FRINGE
     URBANIZED   : CH-2-1C
—INSIDE/OUTSIDE MSA
     U.S.           : CH-2-1*; CH-2-1B; CPH-S-1-1
     REGION/DIV  : CPH-S-1-1
     REGION       : CH-2-1*
     STATE       : CH-2*; CPH-S-1-1
  —RURAL & RURAL FARM
     COUNTY       : CH-2
—URBAN & RURAL & SIZE OF PLACE
     U.S.           : CH-2-1*; CH-2-1C
     REGION       : CH-2-1*
—URBAN, RURAL, SIZE OF PLACE, FARM
     STATE       : CH-2*
SUBDIVISIONS
     use .....       : NUMBER OF COUNTY SUBDIVISIONS AND TYPE OF SUBDIVISION
TELEPHONE IN UNIT
     see also..      : CHARACTERISTICS OF THE BLACK POPULATION

     U.S.           : CH-2-1; CH-2-1B; CH-2-1C; CPH-5-1
     REGION/DIV  : CPH-5-1
     REGION       : CH-2-1
     STATE       : CH-2; CPH-5; CPH-5-1
     COUNTY       : CH-2; CPH-3*; CPH-4; CPH-5
     SUBDIV       : CPH-5
     SELECT SDV  : CH-2; CPH-4
     PLACE        : CPH-5
     PLC 10+      : CH-2; CPH-3*; CPH-4
     MSA           : CH-2-1B; CPH-3*; CPH-5-1
     URBANIZED   : CH-2-1C; CPH-5-1
     CONGRS DIS  : CPH-4
     TRACT       : CPH-3*
—IN CENTRAL CITY/NOT IN CENTRAL CITY
     MSA           : CH-2-1B
—IN CENTRAL PLACE/URBAN FRINGE
     URBANIZED   : CH-2-1C
—INSIDE/OUTSIDE MSA
     U.S.           : CH-2-1; CH-2-1B
     REGION       : CH-2-1
     STATE       : CH-2
```

—URBAN & RURAL & SIZE OF PLACE
  U.S.   : CH-2-1; CH-2-1C
  REGION : CH-2-1
—URBAN, RURAL, SIZE OF PLACE, FARM
  STATE   : CH-2
TELEPHONE IN UNIT (PERCENT)
  use .....   : HOUSING: DETAILED SUMMARY CHARACTERISTICS
TELEPHONE IN UNIT BY HOUSEHOLD COMPOSITION BY AGE OF HOUSEHOLDER FOR OWNER/
RENTER
  use .....   : METROPOLITAN HOUSING CHARACTERISTICS
TELEPHONE IN UNIT BY STRUCTURAL & FINANCIAL HOUSING CHARACTERISTICS
  use .....   : METROPOLITAN HOUSING CHARACTERISTICS
TELEPHONE, TELEVISION, OR RADIO
  OUTLYING : CPH-6
TENURE
  U.S.   : CH-1-1#; CH-1-1B; CH-1-1C; CH-2-1#; CH-2-1B; CH-2-1C; CPH-1-1; CPH-5-1
  REGION/DIV : CPH-1-1; CPH-5-1
  REGION : CH-1-1#; CH-2-1#
  DIVISION : CH-1-1*; CH-2-1*
  STATE   : CH-1#; CH-1-1*; CH-2#; CH-2-1*; CPH-1; CPH-1-1
       : CPH-5; CPH-5-1
  COUNTY : CH-1#; CH-2#; CPH-1; CPH-3*; CPH-4; CPH-5
  SUBDIV : CPH-1; CPH-5
  SELECT SDV : CH-1#; CH-2#; CPH-4
  PLACE   : CPH-1; CPH-5
  PLC 10+ : CH-1#; CH-2#; CPH-3*; CPH-4
  PLC 2.5-9 : CH-1; CH-2#
  PLC 1-2.5 : CH-1
  MSA   : CH-1-1B#; CH-2-1B#; CPH-1-1; CPH-3*; CPH-5-1; CPH-S-1-1
  URBANIZED : CH-1-1C#; CH-2-1C#; CPH-1-1; CPH-5-1
  NATIVE AM : CH-1-1A*; CH-2; CH-2-1A; CPH-1; CPH-1-1; CPH-4; CPH-5; CPH-5-1
  OUTLYING : CPH-6
  CONGRS DIS : CPH-4; CPH-4*; CPH-4*
  TRACT   : CPH-3*
—IN CENTRAL CITY/NOT IN CENTRAL CITY
  U.S.   : CPH-S-1-1
  REGION/DIV : CPH-S-1-1
  STATE   : CPH-S-1-1
  MSA   : CH-1-1B; CH-2-1B; CPH-S-1-1
—IN CENTRAL PLACE/URBAN FRINGE
  URBANIZED : CH-1-1C; CH-2-1C
—INSIDE/OUTSIDE MSA
  U.S.   : CH-1-1*; CH-1-1B; CH-2-1*; CH-2-1B; CPH-S-1-1
  REGION/DIV : CPH-S-1-1
  REGION : CH-1-1*; CH-2-1*
  STATE   : CH-1*; CH-2*; CPH-S-1-1
—POPULATION SIZE CLASS OF MSA
  U.S.   : CH-1-1B

—POPULATION SIZE CLASS OF URBANIZED AREA
    U.S.   : CH-1-1C
—RURAL & RURAL FARM
    COUNTY   : CH-2*
—URBAN & RURAL & SIZE OF PLACE
    U.S.   : CH-1-1*; CH-1-1C; CH-2-1*; CH-2-1C
    REGION   : CH-1-1*; CH-2-1*
    STATE   : CH-1*
—URBAN, RURAL, SIZE OF PLACE, FARM
    STATE   : CH-2*
TENURE BY SELECTED CHARACTERISTICS (BLACKS)
    U.S.   : CP-3-6
    STATE   : CP-3-6 FOR STATES WITH MORE THAN 900,000 BLACKS
    MSA   : CP-3-6 FOR AREAS WITH MORE THAN 400,000 BLACKS
TRACTS
    use .....   : NUMBER OF CENSUS TRACTS AND BLOCK NUMBERING AREAS
TRAVEL TIME TO WORK BY YEAR HOUSEHOLDER MOVED INTO UNIT
    use .....   : METROPOLITAN HOUSING CHARACTERISTICS
TRAVEL TO WORK
    use .....   : JOURNEY TO WORK
TYPE OF CONSTRUCTION
    OUTLYING   : CPH-6
UNEMPLOYMENT STATUS
    use .....   : LABOR FORCE STATUS
UNITS IN STRUCTURE
    see also..   : ANCESTRY: DETAILED CHARACTERISTICS...
                : ASIANS AND PACIFIC ISLANDERS: DETAILED CHARACTERISTICS...
                : CHARACTERISTICS OF THE BLACK POPULATION
                : FOREIGN BORN: DETAILED CHARACTERISTICS...
                : HISPANIC ORIGIN: DETAILED CHARACTERISTICS...
                : HOUSING CHARACTERISTICS OF AMERICAN INDIANS BY TRIBE

    U.S.   : CH-1-1#; CH-1-1B*; CH-1-1C*; CPH-1-1
    REGION/DIV :   CPH-1-1
    REGION   : CH-1-1#
    DIVISION   : CH-1-1*
    STATE   : CH-1#; CH-1-1*; CPH-1; CPH-1-1
    COUNTY   : CH-1#; CPH-1; CPH-3*; CPH-4
    SUBDIV   : CH-1; CPH-1
    SELECT SDV : CH-1#; CPH-4
    PLACE   : CPH-1
    PLC 50+   : CH-1-1
    PLC 10+   : CH-1#; CPH-3*; CPH-4
    PLC 2.5-9   : CH-1#
    PLC 1-2.5   : CH-1*
    MSA   : CH-1-1; CH-1-1B#; CPH-1-1; CPH-3*; CPH-S-1-1
    URBANIZED : CH-1-1; CH-1-1C#; CPH-1-1
    NATIVE AM   : CH-1; CH-1-1; CH-1-1A*

```
        OUTLYING     : CPH-6
        CONGRS DIS   : CPH-4
        TRACT        : CPH-3*
—IN CENTRAL CITY/NOT IN CENTRAL CITY
        U.S.         : CPH-S-1-1
        REGION/DIV   : CPH-S-1-1
        STATE        : CPH-S-1-1
        MSA          : CH-1-1B*; CPH-S-1-1
—IN CENTRAL PLACE/URBAN FRINGE
        URBANIZED    : CH-1-1C*
—INDIVIDUAL CENTRAL CITY
        MSA          : CH-1-1B
—INDIVIDUAL CENTRAL PLACE
        URBANIZED    : CH-1-1C
—INSIDE/OUTSIDE MSA
        U.S.         : CH-1-1*; CH-1-1B*; CPH-S-1-1
        REGION/DIV   : CPH-S-1-1
        REGION       : CH-1-1*
        STATE        : CH-1*; CPH-S-1-1
—POPULATION SIZE CLASS OF MSA
        U.S.         : CH-1-1B*
—POPULATION SIZE CLASS OF URBANIZED AREA
        U.S.         : CH-1-1C*
—URBAN & RURAL & SIZE OF PLACE
        U.S.         : CH-1-1*; CH-1-1C*
        REGION       : CH-1-1*
        STATE        : CH-1*
```

UNITS IN STRUCTURE (PERCENT)
    use .....   : HOUSING: GENERAL SUMMARY CHARACTERISTICS

UNITS IN STRUCTURE BY HOUSEHOLD COMPOSITION BY AGE OF HOUSEHOLDER FOR OWNER/RENTER
    use .....   : METROPOLITAN HOUSING CHARACTERISTICS

UNITS IN STRUCTURE BY STRUCTURAL & FINANCIAL HOUSING CHARACTERISTICS
    use .....   : METROPOLITAN HOUSING CHARACTERISTICS

UNMARRIED PARTNER HOUSEHOLDS
```
        see also..   : ANCESTRY: DETAILED CHARACTERISTICS
                     : ASIANS AND PACIFIC ISLANDERS: DETAILED CHARACTERISTICS...
                     : FOREIGN BORN: DETAILED CHARACTERISTICS...
                     : HISPANIC ORIGIN: DETAILED CHARACTERISTICS...
                     : HOUSEHOLD TYPE AND RELATIONSHIP
                     : POPULATION CHARACTERISTICS OF AMERICAN INDIANS BY TRIBE


        U.S.         : CP-2-1#; CP-2-1B; CP-2-1C
        REGION/DIV   : CP-2-1
        STATE        : CP-2#
        COUNTY       : CP-2*
        SELECT SDV   : CP-2*
        PLC 10+      : CP-2*
```

```
     SELECT SDV    : CH-1
     PLC 50+       : CH-1-1
     PLC 10+       : CH-1
     PLC 2.5-9     : CH-1
     PLC 1-2.5     : CH-1
     MSA           : CH-1-1; CH-1-1B
     URBANIZED     : CH-1-1; CH-1-1C
—IN CENTRAL CITY/NOT IN CENTRAL CITY
     MSA           : CH-1-1B
—IN CENTRAL PLACE/URBAN FRINGE
     URBANIZED     : CH-1-1C
—INDIVIDUAL CENTRAL CITY
     MSA           : CH-1-1B
—INDIVIDUAL CENTRAL PLACE
     URBANIZED     : CH-1-1C
—INSIDE/OUTSIDE MSA
     U.S.          : CH-1-1; CH-1-1B
     REGION        : CH-1-1
     STATE         : CH-1
—POPULATION SIZE CLASS OF MSA
     U.S.          : CH-1-1B
—POPULATION SIZE CLASS OF URBANIZED AREA
     U.S.          : CH-1-1C
—URBAN & RURAL & SIZE OF PLACE
     U.S.          : CH-1-1; CH-1-1C
     REGION        : CH-1-1
     STATE         : CH-1
VACANCY STATUS
     U.S.          : CH-1-1; CH-1-1B; CH-1-1C; CH-2-1; CH-2-1B; CH-2-1C
     REGION        : CH-1-1; CH-2-1
     STATE         : CH-1; CH-2
     COUNTY        : CH-1; CH-2
     SELECT SDV    : CH-1; CH-2
     PLC 10+       : CH-1; CH-2
     PLC 2.5-9     : CH-1
     MSA           : CH-1-1B; CH-2-1B; CPH-S-1-1
     URBANIZED     : CH-1-1C; CH-2-1C
     OUTLYING      : CPH-6
—IN CENTRAL CITY/NOT IN CENTRAL CITY
     U.S.          : CPH-S-1-1
     REGION/DIV    : CPH-S-1-1
     STATE         : CPH-S-1-1
     MSA           : CH-1-1B; CH-2-1B; CPH-S-1-1
—IN CENTRAL PLACE/URBAN FRINGE
     URBANIZED     : CH-1-1C; CH-2-1C
—INSIDE/OUTSIDE MSA
     U.S.          : CH-1-1; CH-1-1B; CH-2-1; CH-2-1B; CPH-S-1-1
     REGION/DIV    : CPH-S-1-1
     REGION        : CH-1-1; CH-2-1
     STATE         : CH-1; CH-2; CPH-S-1-1
```

—POPULATION SIZE CLASS OF MSA
    U.S.   : CH-1-1B
—POPULATION SIZE CLASS OF URBANIZED AREA
    U.S.   : CH-1-1C
—RURAL & RURAL FARM
    COUNTY   : CH-2
—URBAN & RURAL & SIZE OF PLACE
    U.S.   : CH-1-1; CH-1-1C; CH-2-1; CH-2-1C
    REGION   : CH-1-1; CH-2-1
    STATE   : CH-1
—URBAN, RURAL, SIZE OF PLACE, FARM
    STATE   : CH-2
VALUE OF HOUSING UNIT
    see also..   : PURCHASE PRICE FOR HOUSING UNIT

    U.S.   : CH-1-1#; CH-1-1B*; CH-1-1C*; CPH-1-1
    REGION/DIV : CPH-1-1
    REGION   : CH-1-1#
    DIVISION   : CH-1-1*
    STATE   : CH-1#; CH-1-1*; CPH-1; CPH-1-1
    COUNTY   : CH-1#; CPH-1; CPH-3*; CPH-4
    SUBDIV   : CH-1; CPH-1
    SELECT SDV : CH-1#; CPH-4
    PLACE   : CPH-1
    PLC 50+   : CH-1-1
    PLC 10+   : CH-1#; CPH-3*; CPH-4
    PLC 2.5-9 : CH-1#
    PLC 1-2.5 : CH-1*
    MSA   : CH-1-1; CH-1-1B#; CPH-1-1; CPH-3*; CPH-S-1-1
    URBANIZED : CH-1-1; CH-1-1C#; CPH-1-1
    NATIVE AM : CH-1; CH-1-1; CH-1-1A*; CPH-1; CPH-1-1; CPH-4
    OUTLYING   : CPH-6
    CONGRS DIS : CPH-4
    TRACT   : CPH-3*
—IN CENTRAL CITY/NOT IN CENTRAL CITY
    U.S.   : CPH-S-1-1
    REGION/DIV : CPH-S-1-1
    STATE   : CPH-S-1-1
    MSA   : CH-1-1B*; CPH-S-1-1
—IN CENTRAL PLACE/URBAN FRINGE
    URBANIZED : CH-1-1C*
—INDIVIDUAL CENTRAL CITY
    MSA   : CH-1-1B
—INDIVIDUAL CENTRAL PLACE
    URBANIZED : CH-1-1C
—INSIDE/OUTSIDE MSA
    U.S.   : CH-1-1*; CH-1-1B*; CPH-S-1-1
    REGION/DIV : CPH-S-1-1
    REGION   : CH-1-1*
    STATE   : CH-1*; CPH-S-1-1

—POPULATION CLASS OF URBANIZED AREA
    U.S.   : CH-1-1C*
—POPULATION SIZE CLASS OF MSA
    U.S.   : CH-1-1B*
—URBAN & RURAL & SIZE OF PLACE
    U.S.   : CH-1-1*; CH-1-1C*
    REGION   : CH-1-1*
    STATE   : CH-1*
VALUE OF HOUSING UNIT (MEDIAN)
    use .....   : HOUSING: GENERAL SUMMARY CHARACTERISTICS
VALUE OF HOUSING UNIT BY MORTGAGE CHARACTERISTICS
    U.S.   : CH-4-1
    REGION   : CH-4-1
VALUE OF HOUSING UNIT BY SELECTED HOUSEHOLD CHARACTERISTICS (BLACKS)
    use .....   : CHARACTERISTICS OF THE BLACK POPULATION
VALUE OF HOUSING UNIT BY YEAR HOUSEHOLDER MOVED INTO UNIT
    use .....   : METROPOLITAN HOUSING CHARACTERISTICS
VEHICLES AVAILABLE
    see also..   : CHARACTERISTICS OF THE BLACK POPULATION
                    : HOUSING CHARACTERISTICS OF AMERICAN INDIANS BY TRIBE

    U.S.   : CH-2-1#; CH-2-1B; CH-2-1C; CPH-5-1
    REGION/DIV   : CPH-5-1
    REGION   : CH-2-1#
    DIVISION   : CH-2-1*
    STATE   : CH-2#; CH-2-1*; CPH-5; CPH-5-1
    COUNTY   : CH-2#; CPH-3*; CPH-4; CPH-5
    SUBDIV   : CPH-5
    SELECT SDV   : CH-2#; CPH-4
    PLACE   : CPH-5
    PLC 10+   : CH-2#; CPH-3*; CPH-4
    PLC 2.5-9   : CH-2#
    MSA   : CH-2-1B#; CPH-3*; CPH-5-1; CPH-S-1-1
    URBANIZED   : CH-2-1C#; CPH-5-1
    NATIVE AM   : CH-2; CH-2-1A; CPH-4; CPH-5; CPH-5-1
    OUTLYING   : CPH-6
    CONGRS DIS   : CPH-4; CPH-4*
    TRACT   : CPH-3*
—IN CENTRAL CITY/NOT IN CENTRAL CITY
    U.S.   : CPH-S-1-1
    REGION/DIV   : CPH-S-1-1
    STATE   : CPH-S-1-1
    MSA   : CH-2-1B; CPH-S-1-1
—IN CENTRAL PLACE/URBAN FRINGE
    URBANIZED   : CH-2-1C
—INSIDE/OUTSIDE MSA
    U.S.   : CH-2-1*; CH-2-1B; CPH-S-1-1
    REGION/DIV   : CPH-S-1-1
    REGION   : CH-2-1*
    STATE   : CH-2*; CPH-S-1-1

—URBAN, RURAL, SIZE OF PLACE, FARM
    STATE   : CP-2*
VETERAN STATUS FOR PERSONS 60 YEARS AND OLDER
    NATIVE AM   : CP-2-1A*
VETERAN STATUS OF OWNER BY MORTGAGE CHARACTERISTICS
    U.S.   : CH-4-1
    REGION   : CH-4-1
VOCATIONAL TRAINING
    OUTLYING   : CPH-6
VOTING AGE PERSONS
    COUNTY   : CPH-4
    SELECT SDV : CPH-4
    PLC 10+   : CPH-4
    NATIVE AM   : CPH-4
    CONGRS DIS : CPH-4*
WATER
    use .....   : SOURCE OF WATER
WATER AREA
    U.S.   : CPH-2-1
    REGION/DIV : CPH-2-1
    STATE   : CPH-2-1
    OUTLYING   : CPH-2-1
WEEKS WORKED IN 1989
    U.S.   : CPH-5-1
    REGION/DIV : CPH-5-1
    STATE   : CPH-5; CPH-5-1
    COUNTY   : CPH-4; CPH-5
    SUBDIV   : CPH-5
    SELECT SDV : CPH-4
    PLACE   : CPH-5
    PLC 10+   : CPH-4
    MSA   : CPH-5-1
    URBANIZED : CPH-5-1
    CONGRS DIS : CPH-4
WORK STATUS IN 1989
    see also..   : HOURS WORKED PER WEEK IN 1989
                 : LABOR FORCE STATUS
                 : POPULATION CHARACTERISTICS OF AMERICAN INDIANS BY TRIBE
                 : WEEKS WORKED IN 1989

    U.S.   : CP-2-1#; CP-2-1B; CP-2-1C
    REGION/DIV : CP-2-1
    STATE   : CP-2#
    COUNTY   : CP-2#; CPH-3*
    SELECT SDV : CP-2#
    PLC 10+   : CP-2#; CPH-3*
    PLC 2.5-9   : CP-2#
    MSA   : CP-2-1B#; CPH-3*; CPH-S-1-1

—IN CENTRAL CITY/NOT IN CENTRAL CITY
    U.S.   : CPH-S-1-1
    REGION/DIV : CPH-S-1-1
    STATE   : CPH-S-1-1
    MSA   : CP-2-1B; CPH-S-1-1
—IN CENTRAL PLACE/URBAN FRINGE
    URBANIZED   : CP-2-1C
—INDIVIDUAL CENTRAL CITY
    MSA   : CP-2-1B
—INDIVIDUAL CENTRAL PLACE
    URBANIZED   : CP-2-1C
—INSIDE/OUTSIDE MSA
    U.S.   : CP-2-1*; CP-2-1B; CPH-S-1-1
    REGION/DIV : CPH-S-1-1
    STATE   : CP-2*; CPH-S-1-1
—RURAL OR RURAL FARM
    COUNTY   : CP-2
—URBAN, RURAL & SIZE OF PLACE
    U.S.   : CP-2-1*; CP-2-1C
—URBAN, RURAL, SIZE OF PLACE, FARM
    STATE   : CP-2*
WORKERS IN HOUSEHOLDS IN 1989 BY YEAR HOUSEHOLDER MOVED INTO UNIT BY OWNER/ RENTER
    use .....   : METROPOLITAN HOUSING CHARACTERISTICS
YEAR HOUSEHOLDER MOVED INTO UNIT
    see also..   : ANCESTRY: DETAILED CHARACTERISTICS...
                  : ASIANS AND PACIFIC ISLANDERS: DETAILED CHARACTERISTICS...
                  : CHARACTERISTICS OF THE BLACK POPULATION
                  : FOREIGN BORN: DETAILED CHARACTERISTICS...
                  : HISPANIC ORIGIN: DETAILED CHARACTERISTICS...
                  : HOUSING CHARACTERISTICS OF AMERICAN INDIANS BY TRIBE
                  : RESIDENCE IN 1985

    U.S.   : CH-2-1#; CH-2-1B; CH-2-1C; CPH-5-1
    REGION/DIV : CPH-5-1
    REGION   : CH-2-1#
    DIVISION   : CH-2-1*
    STATE   : CH-2#; CH-2-1*; CPH-5; CPH-5-1
    COUNTY   : CH-2#; CPH-3*; CPH-4; CPH-5
    SUBDIV   : CPH-5
    SELECT SDV : CH-2#; CPH-4
    PLACE   : CPH-5
    PLC 10+   : CH-2#; CPH-3*; CPH-4
    PLC 2.5-9   : CH-2#
    MSA   : CH-2-1B#; CPH-3*; CPH-5-1; CPH-S-1-1
    URBANIZED   : CH-2-1C#; CPH-5-1
    NATIVE AM   : CH-2; CH-2-1A
    OUTLYING   : CPH-6
    CONGRS DIS : CPH-4
    TRACT   : CPH-3*

—IN CENTRAL CITY/NOT IN CENTRAL CITY
    U.S.   : CPH-S-1-1
    REGION/DIV : CPH-S-1-1
    STATE   : CPH-S-1-1
    MSA   : CH-2-1B; CPH-S-1-1
—IN CENTRAL PLACE/URBAN FRINGE
    URBANIZED   : CH-2-1C
—INSIDE/OUTSIDE MSA
    U.S.   : CH-2-1*; CH-2-1B; CPH-S-1-1
    REGION/DIV : CPH-S-1-1
    REGION   : CH-2-1*
    STATE   : CH-2*; CPH-S-1-1
—RURAL & RURAL FARM
    COUNTY   : CH-2
—URBAN & RURAL & SIZE OF PLACE
    U.S.   : CH-2-1*; CH-2-1C
    REGION   : CH-2-1*
—URBAN, RURAL, SIZE OF PLACE, FARM
    STATE   : CH-2*
YEAR HOUSEHOLDER MOVED INTO UNIT (PERCENT)
    use .....   : HOUSING: DETAILED SUMMARY CHARACTERISTICS
YEAR HOUSEHOLDER MOVED INTO UNIT BY HOUSEHOLD COMPOSITION BY AGE OF HOUSE-
HOLDER FOR OWNER/RENTER
    use .....   : METROPOLITAN HOUSING CHARACTERISTICS
YEAR HOUSEHOLDER MOVED INTO UNIT BY STRUCTURAL & FINANCIAL HOUSING CHARAC-
TERISTICS
    use .....   : METROPOLITAN HOUSING CHARACTERISTICS
YEAR OF ENTRY
    MSA   : CPH-S-1-1
—IN CENTRAL CITY/NOT IN CENTRAL CITY
    U.S.   : CPH-S-1-1
    REGION/DIV : CPH-S-1-1
    STATE   : CPH-S-1-1
    MSA   : CPH-S-1-1
—INSIDE/OUTSIDE MSA
    U.S.   : CPH-S-1-1
    REGION/DIV : CPH-S-1-1
    STATE   : CPH-S-1-1
YEAR OF ENTRY TO AREA
    OUTLYING   : CPH-6
YEAR OF ENTRY, AREA OF BIRTH FOR FOREIGN BORN
    U.S.   : CP-2-1; CP-2-1B; CP-2-1C
    REGION/DIV : CP-2-1
    STATE   : CP-2
    COUNTY   : CP-2
    SELECT SDV : CP-2
    PLC 10+   : CP-2
    PLC 2.5-9   : CP-2
    MSA   : CP-2-1B
    URBANIZED   : CP-2-1C

—IN CENTRAL CITY/NOT IN CENTRAL CITY
  MSA   : CP-2-1B
—IN CENTRAL PLACE/URBAN FRINGE
  URBANIZED : CP-2-1C
—INDIVIDUAL CENTRAL CITY
  MSA   : CP-2-1B
—INDIVIDUAL CENTRAL PLACE
  URBANIZED : CP-2-1C
—INSIDE/OUTSIDE MSA
  U.S.   : CP-2-1; CP-2-1B
  STATE   : CP-2
—URBAN, RURAL & SIZE OF PLACE
  U.S.   : CP-2-1; CP-2-1C
—URBAN, RURAL, SIZE OF PLACE, FARM
  STATE   : CP-2
YEAR PROPERTY ACQUIRED BY MORTGAGE CHARACTERISTICS
  U.S.   : CH-4-1
  REGION   : CH-4-1
YEAR STRUCTURE BUILT
  see also..   : CHARACTERISTICS OF THE BLACK POPULATION
         : HOUSING CHARACTERISTICS OF AMERICAN INDIANS BY TRIBE

  U.S.   : CH-2-1#; CH-2-1B; CH-2-1C; CPH-5-1
  REGION/DIV : CPH-5-1
  REGION   : CH-2-1#
  DIVISION : CH-2-1*
  STATE   : CH-2#; CH-2-1*; CPH-5; CPH-5-1
  COUNTY   : CH-2#; CPH-3*; CPH-4; CPH-5
  SUBDIV   : CPH-5
  SELECT SDV : CH-2#; CPH-4
  PLACE   : CPH-5
  PLC 10+   : CH-2#; CPH-3*; CPH-4
  PLC 2.5-9 : CH-2#
  MSA   : CH-2-1B#; CPH-3*; CPH-5-1; CPH-S-1-1
  URBANIZED : CH-2-1C#; CPH-5-1
  NATIVE AM : CH-2; CH-2-1A
  OUTLYING : CPH-6
  CONGRS DIS : CPH-4
  TRACT   : CPH-3*
—IN CENTRAL CITY/NOT IN CENTRAL CITY
  U.S.   : CPH-S-1-1
  REGION/DIV : CPH-S-1-1
  STATE   : CPH-S-1-1
  MSA   : CH-2-1B; CPH-S-1-1
—IN CENTRAL PLACE/URBAN FRINGE
  URBANIZED : CH-2-1C
—INSIDE/OUTSIDE MSA
  U.S.   : CH-2-1*; CH-2-1B; CPH-S-1-1
  REGION/DIV : CPH-S-1-1

Part II:

Table-Finding Guide to *STF 1* and *STF 3* on CD-ROM

Compiled by Michael Lavin and Cynthia Cornelius

Part II
Section 1

How to Use Part II

How to Use Part Two: Indexes to Major CD-ROM Products

Coverage

PART II OF the *Subject Index to the 1990 Census* provides a series of reference tools created to help Census users locate needed data on the Census Bureau's major 1990 CD-ROM products. These CD-ROM publications are called Summary Tape Files, and they appear as two main series: *STF 1*, containing "complete-count" data from every 1990 Census Questionnaire received by the Bureau; and *STF 3*, containing sample data taken from the Long-Form Questionnaires only. Approximately 17% of the U.S. population received a Long-Form. In other words, *STF 1* reports the results of the actual Census enumeration, while *STF 3* represents estimates taken from the decennial sample survey. *STF 3* is much more detailed, however. It contains 262 tables, compared with the 92 found in *STF 1*.

The following specialized 1990 Summary File CD-ROM products have been excluded from the indexes in Part II: the *Equal Employment Opportunity File* (*EEO*); the *County-to-County Migration Files*; the *Comprehensive Housing Affordability Strategy*; the *Special Tabulation on Aging* (also called the *AOA* files), and the 21 titles in the *Subject Summary Tape File* series (*SSTF*s). These were excluded because the subject coverage of each product is narrowly defined (as with the *EEO* and *County Migration* files), or because the extensive amount of cross-tabulation made it too difficult to incorporate into the structure of a detailed subject index (as with the *SSTF* and *AOA* files). In any event, *STF 1* and *STF 3* are the most heavily used CD-ROM products from the 1990 Census.

Organization

Part II consists of several sections, each of which provides a different type of guide to the CD-ROM products:

▶ a list of 1990 Census CD-ROM products
▶ a guide to the geographic levels covered by the *STF* subfiles
▶ a detailed subject index to *STF 1* and *STF 3*
▶ a numerical list of tables appearing in *STF 1* and *STF 3*
▶ and a guide to the special Universes (domains) to which individual *STF* tables are limited.

The latter guide can be helpful in reminding users that many tables appearing in *STF 1* and *STF 3* are limited to a particular subgroup of the total population, such as Hispanic Households, or Persons Age 16-19.

Indexing Methodology

The main feature of Part II is found in Section 4, the alphabetical index to subjects covered by *STF 1* and *STF 3*. The subject index incorporates nearly 1,500 index terms, plus an additional 500 cross-references to guide users to proper Census terminology or to related concepts. The intent was to provide extremely detailed access to the *Summary Tape Files*. In addition to indexing the topic of each table, individual tabulation categories have been indexed, where appropriate. For example, only two tables provide information on the number of step-children in the United States, but the information is "hidden" under the broader table name of "Household Type and Relationship." The subject index lists "Step- Children" as well as the broader category of "Household Relationship."

Each table is represented by an average of five index entries. Extremely detailed tables may have 20 or more entries in the subject index.

The subject index provides a dual approach to the topics covered. Specific topics appear in the index alphabetically under the name of the topic itself, but they also appear as subtopics under the broader concepts to which they relate. For example, "Place of Work" and "Travel Time to Work" each receive individual index entries, but they also appear as subtopics under the broader subject of "Commuting." In this way, users can quickly locate a needed topic, but they can also see how similar topics are related to one another.

Great care has been taken to distinguish between subtle differences in the types of data being reported in similar tables. For example, statistics about income appear in numerous *STF 3* tables. Some tabulate Household Income, others tabulate Family Income, and a few report Personal (Individual) Income. The subject index utilizes separate headings for each income concept. Furthermore, most income tables show frequency distributions for various dollar ranges of income, but others sum the total of all incomes for every person, family, or household in the geographic area. The latter tables are shown in the index under separate entries -- "Household Income (Aggregate)," for example.

A more subtle distinction involves determining who or what is actually being counted in the table. Many tables provide information about children. Some count the children themselves, while others count the number of households where children are present. Similarly, many tables provide information about the racial characteris-

tics of individuals, while others focus on the race of the Householder only. To avoid confusion, the subject index uses phrases such as "Children Present in Household," and "Race of Householder," to differentiate them from basic tables about "Children" or "Race."

Indexing for *STF 1* and *STF 3* appear together in a single alphabet. This saves the user from trying to guess which file a topic appears in. It also allows the user to see at a glance which topics are covered in both files. In this way, users can turn to *STF 1* for complete-count tabulations before examining the estimates shown in *STF 3*.

Tips on Locating Census Data on CD-ROM

STF 1 and *STF 3* are each divided into four subfiles, designated by the suffixes A through D. Table numbering for all subfiles in *STF 3* are identical. For example, Table H23 reports "Source of Water" for Housing Units. The table structure for H23 is exactly the same in *STF 3A*, *STF 3B*, *STF 3C*, and *STF 3D*. The difference among the subfiles lies in the type of geography covered by each. For example, *STF 3D* focuses on Congressional Districts, while *STF 3B* covers Zip Code Areas. A comparative guide to the geographic coverage of the various subfiles can be seen in Part II, Section 3 of this book.

The topics covered in *STF 1* differ from those of *STF 3*, but the geographic coverage of the subfiles are similar. *STF 1A* and *STF 3A* both focus on Census Tracts and Block Groups, for example. As noted above, Table H23 in *STF 3* deals the Source of Water in Housing Units. Table 23 in *STF 1* reports "Value of Specified Owner Occupied Housing Units."

STF 1B offers the only exception to the above-mentioned pattern of table numbering. STF 1A, STF 1C, and STF 1D each contain the same 92 tables. In contrast, *STF 1B* contains a single table which summarizes a variety of key population and housing measures. The table is repeated approximately six million times, once for each Census Block in the United States.

Population tables are always preceded by the letter P (e.g., Table P1, Table P35). Housing tables are designated with an H prefix (Table H2, Table H56).

Follow these simple steps to locate needed information from the 1990 Census *Summary Tape Files*.

1. Consult the subject index to determine whether the needed data are reported in *STF 1* or *STF 3*.

2. If the same topic is found in both *Summary Tape Files*, use the complete-count data from *STF 1*, unless you are calculating percentages for other topics found in *STF 3*.

3. Consult the guide shown in Part II, Section 3 of the *Subject Index* to determine which subfile focuses on the type of geography you want to analyze. For example, *STF 1C* provides data for the nation and for each of the 50 states; *STF 1A* provides the same data, but for Census Tracts and Block Groups.

How to Read the Subject Index

Within each subject entry in Part II, Section 4, information for *STF 1* and *STF 3* are shown on separate lines. In some cases, a third line is shown, indicating the single table unique to *STF 1B*.

The designation "GenProfile" indicates one of the unnumbered General Profile tables which appear at the beginning of every file. *STF 1* contains a single General Profile, while *STF 3* contains four separate Profiles for each geographic entity. The designation "Geographic Identifiers" refers to the other unnumbered table found at the beginning of every file. The index identifies all other tables by their table numbers (e.g., P33, H51).

The following examples show how to interpret the entries found in the subject index.

Age 65 or Older (Persons)
    Distribution (by Age Group)
        STF1: P11
        STF3: P13
    in Single-Person Households
        STF1: GenProfile, P23, P25
        STF3: P18
    Total Persons
        STF1: GenProfile
        STF1B
        STF3: GenProfile3
    x Veteran Status
        STF3: GenProfile2

The number of persons age 65 or older who live alone (i.e., in single-person households), can be found in four different tables--three in *STF 1* and one in *STF 3*. The relevant information in *STF 1* can be located in the unnumbered General Profile table, as well as Tables P23 and P25. Sample data on the number of senior citizens

living alone are located in Table P18 of *STF 3*.

To take a second example, the total number of persons age 65 or older can be located in three tables: the unnumbered General Profile in *STF 1*, the single unique table in *STF 1B*, and the third unnumbered Profile Table in *STF 3*. A breakdown (distribution) of the elderly population by age group (in five-year age groups) can be seen in *STF 1* Table P11 and *STF 3* Table P13.

A point of confusion may arise from the way in which specific topics are indexed under their particular subject term, but also as a subtopic under a broader category. If the subtopic is too complex to be summarized within a broader category, the subtopic will appear as a "Use" reference. The following example shows how this technique is employed in the index.

Households
    x Language Spoken
        Use: Language Spoken at Home
    x Nonrelatives Present
        STF1: P26
    Persons in Households x Household Relationship
        STF1: P15, P21, P22, P23
        STF3: P17, P18
    x Poverty Status
        STF3: 127
    x Race of Householder
        STF1: P19
        STF3: P20

Different types of data pertaining to Households can be found as subtopics under the "Households" entry in the index-- Nonrelatives Present, Poverty Status, and so on. The tables dealing with Household Language are too complicated to summarize as a subtopic, because they have subtopics of their own. In this case, the user is referred to the "L" section of the index to consult "Language Spoken at Home."

Part II
Section 2

List of 1990 CD-ROM Products

List of 1990 CD-ROM Products

PRIMARY TITLE	UNIVERSE	GEOGRAPHY	# OF DISCS	ON-DISC SOFTWARE
STF 1A	100%	Block Group	17	GO
STF 1B	100%	Blocks	10	GO
STF 1C	100%	nation	1	GO
STF 1D [a]	100%	CDs	1	GO
STF 3A	sample	Block Group	61	GO
STF 3B	sample	ZIP Codes	3	GO
STF 3C	sample	national	2	GO
STF 3D [a]	sample	CDs	1	GO
PL P4-171	100%	Blocks	10	GO
EEO File	sample	national	2	GO
Subject Summary Tape Files [b]	sample	national, some MSAs	33	GO
Special Tabulation on Aging	sample	various	21	GO
PUMS A (5%)	sample	PUMAs	7	CrossTab
PUMS B (1%)	sample	PUMAs	2	CrossTab
1994 TIGER /Line [c]	---	all	44	LandView
GICS	---	all	1	GO
Census Tract Street Index	---	Tracts	6	GO

[a] STF 1D and STF 3D issued together on single disc.
[b] See next page for detailed list
[c] 1995 and 1996 revisions issued by U.S. Dept. of Transportation

Subject Summary Tape Files

File	Discs	Title
SSTF 1	1	Foreign Born Population of the U.S.
SSTF 2	1	Ancestry of the Population in the U.S.
SSTF 3	1	Persons of Hispanic Origin in the U.S.
SSTF 4	3	Characteristics of Adults with Work Disabilities, Mobility Limitations, or Self-Care Limitations.
SSTF 5	1	Characteristics of the Asian and Pacific Islander population of the U.S.
SSTF 6	1	Education in the United States.[1]
SSTF 7	8	Metropolitan Housing Characteristics.
SSTF 8	1	Housing of the Elderly.
SSTF 9	1	Housing Characteristics of New Units.
SSTF 10	1	Mobile Homes.
SSTF 11	0	(publication canceled)
SSTF 12	1	Employment Status, Work Experience, and Veteran Status.[1]
SSTF 13	1	Characteristics of American Indians by Tribe and Language.
SSTF 14	1	Occupation and Industry
SSTF 15	1	Geographic Mobility in the United States
SSTF 16	1	Fertility.
SSTF 17	1	Poverty Areas in the United States.
SSTF 18	1	Condominium Housing.
SSTF 19	1	The Older Population in the United States.
SSTF 20	1	Journey to Work in the United States.
SSTF 21	3	Characteristics of the Black Population.
SSTF 22	3	Earnings by Occupation and Education.

[1] SSTF 6 and SSTF 12 issued together on a single disc

Part II
Section 3

Guide to Geographic Coverage in *STF 1* and *STF 3*

Guide to Geographic Coverage in *STF 1* and *STF 3*

Summary Level	STF 1	STF 3
United States/Regions/Divisions	C	C
Amer. Indian/Alaska Native Areas[1]	A B C D	A C D
States	A B C D	A B C D
Congressional Districts		
101st Congress	A B	--
103rd Congress	D	D
Metropolitan Areas[1]	B C	A C
Urbanized Areas[1]	B C	A C
Urban/Rural	B C	A C
Counties	A B C D	A B C D
Places (by population size)		
10,000 or more	A B C D	A C D
less than 10,000	A B	A
County Subdivisions		
all MCDs and CCDs	A B	A
MCDs of 10,000 or more[2]	C D	C D
MCDs under 10,000[3]	C	--
Census Tracts or BNAs	A B	A
Block Groups	A B	A
Blocks	B	--
ZIP Code Areas	--	B

[1] Data for that part of Area within state boundary only, except for C subfiles, which provide Area totals.
[2] 12 states where MCDs serve as general purpose governments.
[3] MCDs in Metropolitan Areas of New England states only.

Part II
Section 4

Subject Index to *STF 1* and *STF 3*

-A-

Ability to Speak English
Use: English Language Proficiency
Administrative and Managerial Occupations (Persons Employed)
STF3: GenProfile2, P78
Administrative Support Occupations (Persons Employed)
STF3: GenProfile2, P78
Adopted or Naturally-Born Children
STF1: P15
STF3: P17
Adult Children (Age 18 or Older) in Family (Number of Families)
STF3: P22
African Ancestry, Subsaharan
Use: Subsaharan African Ancestry
Age
See Also: Age of Household Member (Number of Households)
See Also: Age of Householder
See Also: Age 65 or Older (Persons)
See Also: Children
Children Ever Born x Age of Mother x Marital History
STF3: P39
Citizenship x ...
STF3: P37
Disability Status x Sex x ...
STF3: P66, P67, P68, P69

Age
 Distribution (by Single Year or Age Group)
  STF1: GenProfile, P11
  STF3: P13
 Employment Status and Disability Status x Sex
  STF3: P66, P67
 Group Quarters Population x ...
  STF1: P21, P22, P23
  STF3: P41
 Hispanic Origin x Sex x ...
  STF1: P13
  STF3: P15
 Household Members Age 17 or Younger x Household Relationship x ...
  STF1: P22
 Imputation
  STF1: P33
  STF3: P131
 Institutionalized Population x ... (Age 17 or Younger)
  STF1: P22
 Language Spoken at Home and Ability to Speak English x ...
  STF3: P28, P30
 Marital History x ... (Females Only)
  STF3: P38
 Median Age
  STF1: GenProfile
 Mobility Limitation Status x Sex x ...
  STF3: P67, P68, P69
 Poverty Status x ...
  STF3: P117, P118, P119, P120, P126
 Public Assistance Income (Aggregate Persons in Households) x ...
  STF3: P106
 Race x Sex x ...
  STF1: P12
  STF3: P14
 Sex x Disability Status x ...
  STF3: P66, P67, P68, P69
 Sex x Hispanic Origin x ...
  STF1: P13
  STF3: P15
 Sex x Poverty Status x ...
  STF3: P118
 Sex x Race x ...
  STF1: P12
  STF3: P14
 Sex x Veteran Status x ...
  STF3: P64
 Veteran Status x Sex x ...
  STF3: P64

Age of Building
   Use: Year Structure Built
Age of Household Member (Number of Households)
   Adult Child (Age 18 or Older) in Household
      STF3: P22
   Age 17 or Younger x Household Type
      STF1: P18
      See Also: Age 17 or Younger (Persons)
      See Also: Children Present in Household
      See Also: Householder or Spouse Age 17 or Younger
   Age 60 or Older x Household Type
      STF1: P24
   Age 65 or Older x Household Type
      STF1: P25
      See Also: Age 65 or Older (Persons)
      See Also: Householder Age 65 or Older (Number of Households)
Age of Householder
   Age 17 or Younger
      Use: Householder or Spouse Age 17 or Younger
   Age 65 or Older
      Use: Householder Age 65 or Older (Number of Households)
   Gross Rent as a Percentage of Household Income x ...
      STF3: H51
   Hispanic Origin of Householder x Household Income x ...
      STF3: P88
   Household Income x ...
      STF3: P86
   Household Income x Hispanic Origin of Householder x ...
      STF3: P88
   Household Income x Race of Householder x ...
      STF3: P87
   Household Type x ...
      STF3: P24
   Housing Tenure x ...
      STF1: H12
      STF3: H13
   Meals Included in Rent x ...
      STF1: H39
   Monthly Owner Costs as Percentage of Household Income x ...
      STF3: H60
   Plumbing Facilities x ...
      STF3: H68
   Poverty Status x ... x Household Type
      STF3: P127
   Race x ... x Household Income
      STF3: P87
   Telephone Availability x ...
      STF3: H36

Age of Householder
    Vehicle Availability x ...
        STF3: H41
Age 16-19 (Persons)
    x Employment Status, School Enrollment, and Educational Attainment
        STF3: GenProfile2, P61, P62, P63
    Hispanic Origin x Employment Status and School Enrollment
        STF3: P63
    Race x Employment Status and School Enrollment
        STF3: P62
    Total Persons
        STF3: GenProfile2
Age 16 or Older (Persons)
    x Employment Status
        Use: Employment Status
    x Sex
        STF3: GenProfile2
    Total Persons
        STF3: GenProfile2
    Workers (Person Working During Reference Week)
        STF3: GenProfile2
Age 17 or Younger (Persons)
    See Also: Age of Household Member -- Age 17 or Younger
    See Also: Householder or Spouse Age 17 or Younger
    x Citizenship
        STF3: P37
    Group Quarters Population
        STF1: P21, P22
        STF3: P41
    x Household Relationship
        STF1: P21, P22
        See Also: Children Present in Household
    Percentage of Total Population
        STF1: GenProfile
    Total Persons
        STF1: GenProfile
        STF1B
Age 65 or Older (Persons)
    See Also: Age of Household Member -- Age 65 or Older
    See Also: Householder Age 65 or Older
    Disability Status x Sex
        STF3: P66, P67, P68, P69
    Distribution (by Age Group)
        STF1: P11
        STF3: P13
    Employment Status and Disability Status x Sex
        STF3: P66, P67

Age 65 or Older (Persons)
    Group Quarters Population
        STF1: P23
        STF3: P41
    Hispanic Origin x Sex x Age Group
        STF1: P13
        STF3: P15
    x Household Type and Relationship
        STF1: P23
        STF3: P18
    x Language Spoken and Ability to Speak English
        STF3: P28, P30
    x Linguistic Isolation
        STF3: P30
    Living Alone
        STF1: GenProfile, P23, P25
        STF3: P18
    x Mobility Limitation Status
        STF3: GenProfile1, P67, P68, P69
    Percentage Below Poverty Level
        STF3: GenProfile3
    Percentage of Total Population
        STF1: GenProfile
    x Poverty Status
        STF3: GenProfile3, P117
    Poverty Status x Hispanic Origin
        STF3: P120
    Poverty Status x Household Type and Relationship
        STF3: P122
    Poverty Status x Race
        STF3: P119
    Poverty Status x Sex
        STF3: P118
    Public Assistance Income (Aggregate Persons in Household x Age)
        STF3: P106
    Race x Sex x Age Group
        STF1: P12
        STF3: P14
    x Relationship (Persons in Households)
        STF1: P23
        STF3: P18
    x Self-Care Limitation Status
        STF3: GenProfile1, P68, P69
    Sex x Disability Status
        STF3: P66, P67, P68, P69
    Sex x Veteran Status
        STF3: P64

Age 65 or Older (Persons)
   in Single-Person Households
      STF1: GenProfile, P23, P25
      STF3: P18
   Total Persons
      STF1: GenProfile
      STF1B
      STF3: GenProfile3
   x Veteran Status
      STF3: GenProfile2
   Veteran Status x Sex
      STF3: P64
   x Work Disability Status
      STF3: P66, P68
Aggregate Income (Families)
   Use: Family Income, Aggregate Amount
Aggregate Income (Households)
   Use: Household Income, Aggregate Amount
Aggregate Income (Individuals)
   Use: Personal Income, Aggregate Amount
Agriculture, Forestry, and Fishery Industries (Persons Employed)
   STF3: GenProfile2, P77
Aleuts (Race)
   STF1: P7
   STF3: P9
   See Also: American Indians, Eskimos, and Aleuts (Racial Group)
   See Also: Race
Allocation Rates
   See Also: Imputation Values
   See Also: Substitution Rates
   Housing Units with at Least One Item Allocated
      STF1: H46
      STF3: H72
   Persons with at Least One Item Allocated
      STF1: P30
      STF3: P128
American Ancestry
   Use: United States Ancestry
American Indian Languages Spoken
   STF3: P31
American Indians (Race)
   See Also: American Indians, Eskimos, and Aleuts (Racial Group)
   See Also: Race
   Percentage of Total Population
      STF1: GenProfile
   Total Persons
      STF1: GenProfile, P7
      STF3: P9

American Indians, Eskimos, and Aleuts (Racial Group)
    See Also: Aleuts
    See Also: American Indians
    See Also: Eskimos
    See Also: Race of Householder
    Age x Poverty Status
        STF3: P119
    Age x Sex
        STF1: P12
        STF3: P14E, P14F
    Distribution (by Racial Subgroups)
        STF1: P7
        STF3: P9
    x Educational Attainment (Age 25 or Older)
        STF3: P58
    x Educational Attainment and Employment Status (Age 16-19)
        STF3: P62
    Employment Status x Sex (Age 16 or Older)
        STF3: P71
    x Employment Status and Educational Attainment (Age 16-19)
        STF3: P62
    x Hispanic Origin
        STF1: P10
        STF3: P12
    Imputation
        STF1: P34
        STF3: P132
    Income, Per Capita
        STF3: P115A
    Income, Personal (Aggregate)
        STF3: P115
        See Also: Race of Householder x Household Income
    Poverty Status x Age
        STF3: P119
    x School Enrollment
        STF3: P55
    x School Enrollment or Educational Attainment (Age 16-19)
        STF3: P62
    Sex x Age
        STF1: P12
        STF3: P14E, P14F
    Sex x Employment Status (Age 16 or Older)
        STF3: P71
    x Subgroup
        STF1: P7
        STF3: P9
    Total Persons
        STF1: GenProfile, P6

American Indians, Eskimos, and Aleuts (Racial Group)
    Total Persons
        STF1B
        STF3: P8
Ancestry
    See Also: Hispanic Origin x Subgroup
    See Also: Place of Birth
    See Also: Race -- Distribution (by 25 Racial Subgroups)
    x First Ancestry Group
        STF3: P33
    Imputation
        STF3: P142
    Persons Reporting Multiple Ancestries
        STF3: P32
    Persons Reporting Single Ancestry
        STF3: P32
    x Second Ancestry Group
        STF3: P34
    x Single Ancestry Group
        STF3: P35
    x Total Ancestry Groups Reported (First or Second)
        STF3: GenProfile1
Apartment Buildings
    Use: Multi-Unit Structures
Apartments
    Use: Units in Structure (Housing)
Arab Ancestry
    STF3: GenProfile1, P33, P34, P35
Arabic Language Spoken
    STF3: P31
Area, Land
    Use: Land Area (Square Kilometers)
Area, Water
    Use: Water Area (Square Kilometers)
Armed Forces Employment
    See Also: Civilian Labor Force
    See Also: Employment Status
    See Also: Veteran Status
    Age 16-19
        STF3: P61, P62, P63
    x Hispanic Origin (Age 16-19)
        STF3: P63
    Hispanic Origin x Sex (Age 16 or Older)
        STF3: P72
    x Race (Age 16-19)
        STF3: P62
    Race x Sex (Age 16 or Older)
        STF3: P71
    x Sex (Age 16 or Older)
        STF3: GenProfile2, P70

Asians and Pacific Islanders (Racial Group)
    Imputation
        STF1: P34
        STF3: P132
    Income, Per Capita
        STF3: P115A
    Income, Personal (Aggregate)
        STF3: P115
        See Also: Race of Householder x Household Income
    Poverty Status x Age
        STF3: P119
    x School Enrollment
        STF3: P55
    x School Enrollment or Educational Attainment (Age 16-19)
        STF3: P62
    Sex x Age
        STF1: P12
        STF3: P14G, P14H
    Sex x Employment Status (Age 16 or Older)
        STF3: P71
    x Subgroup
        STF1: P7
        STF3: P9
    Total Persons
        STF1: GenProfile, P6
        STF1B
        STF3: P8
Austrian Ancestry
    STF3: GenProfile1, P33, P34, P35
Averages (Values Calculated)
    See Also: Ratios (Values Calculated)
    Means
        Use: Means (Values Calculated)
    Medians
        Use: Medians (Values Calculated)
    Per Capita Income
        Use: Per Capita Income
    Persons Per Family
        STF1: P17A
    Persons Per Household
        STF1: GenProfile
    Persons Per Occupied Housing Unit
        STF1: GenProfile, H17A, H18A

-B-

Bedrooms
    See Also: Rooms in Housing Unit

Bedrooms
    Distribution (by Number of Rooms)
        STF3: GenProfile4, H31
    Gross Rent x ...
        STF3: H34
    Housing Tenure x ...
        STF3: H33
    Imputation
        STF3: H81
    Vacant Housing Units x ...
        STF3: H32
Belgian Ancestry
    STF3: GenProfile1, P33, P34, P35
Birth Rate (Children Ever Born)
    STF3: GenProfile1
    See Also: Children Ever Born (Aggregate Number)
Blacks (Race)
    See Also: Race of Householder
    Age x Poverty Status
        STF3: P119
    Age x Sex
        STF1: P12
        STF3: P14C, P14D
    x Educational Attainment (Age 25 or Older)
        STF3: P58
    x Educational Attainment and Employment Status (Age 16-19)
        STF3: P62
    Employment Status x Sex (Age 16 or Older)
        STF3: P71
    x Employment Status and Educational Attainment (Age 16-19)
        STF3: P62
    x Hispanic Origin
        STF1: P10
        STF3: P12
    Imputation
        STF1: P34
        STF3: P132
    Income, Per Capita
        STF3: P115A
    Income, Personal (Aggregate)
        STF3: P115
        See Also: Race of Householder x Household Income
    Poverty Status x Age
        STF3: P119
    x School Enrollment
        STF3: P55
    x School Enrollment or Educational Attainment (Age 16-19)
        STF3: P62

Blacks (Race)
    Sex x Age
        STF1: P12
        STF3: P14C, P14D
    Sex x Employment Status (Age 16 or Older)
        STF3: P71
    Total Persons
        STF1: GenProfile, P6
        STF1B
        STF3: P8
Boarded-Up Housing
    STF1: H6
Buildings, Age of
    Use: Year Structure Built
Buildings, Apartment
    Use: Multi-Unit Structures
Buildings, Size of
    Use: Units in Structure (Housing)
Business Services Industries (Persons Employed)
    STF3: GenProfile2, P77

-C-

Cambodians (Race)
    STF1: P7
    STF3: P9
    See Also: Asians
Canadian Ancestry
    STF3: GenProfile1, P33, P34, P35
Carpooling
    Use: Vehicle Occupancy (Commuting)
Childless Families
    See Also: Family Households x Children Present
    x Family Type
        STF1: P16
        STF3: P19
    Hispanic Origin x Family Type
        STF1: P20
        STF3: P21
    x Poverty Status (Without Own Children)
        STF3: P123, P124, P125
    x Race x Family Type
        STF1: P19
        STF3: P20
    Without Own Children
        STF3: P19, P20, P21
    Without Related Children
        STF1: P16, P19, P20

Children
    Related Children
        Use: Related Children
    Step Children
        STF1: P15
        STF3: P17
    x Subfamily Type
        STF3: P26
        See Also: Children Present in Household x Subfamily Type
Children Ever Born (Aggregate Number)
    Age of Mother x Marital History
        STF3: GenProfile1, P38
    Birth Rate (Per 1,000 Women)
        STF3: GenProfile1
    Imputation
        STF3: P153
Children Present in Household
    See Also: Age of Household Member -- Age 17 or Younger
    See Also: Childless Families
    See Also: Children
    See Also: Household Relationship
    See Also: Own Children Present in Family
    See Also: Related Children Present in Family
    Adult Children (Age 18 or Older) x Family Type
        STF3: P22
    Employment Status of Mother (Number of Women) x ...
        STF3: P73
        See Also: Children x Employment Status of Parent(s)
    Family Householder, No Spouse Present x ...
        STF1B
        See Also: Children Present in Household x Family Type
    Family Type x ...
        STF1: P16, P18
        STF3: P19
    Family Type x Aggregate Family Income (Number of Families)
        STF3: P109
    Family Type x Hispanic Origin of Householder
        STF1: P20
        STF3: P21
    Family Type x Race of Householder
        STF1: P19
        STF3: P20
    Female Householder, No Husband Present x ...
        Use: Children Present in Household x Family Type
    Hispanic Origin of Householder x Household Type
        STF1: P20
        STF3: P21
    Hispanic Origin of Householder x Poverty Status of Family
        STF3: P125

Children Present in Household
    Household Type x ...
        STF1: P16, P18
        STF3: P19
    Household Type x Hispanic Origin of Householder
        STF1: P20
        STF3: P21
    Household Type x Race of Householder
        STF1: P19
        STF3: P20
    Income, Family (Aggregate) x Family Type
        STF3: P109
    Male Householder, No Wife Present x ...
        Use: Children Present in Household x Family Type
    Poverty Status (Families) x ...
        STF3: P123, P124, P125
        See Also: Children x Poverty Status
    Race of Householder x Household Type
        STF1: P19
        STF3: P20
    Race of Householder x Poverty Status of Family
        STF3: P124
    Subfamily Type x ...
        STF3: P25
        See Also: Children x Subfamily Type
Chinese (Race)
    STF1: P7
    STF3: P9
    See Also: Asians
Chinese Language Spoken
    STF3: P31
Citizenship
    x Age
        STF3: P37
    Imputation
        STF3: P137
Civilian Labor Force
    See Also: Armed Forces Employment
    See Also: Employment Status
    See Also: Labor Force Status
    x Employment Status
        STF3: GenProfile2
    Percentage Unemployed
        STF3: GenProfile2
    x Sex
        STF3: GenProfile2
    Total Persons
        STF3: GenProfile2

Class of Worker
   x Category
      STF3: P79
   Imputation
      STF3: P165
Cleaners, Laborers, and Related Occupations
   STF3: GenProfile2, P78
Clerical Occupations (Persons Employed)
   STF3: GenProfile2, P78
Coal (Source of Home Heating Fuel)
   STF3: H30
College Dormitories Population
   STF1: P28
   STF3: P40
   See Also: Group Quarters Population
College Enrollment
   Use: School Enrollment -- Distribution (by Grade Level)
College Graduates
   Use: Educational Attainment
Colombians (Hispanic Origin)
   STF3: P11
   See Also: Hispanic Origin
Communications and Public Utilities Industries (Persons Employed)
   STF3: GenProfile2, P77
Commuting to Work
   Imputation
      STF3: P155, P156, P157, P158
   Place of Work
      STF3: P45, P46, P47, P48
   Time Leaving Home to Go to Work
      STF3: P52
   Transportation Mode
      STF3: GenProfile2, P49
   Travel Time (Aggregate)
      STF3: P51
   Travel Time (Distribution)
      STF3: P50
   Vehicle Occupancy
      STF3: P53
Complete-Count (Housing Units)
   Use: Housing Units -- Total Number
Complete-Count (Population)
   Use: Total Population -- Complete Count
Condominium Status
   Imputation
      STF3: H73
   x Monthly Owner Costs (Aggregate) x Mortgage Status
      STF3: H57

Crowded Housing Units (More Than 1 Person Per Room)
    STF1B
    See Also: Persons Per Room
Cubans (Hispanic Origin)
    STF1: P9
    STF3: P11
    See Also: Hispanic Origin
Czech Ancestry
    STF3: GenProfile1, P33, P34, P35

-D-

Danish Ancestry
    STF3: GenProfile1, P33, P34, P35
Disability Status (Employment)
    Use: Work Disability Status
Disability Status (Mobility Limitations)
    Use: Mobility Limitation Status
Disability Status (Self-Care Limitations)
    Use: Self-Care Limitation Status
Dividend, Interest, or Net Rental Income
    See Also: Household Income x Source of Income
    Aggregate Amount
        STF3: P101
    Households Receiving
        STF3: P93
Divorced Persons (Marital Status) x Sex
    STF1: P14
    STF3: P27
Dominicans (Hispanic Origin)
    STF3: P11
    See Also: Hispanic Origin
Dormitory Population
    STF1: P28
    STF3: P40
Duration of Vacancy (Housing Units)
    Distribution (by Duration)
        STF1: H40
    Imputation
        STF1: H48
Dutch Ancestry
    STF3: GenProfile1, P33, P34, P35

-E-

Earnings (Households Receiving)
    STF3: P89

Employment Status
   Children x Employment Status of Parents
      STF3: P74
   x Educational Attainment (Age 16-19)
      STF3: GenProfile2, P61, P62, P63
   Females x Own Children Present x ...
      STF3: P73
   x Hispanic Origin (Age 16-19)
      STF3: P63
   Imputation
      STF3: P159
   x Mobility Limitation Status
      STF3: P67
   Mothers x ...
      STF3: P73
   Percentage of Labor Force Unemployed
      STF3: GenProfile2
   x Race (Age 16-19)
      STF3: P62
   Race x Sex
      STF3: P71
   x Sex
      STF3: GenProfile2, P70
      See Also: Work Status x Sex
   Sex x Age x Work Disability Status
      STF3: P66
   Sex x Race
      STF3: P71
   Teenagers x ...
      Use: Employment Status -- Age 16-19
   Unemployment Rate
      STF3: GenProfile2
   x Work Disability Status
      STF3: P66
English Ancestry
   STF3: GenProfile1, P33, P34, P35
English Language Proficiency
   See Also: Language Spoken at Home
   See Also: Linguistic Isolation
   Age x Language Spoken x ...
      STF3: P28
   Imputation
      STF3: P147
   Summary Data
      STF3: GenProfile1
English Language Spoken
   STF3: P31
Entertainment and Recreation Services Industries (Persons Employed)
   STF3: GenProfile2, P77

Entry into United States
    Use: Year of Entry
Eskimos (Race)
    STF1: P7
    STF3: P9
    See Also: American Indians, Eskimos, and Aleuts (Racial Group)
    See Also: Race
Ethnic Heritage
    Use: Ancestry
Executives (Occupation)
    STF3: GenProfile2, P78

-F-

Families
    Use: Family Households
Family Householder with Children, No Spouse Present
    STF1B
    See Also: Family Households x Family Type
Family Households
    See Also: Female Householder, No Husband Present
    See Also: Male Householder, No Wife Present
    See Also: Married Couple Families
    See Also: Subfamilies
    See Also: Workers in Family
    x Adult Children Present (Age 18 or Older)
        STF3: P22
        See Also: Family Households x Children Present
    x Age of Householder
        STF3: P24
    Children in Household (Aggregate Number of Children)
        STF1: P21
    Children in Household x Age (Own Children)
        STF3: P23
    x Children Not Present
        Use: Childless Families
    x Children Present
        STF1: P16
        STF3: GenProfile3, P19
        See Also: Family Households x Adult Children Present
        See Also: Family Households -- Household Member Age 17 or Younger
    Children Present x Aggregate Family Income
        STF3: P109
    Children Present x Hispanic Origin of Householder
        STF1: P20
        STF3: P21
    Children Present x Poverty Status
        STF3: P123

Family Households
    Children Present x Race of Householder
        STF1: P19
        STF3: P20
    x Family Type
        STF1: GenProfile, P16,
        STF3: P19
    Family Type x Hispanic Origin of Householder
        STF1: P20
        STF3: P21
    Family Type x Household Member Age 17 or Younger
        STF1: P18
    Family Type x Poverty Status
        STF3: P123, P127
    Family Type x Race of Householder
        STF1: P19
        STF3: P20
    Hispanic Origin of Householder x Family Type
        STF1: P20
        STF3: P21
    Household Member Age 17 or Younger
        STF1: P18
        See Also: Family Households x Children Present
    Household Member Age 60 or Older
        STF1: P24
    Household Member Age 65 or Older
        STF1: P25
    x Household Size (Distribution by Number of Persons)
        STF1: P27
    x Household Type
        Use: Family Households x Family Type
    Householder with Children, No Spouse Present
        STF1Bp125
        See Also: Family Households x Family Type
    Income
        Use: Family Income
    Percentage Below Poverty Level
        STF3: GenProfile3
    Persons in Families (Aggregate)
        STF1: P17
    Persons in Families x Household Relationship
        STF1: P15, P21, P23
        STF3: P17, P18, P23
    Persons Per Family
        STF1: P17A
    x Poverty Status
        STF3: GenProfile3, P123, P124, P125, P127
    Poverty Status x Age of Householder x Family Type
        STF3: P127

Family Type
    Poverty Status x Hispanic Origin of Householder x ...
        STF3: P125
    Poverty Status x Race of Householder x ...
        STF3: P124
Family Workers, Unpaid
    STF3: P79
Farm Housing Units
    STF3: H5
Farm Population
    STF3: GenProfile1, P6
Farm Self-Employment Income
    See Also: Household Income x Source of Income
    See Also: Nonfarm Self-Employment Income
    Aggregate Amount
        STF3: P100
    Average (Mean) Household Income
        STF3: GenProfile3
    Households Receiving
        STF3: GenProfile3, P92
Farming, Forestry, and Fishing Occupations (Persons Employed)
    STF3: GenProfile2, P78
Father-Child Families
    Use: Male Householder, No Wife Present
Father-Child Subfamilies
    Use: Subfamilies
Female Householder
    See Also: Female Householder, No Husband Present
    See Also: Householder x Sex
    Age 65 or Older
        STF1: P23
        STF3: P18
    x Household Member Age 17 or Younger
        STF1: P18
    x Household Type
        STF1: P16
        STF3: P17, P18
Female Householder, No Husband Present
    See Also: Nonfamily Households
    See Also: Family Households
    See Also: Working Mothers
    x Adult Children (Age 18 or Older) Present
        STF3: P22
        See Also: Female Householder, No Husband Present x Children Present
    Children in Household (Aggregate Number of Children)
        STF1: P21
    Children in Household x Age (Own Children)
        STF3: P23

Female Householder, No Husband Present
    x Children Present (Number of Households)
        STF1: P16
        STF3: GenProfile3, P19
        See Also: Female Householder, No Husband Present x Adult Children Present
        See Also: Female Householder, No Husband Present -- Household Member Age 17 or Younger
    Children Present x Aggregate Family Income
        STF3: P109
    Children Present x Hispanic Origin of Householder
        STF1: P20
        STF3: P21
    Children Present x Poverty Status
        STF3: P123
    Children Present x Race of Householder
        STF1: P19
        STF3: P20
    Family Income (Aggregate) x Children Present
        STF3: P109
    Hispanic Origin of Householder x Children Present
        STF1: P20
        STF3: P21
    Household Member Age 17 or Younger (Aggregate Children)
        STF1: P21
    Household Member Age 17 or Younger (Households)
        STF1: P18
        See Also: Family Householder with Children, No Spouse Present
        See Also: Female Householder, No Husband Present x Children Present
    Households (Total Number)
        STF3: GenProfile3
    Percentage of Households Below Poverty Level
        STF3: GenProfile3
    Persons Age 17 or Younger in Household (Aggregate Persons)
        STF1: P21
    x Poverty Status
        STF3: GenProfile3
    Poverty Status x Age of Householder
        STF3: P127
    Poverty Status x Family Type and Presence of Children
        STF3: P123
    Poverty Status x Hispanic Origin of Householder
        STF3: P125
    Poverty Status x Race of Householder
        STF3: P124
    Poverty Status of Children in Household x Age
        STF3: P126
    Poverty Status of Persons in Household (Age 65 or Older)
        STF3: P122

Female Householder, No Husband Present
    Race of Householder x Children Present
        STF1: P19
        STF3: P20
Fertility
    Use: Children Ever Born
Filipinos (Race)
    STF1: P7
    See Also: Asians
Finance, Insurance, and Real Estate Industries (Persons Employed)
    STF3: GenProfile2, P77
Finnish Ancestry
    STF3: GenProfile1, P33, P34, P35
Foreign Born Population
    See Also: Place of Birth
    x Citizenship
        STF3: P37
    Total Persons
        STF3: P42
    x Year of Entry to U.S.
        STF3: GenProfile1, P36
French Ancestry (except Basque)
    STF3: GenProfile1, P33, P34, P35
French Canadian Ancestry
    STF3: GenProfile1, P33, P34, P35
French Creole Language Spoken
    STF3: P31
French Language Spoken
    STF3: P31
Fuel, Home Heating
    Use: Heating Fuel

-G-

Gender
    Use: Sex
German Ancestry
    STF3: GenProfile1, P33, P34, P35
German Language Spoken
    STF3: P31
Government Workers
    STF3: GenProfile2, P79
    See Also: Public Administration Industries (Persons Employed)
Grandchildren
    STF1: P15
    STF3: P17
Greek Ancestry
    STF3: GenProfile1, P33, P34, P35

Group Quarters Population
    x Income, Per Capita
        STF3: P114B
    x Income, Personal (Aggregate)
        STF3: P114
    Poverty Status (Age 65 or Older)
        STF3: P122
    Total Persons
        STF1: GenProfile
    x Type of Group Quarters
        STF1: P28
        STF3: P40
Grown Children in Household
    Use: Adult Children in Household
Guamanians (Race)
    STF1: P7
    STF3: P9
    See Also: Pacific Islanders
Guatemalans (Hispanic Origin)
    STF3: P11
    See Also: Hispanic Origin

-H-

Handlers, Equipment Cleaners, and Related Occupations
    STF3: GenProfile2, P78
Hawaiians (Race)
    STF1: P7
    STF3: P9
    See Also: Pacific Islanders
Health Service Industries (Persons Employed)
    STF3: GenProfile2, P77
Heating Fuel
    Imputation
        STF3: H79
    x Type Used
        STF3: GenProfile4, H30
High School Enrollment
    Use: School Enrollment -- Distribution (by Grade Level)
High School Graduates
    Use: Educational Attainment
Hispanic Origin
    See Also: Hispanic Origin of Householder
    See Also: Spanish Language Spoken
    Age x Sex
        STF1: P13
        STF3: P15

Hispanic Origin of Householder
    Aggregate Persons in Housing Units x Housing Tenure x ...
        STF3: H15
    x Children Present in Household
        STF1: P20
        STF3: P21
    Contract Rent (Aggregate) x ...
        STF1: H37
    Gross Rent x ...
        STF3: H46
    Household Income (Aggregate) x ...
        STF3: P85
    x Household Income (Distribution)
        STF3: P83
    Household Income x ... x Age of Householder
        STF3: P88
    x Household Type
        STF1: P20
        STF3: P21
    Housing Tenure x Race of Householder x ...
        STF1: H11
        STF3: H12
    Housing Value (Aggregate) x ...
        STF1: H28
    x Monthly Owner Costs x Mortgage Status
        STF3: H55
    Mortgage Status x Monthly Owner Costs
        STF3: H55
    Owner Occupied Housing Units (Specified) x ...
        STF1: H27
    Percentage x Housing Tenure
        STF1: GenProfile
    x Plumbing Facilities in Housing Unit
        STF3: H67
    Poverty Status x Family Type and Presence of Children
        STF3: P125
    x Race of Householder
        STF1: H10
        STF3: H11
    Race of Householder x Housing Tenure
        STF1: H11
        STF3: H12
    Renter Occupied Housing Units (Specified) x ...
        STF1: H36
    x Vehicles Available
        STF3: H40
Hmongs (Race)
    STF1: P7
    STF3: P9

Hmongs (Race)
    See Also: Asians
Home Heating Fuel
    Use: Heating Fuel
Home Workers
    Use: Working at Home (Number of Persons)
Homeless Population (Emergency Shelters and Visible in Street Locations)
    STF1: P28
    STF3: P40
    See Also: Group Quarters Population
Homeowner Costs
    Use: Monthly Owner Costs (Specified Owner Occupied Units)
Hondurans (Hispanic Origin)
    STF3: P11
    See Also: Hispanic Origin
Hours Worked
    Use: Usual Hours Worked Per Week
House Heating Fuel
    Use: Heating Fuel
Household Income
    See Also: Family Income
    See Also: Nonfamily Household Income
    See Also: Per Capita Income
    See Also: Personal Income (Individuals)
    x Age of Householder
        STF3: P86
    Aggregate
        Use: Household Income, Aggregate Amount
    Average (Mean) Income x Income Type
        STF3: GenProfile3
    Distribution (Households by Income Level)
        STF3: GenProfile3, P80
    Earnings
        STF3: P89
    Farm Self-Employment Income
        STF3: GenProfile3, P92
    x Gross Rent as Percentage of Household Income
        STF3: H50
        See Also: Gross Rent as Percentage of Income
    x Hispanic Origin of Householder
        STF3: P83
    Hispanic Origin of Householder x Age of Householder
        STF3: P88
    Housing Tenure x Mortgage Status
        Use: Household Income - Mortgage Status x Housing Tenure
    Imputation
        STF3: P167
    Interest, Dividend, or Net Rental Income
        STF3: P93

Household Income, Aggregate Amount
   x Race of Householder
      STF3: P84
   Retirement Income
      STF3: P104
   Social Security Income
      STF3: P102
   x Source of Income
      STF3: P98, P99, P100, P101, P102, P103, P104, P105
   Total Population x ...
      STF3: P81
      See Also: Personal Income, Aggregate Amount -- Persons in Households
   Wage or Salary Income
      STF3: P98
Household Language
   Use: Language Spoken at Home
Household Relationship
   Age 17 or Younger (Total Persons) x ...
      STF1: P21
   Age 17 or Younger x Age x ...
      STF1: P22
   Age 65 or Older (Total Persons) x ...
      STF1: P23
      STF3: P18
   x Household Type
      STF1: P15, P21, P23
      STF3: P17, P18
   Imputation
      STF1: P31
      STF3: P129
   Poverty Status x Age Group x Household Type x ...
      STF3: P122
   x Subfamily Type
      STF3: P26
Household Service Occupations (Persons Employed)
   STF3: GenProfile2, P78
Household Size
   Distribution (by Number of Persons)
      STF1: GenProfile, P27, H17
      STF3: P16
   x Household Type
      STF1: P16, P27
   x Housing Tenure
      STF1: H18
      STF3: H18
Household Type
   See Also: Family Households
   See Also: Nonfamily Households

Household Type
  See Also: Group Quarters Population
  x Adult Children (Age 18 or Older) Present
      STF3: P22
  x Age of Householder
      STF3: P24
  x Children Present
      STF1: P16, P19, P20
      STF3: P19, P20, P21
  x Hispanic Origin
      STF1: P20
      STF3: P21
  Household Member Age 17 or Younger x ...
      STF1: P18, P21
  Household Member Age 60 or Older x ...
      STF1: P24
  Household Member Age 65 or Older x ...
      STF1: P25
  x Household Size
      STF1: P27
  Poverty Status x Relationship x ... (Persons in Households)
      STF3: P122
  Poverty Status x Age of Householder
      STF3: P127
  x Race of Householder
      STF1: P19
  x Relationship of Household Member
      STF1: GenProfile, P15, P21, P23
      STF3: P17, P18
Householder
  See Also: Female Householder, No Husband Present
  See Also: Male Householder, No Wife Present
  x Age
      Use: Age of Householder
  Age 17 or Younger
      Use: Householder or Spouse Age 17 or Younger
  Age 65 or Older
      Use: Householder Age 65 or Older
  Gross Rent x Age
      Use: Gross Rent as a Percentage of Household Income x Age of Householder
  x Hispanic Origin
      Use: Hispanic Origin of Householder
  x Household Type
      STF1: P15
      STF3: P17
  Poverty Status x Age
      STF3: P127
  x Race
      Use: Race of Householder

Households
    See Also: Single-Person Households
    x Age of Householder
        STF3: P24
    x Children Present
        STF1: P16, P19, P20
        STF3: P19, P20, P21
        See Also: Households -- Household Member Age 17 or Younger
    x Hispanic Origin of Householder
        STF1: P20
        STF3: P21
        See Also: Hispanic Origin of Householder
    Household Member Age 17 or Younger
        STF1: P18
        See Also: Age 17 or Younger (Persons)
        See Also: Children Present in Household
    Household Member Age 60 or Older
        STF1: P24
    Household Member Age 65 or Older
        STF1: P25
        See Also: Age 65 or Older (Persons)
    Income
        Use: Household Income
    x Language Spoken
        Use: Language Spoken at Home
    x Nonrelatives Present
        STF1: P26
    Persons in Household (Aggregate)
        Use: Household Size
    Persons in Households x Household Relationship
        STF1: P15, P21, P22, P23
        STF3: P17, P18
    x Poverty Status
        STF3: 127
    x Race of Householder
        STF1: P19
        STF3: P20
        See Also: Race of Householder
    Relationship of Household Members
        Use: Household Relationship
    x Size
        Use: Household Size
    x Telephone Availability
        STF3: GenProfile4, H35, H36
    Total Number
        STF1: GenProfile, P3
        STF3: GenProfile3, P5
    x Type
        Use: Household Type

Housing Tenure
    Race of Householder x Hispanic Origin
        STF1: H11
        STF3: H12
    Rooms (Aggregate) x ...
        STF1: H15
    x Size of Household
        STF1: H18
        STF3: H18
    Summary Data
        STF1: GenProfile, H3
        STF3: H8
    x Telephone Availability
        STF3: H35
    x Units in Structure
        STF1: H43, H44
        STF3: H22
    Vacancy Rate x ...
        STF1: GenProfile
    x Vehicles Available
        STF3: H37, H38
    x Year Householder Moved into Unit
        STF3: H29
    x Year Structure Built
        STF3: H27
Housing Turnover
    Use: Year Householder Moved into Unit
Housing Unit Count
    Use: Housing Units -- Total Number
Housing Units
    See Also: Group Quarters Population
    See Also: Occupied Housing Units
    See Also: Vacant Housing Units
    Bedrooms in Unit
        Use: Bedrooms
    Boarded-Up
        STF1: H6
    Complete Count
        STF1: GenProfile, Geographic Identifiers, H1
        STF3: Geographic Identifiers, H3
    Condominiums
        Use: Condominium Status
    Estimated Number
        STF3: GenProfile4, H1
    Farm Units
        STF3: H5
    For Rent
        Use: Vacant Housing Units -- For Rent

Housing Units
  For Sale
      Use: Vacant Housing Units -- For Sale
  Imputation
      STF1: H46
      STF3: H72
  x Kitchen Facilities
      STF3: H42
  Migrant Worker Units (Vacancy Status)
      STF1: H5, H16
      See Also: Vacant Housing Units
  Nonfarm Rural Units
      STF3: H5
  x Number of Units in Structure
      Use: Units in Structure (Housing)
  Occupied Housing Units
      Use: Occupied Housing Units
  Owner Occupied
      Use: Owner Occupied Housing Units
  Persons Living in Housing Unit (Distribution by Number of Persons)
      STF1: H17, H18
      STF3: H18
  Persons Living in Housing Units (Aggregate Persons)
      STF1: H19, H20
      STF1B
      STF3: H19
      See Also: Group Quarters Population
  Persons Living in Housing Units (Aggregate) x Hispanic Origin of Householder
      STF3: H15
  Persons Living in Housing Units (Aggregate) x Race of Householder
      STF3: H14
  Persons Per Unit (Occupied Units)
      STF1: GenProfile, H17A, H18A
  x Plumbing Facilities
      Use: Plumbing Facilities
  Renter Occupied
      Use: Renter Occupied Housing Units
  x Rooms
      Use: Rooms in Housing Unit
  Rural Units
      STF1: H4
      STF3: H5
      See Also: Housing Units -- Farm Units
  Sampling Rate
      STF3: H3A
  Seasonal, Recreational or Occasional Use Units (Vacant Units)
      STF1: H5, H16
      STF3: H6
      See Also: Vacant Housing Units

Housing Units
    x Size (Number of Persons in Occupied Units)
        STF1: H17, H18
        STF3: H18
        See Also: Occupied Housing Units -- Persons Per Unit
    x Size (Number of Rooms)
        STF1: H13
        STF3: H16
    Substituted Units (Imputation Method)
        STF1: H45
    x Tenure
        Use: Housing Tenure
    Total Number (Complete Count)
        STF1: GenProfile, Geographic Identifiers, H1
        STF1B
        STF3: Geographic Identifiers, H3
    Total Number (Estimate)
        STF3: GenProfile4, H1
    x Units in Structure
        Use: Units in Structure (Housing)
    Unweighted Sample Count
        STF3: H2
    Urban Units
        STF1: H4
        STF3: H5
    Urbanized Units
        STF1: H4
        STF3: H5
    Vacant Units
        Use: Vacant Housing Units
    x Value (Specified Owner Occupied Units)
        Use: Housing Value (Specified Owner Occupied Units)
    Value, Aggregate (All Owner Occupied Units)
        STF1: H29
Housing Value (Specified Owner Occupied Units)
    Distribution (by Dollar Amount)
        STF1: GenProfile, H23
        STF3: H61
    Imputation
        STF1: H52
        STF3: H89
    Mean (Average)
        STF1B
    Median
        STF1: GenProfile, H23B
        STF3: H61A

Housing Value (Specified Owner Occupied Units)
    Quartile Values
        STF1: H23A, H23C
        See Also: Price Asked (Specified Vacant For Sale Housing Units)
Housing Value, Aggregate (All Owner Occupied Housing Units)
    Imputation
        STF1: H52
    x Units in Structure
        STF1: H29
Housing Value, Aggregate (Specified Owner Occupied Units Only)
    x Hispanic Origin of Householder
        STF1: H28
    x Mortgage Status
        STF3: H62
    x Race of Householder
        STF1: H26
    Total Amount
        STF1: H24
Hungarian Ancestry
    STF3: GenProfile1, P33, P34, P35
Hungarian Language Spoken
    STF3: P31
Husbands or Wives
    Use: Spouses (Household Relationship)

-I-

Immigration
    Use: Year of Entry
Imputation Values
    See Also: Allocation Rates
    See Also: Substitution Rates
    Ability to Speak English
        STF3: P147
    Age
        STF1: P33
        STF3: P131
    Ancestry
        STF3: P142
    Bedrooms
        STF3: H81
    Children Ever Born
        STF3: P153
    Citizenship
        STF3: P137
    Class of Worker
        STF3: P165

Imputation Values
    Contract Rent
        STF1: H54
    Condominium Status
        STF3: H73
    Disability Status
        STF3: P150, P151, P152
    Duration of Vacancy
        STF1: H48
    Educational Attainment
        STF3: P140, P141
    Employment Status
        STF3: P159
    Family Income
        STF3: P168
    Gross Rent
        STF3: H91
    Group Quarters Population
        STF3: P135
    Hispanic Origin
        STF1: P35
        STF3: P134
    Home Heating Fuel
        STF3: H79
    Household Income
        STF3: P167
    Household Relationship
        STF1: P31
        STF3: P129
    Housing Tenure
        STF1: H51
        STF3: H85
    Housing Units with at Least One Item Allocated
        STF1: H46
        STF3: H72
    Housing Units Substituted
        STF1: H45
    Housing Value
        STF1: H52
        STF3: H89
    Income
        STF3: P166, P167, P168, P169
    Industry
        STF3: P163
    Kitchen Facilities
        STF3: H80
    Language Spoken at Home
        STF3: P145, P146

Imputation Values
    Renter Occupied Housing Units
        STF1: H51
        STF3: H85
    Residence in 1985
        STF3: P143, P144
    Rooms in Unit
        STF1: H50
        STF3: H87
    Self-Care Limitation Status
        STF3: P152
    School Enrollment
        STF3: P139
    Sewage Disposal
        STF3: H76
    Sex
        STF1: P32
        STF3: P130
    Telephone in Unit
        STF3: H82
    Tenure
        Use: Imputation -- Housing Tenure
    Transportation to Work (Mode of Travel)
        STF3: P155, P156
    Travel Time to Work
        STF3: P157, P158
    Units in Structure
        STF1: H49
        STF3: H88
    Usual Hours Worked Per Week
        STF3: P161
    Vacant Housing Units
        STF1: H47, H48
        STF3: H86
    Value
        Use: Imputation -- Housing Value
    Vehicles Available
        STF3: H83
    Veteran Status
        STF3: P148
    Water Source
        STF3: H75
    Weeks Worked in 1989
        STF3: P162
    Work Disability Status
        STF3: P150
    Work Status in 1989
        STF3: P160

Imputation Values
>   Year Householder Moved into Unit
>   STF3: H78
>   Year of Entry to United States
>   STF3: P138
>   Year Structure Built
>   STF3: H77

Income, Family
>   *Use: Family Income*

Income, Household
>   *Use: Household Income*

Income, Per Capita
>   *Use: Per Capita Income*

Income, Personal
>   *Use: Personal Income (Individuals)*

Indians, American
>   *Use: American Indians (Race)*

Indians, Asian
>   *Use: Asian Indians (Race)*

Indic Language Spoken
>   STF3: P31

Indo-European Languages Spoken
>   STF3: P31

Industry (Persons Employed)
>   *See Also: Occupation*
>   Imputation
>   STF3: P163
>   x Industry Type
>   STF3: GenProfile2, P77

Inhabitants, Number of
>   *Use: Total Population*

Institutionalized Persons
>   *See Also: Group Quarters Population*
>   Age 17 or Younger
>   STF1: P21, P22
>   STF3: P41
>   Age 65 or Older
>   STF1: P23
>   STF3: P18, P41
>   x Age Group
>   STF3: P41
>   x Income, Aggregate Amount
>   STF3: P114
>   x Income, Per Capita
>   STF3: P114B
>   Total Persons
>   STF1: GenProfile, P15
>   STF3: P17

Institutionalized Persons
    x Type of Institution
        STF1: P28
        STF3: P40
Insurance, Finance, and Real Estate Industries (Persons Employed)
    STF3: GenProfile2, P77
Interest, Dividend, or Net Rental Income
    See Also: Household Income x Source of Income
    Aggregate Amount
        STF3: P101
    Households Receiving
        STF3: P93
Irish Ancestry
    STF3: GenProfile1, P33, P34, P35
Italian Ancestry
    STF3: GenProfile1, P33, P34, P35
Italian Language Spoken
    STF3: P31

-J-

Japanese (Race)
    STF1: P7
    STF3: P9
    See Also: Asians
Japanese Language Spoken
    STF3: P31
Journey to Work
    Use: Commuting
Juvenile Institution Population
    STF1: P28
    STF3: P40
    See Also: Group Quarters Population

-K-

Kitchen Facilities
    Availability
        STF3: GenProfile4, H42
    Imputation
        STF3: H80
Korean Conflict Veterans
    Use: Military Service Time Period
Korean Language Spoken
    STF3: P31

Koreans (Race)
    STF1: P7
    STF3: P9
    See Also: Asians

-L-

Labor Force Status
    See Also: Employment Status
    Percentage of Persons in Labor Force
        STF3: GenProfile2
    x Sex
        STF3: GenProfile2
    Total Persons x ...
        STF3: GenProfile2
Laborers, Cleaners, and Related Occupations
    STF3: GenProfile2, P78
Land Area (Square Kilometers)
    STF1: Geographic Identifiers
    STF3: Geographic Identifiers
Language Spoken at Home
    See Also: English Language Proficiency
    See Also: Linguistic Isolation
    x Ability To Speak English
        STF3: GenProfile1, P28
    Age x ... x Ability to Speak English
        STF3: P28
    Age x ... x Linguistic Isolation
        STF3: P30
    Distribution (by Language Spoken)
        STF3: P31
    Households x ... x Linguistic Isolation
        STF3: P29
    Imputation
        STF3: P145, P146
    x Linguistic Isolation (Households)
        STF3: P29
    x Linguistic Isolation (Persons)
        STF3: P30
    Persons x ...
        STF3: P28, P30, P31
    Summary Data
        STF3: GenProfile1
Laotians (Race)
    STF1: P7
    STF3: P9
    See Also: Asians

Linguistic Isolation
    See Also: Language Spoken at Home
    Households x ... x Language Spoken
        STF3: P30
    Persons x ... x Language Spoken
        STF3: P29
Lithuanian Ancestry
    STF3: GenProfile1, P33, P34, P35
Living Quarters (Group Quarters)
    Use: Group Quarters Population
Living Quarters (Housing Units)
    Use: Housing Units

-M-

Machine Operators, Assemblers, and Inspectors (Occupation)
    STF3: GenProfile2, P78
Male Householder, No Wife Present
    See Also: Nonfamily Households
    See Also: Family Households
    See Also: Subfamilies
    See Also: Working Parents
    x Adult Children (Age 18 or Older) Present
        STF3: P22
        See Also: Male Householder, No Wife Present x Children Present
    Children in Household (Aggregate Number of Children)
        STF1: P21
    Children in Household x Age (Own Children)
        STF3: P23
    x Children Not Present
        Use: Childless Families
    x Children Present (Number of Households)
        See Also: Male Householder, No Wife Present -- Adult Children Present
        See Also: Male Householder, No Husband Present -- Household Member Age 17 or Younger
        STF1: P16
        STF3: P19
    Children Present x Aggregate Family Income
        STF3: P109
    Children Present x Hispanic Origin of Householder
        STF1: P20
        STF3: P21
    Children Present x Poverty Status
        STF3: P123
    Children Present x Race of Householder
        STF1: P19
        STF3: P20
    Family Income (Aggregate) x Own Children Present
        STF3: P109

Married Couple Families
    x Age of Children (Own Children)
        STF3: P23
    Children in Family (Aggregate Number of Children)
        STF1: P21
    x Children Not Present
        Use: Childless Families
    x Children Present (Number of Families)
        See Also: Married Couple Families x Adult Children Present
        See Also: Married Couple Families -- Household Member Age 17 or Younger
        STF1: P16
        STF3: P19
    Children Present x Aggregate Family Income
        STF3: P109
    Children Present x Hispanic Origin of Householder
        STF1: P20
        STF3: P21
    Children Present x Poverty Status
        STF3: P123
    Children Present x Race of Householder
        STF1: P19
        STF3: P20
    Family Income (Aggregate) x Children Present
        STF3: P109
    Hispanic Origin of Householder x Children Present
        STF1: P20
        STF3: P21
    Household Member Age 17 or Younger x Household Relationship
        STF1: P18
    Percentage of All Households
        STF1: GenProfile
    Poverty Status x Age of Householder
        STF3: P127
    Poverty Status x Family Type and Presence of Children
        STF3: P123
    Poverty Status x Hispanic Origin of Householder
        STF3: P125
    Poverty Status x Race of Householder
        STF3: P124
    Poverty Status of Children in Households x Age
        STF3: P126
    Poverty Status of Persons in Households (Age 65 or Older)
        STF3: P122
    x Race of Householder x Children Present
        STF1: P19
        STF3: P20
    Total Number
        STF1: GenProfile

Married Couple Subfamilies
   Use: Subfamilies
Material Moving Occupations (Persons Employed)
   STF3: GenProfile2, P78
Meals Included in Rent
   Age of Householder x ...
      STF1: H39
   Gross Rent (Aggregate) x ...
      STF3: H48
   Housing Units x ...
      STF1: H39
      STF3: H47
   Imputation
      STF1: H55
      STF3: H90
Means (Values Calculated)
   Mean Contract Rent (Specified Renter Occupied Units)
      STF1B
      See Also: Medians (Values Calculated) -- Median Contract Rent
   Mean Household Income x Income Type
      STF3: GenProfile3
   Mean Housing Value (Specified Owner Occupied Units)
      STF1B
      See Also: Medians (Values Calculated) -- Median Housing Value
   Mean Rooms in Housing Unit
      STF1B
   Mean Travel Time to Work (in Minutes)
      STF3: GenProfile2
Medians (Values Calculated)
   See Also: Averages (Values Calculated)
   Median Age of Population
      STF1: GenProfile
   Median Contract Rent (Specified Renter Occupied Housing Units)
      STF1: GenProfile, H32B
      See Also: Means (Values Calculated) -- Mean Contract Rent
   Median Gross Rent (Specified Renter Occupied Housing Units)
      STF3: GenProfile4, H43, H50A
   Median Housing Value (Specified Owner Occupied Units)
      STF1: GenProfile, H23B
      STF3: H61A
      See Also: Means (Values Calculated) -- Mean Housing Value
   Median Income
      STF3: GenProfile3, P80A, P107A, P110A
   Median Monthly Owner Costs (Specified Owner Occupied Units)
      STF3: H52A, H58A
   Median Year Structure Built
      STF3: H25A

Melanesians (Race)
    STF1: P7
    STF3: P9
    See Also: Pacific Islanders
Mental Hospitals Population
    STF1: P28
    STF3: P40
    See Also: Group Quarters Population
Mexicans (Hispanic Origin)
    STF1: P9
    STF3: P11
    See Also: Hispanic Origin
Micronesians (Race)
    STF1: P7
    STF3: P9
    See Also: Pacific Islanders
Migrant Worker Housing (Vacancy Status)
    STF1: H5, H16
Migration
    Use: Residence in 1985
Military Quarters Population
    STF1: P28
    STF3: P40
    See Also: Group Quarters Population
Military Service Time Period
    See Also: Armed Forces Employment
    See Also: Veteran Status
    Distribution (by Time Period)
        STF3: P65
    Imputation
        STF3: P149
Mining Industry (Persons Employed)
    STF3: GenProfile2, P77
Mobile Homes or Trailers
    x Housing Tenure
        STF1: H43, H44
        STF3: H22
    Imputation
        STF1: H49
        STF3: H88
    Inhabitants (Aggregate) x Housing Tenure
        STF1: H44
    Monthly Owner Costs (Aggregate)
        STF3: H56
    x Plumbing Facilities
        STF3: H70
    Total Number
        STF1: GenProfile, H41
        STF3: H20

Monthly Owner Costs as a Percentage of Household Income
    Median Percentage x Mortgage Status
        STF3: H58A
    Mortgage Status x ...
        STF3: H58
Mortgage Status
    Condominium Status x Housing Tenure x ...
        STF3: H7
    Condominium Status x Monthly Owner Costs (Aggregate)
        STF3: H57
    Hispanic Origin x Monthly Owner Costs
        STF3: H55
    x Housing Tenure and Household Income (Aggregate)
        STF3: H63
    x Housing Value (Aggregate)
        STF3: H62
    Imputation
        STF3: H84
    Mobile Homes x Monthly Owner Costs (Aggregate)
        STF3: H56
    Monthly Owner Costs x ...
        STF3: H52, H53, H54, H55, H56, H57, H58
    Race of Householder x Monthly Owner Costs
        STF3: H54
Mother-Child Families
    Use: Female Householder, No Husband Present
Mother-Child Subfamilies
    Use: Subfamilies
Mothers, Working
    Employment Status
        STF3: P73
    Children in Household x Age
        STF3: P74
Movers
    Use: Residence in 1985
Multi-Unit Structures (Housing Units)
    Distribution (by Number of Units)
        STF1: GenProfile, H41
        STF3: H20
    x Housing Tenure (for individual Units)
        STF1: H43, H44
        STF3: H22
    Imputation
        STF1: H49
        STF3: H88
    Inhabitants (Aggregate) x Housing Tenure
        STF1: H44
    x Plumbing Facilities (for Individual Units)
        STF3: H70

Multi-Unit Structures (Housing Units)
    Ten Units or More in Structure
        STF1: GenProfile
        STF1B
    Vacant Units x ...
        STF1: H42
        STF3: H21
    Value (Aggregate)
        STF1: H29

-N-

National Heritage
    Use: Ancestry
Native Americans
    Use: American Indians
Native Born
    Use: Place of Birth
Native North American Languages Spoken
    STF3: P31
Nativity
    Use: Place of Birth
Natural Gas (Source of Home Heating Fuel)
    STF3: H30
Naturalized Citizens
    STF3: P37
Neighborhood Stability
    Use: Year Householder Moved into Unit
Net Rental Income
    Use: Interest, Dividend, or Net Rental Income
Nicaraguans (Hispanic Origin)
    STF3: P11
    See Also: Hispanic Origin
Nonfamily Household Income
    See Also: Family Income
    See Also: Household Income
    See Also: Personal Income (Individuals)
    Distribution (Households by Income Level)
        STF3: GenProfile3, P110
    Imputation
        STF3: P169
    Median
        STF3: GenProfile3, P110A
Nonfamily Household Income, Aggregate
    STF3: P111
Nonfamily Households
    See Also: Family Households
    See Also: Single-Person Households

Nonfamily Households
    x Age of Householder
        STF3: P24
    x Hispanic Origin of Householder
        STF1: P20
        STF3: P21
    Household Member Age 17 or Younger
        STF1: P18
    Household Member Age 60 or Older
        STF1: P24
    Household Member Age 65 or Older
        STF1: P25
    x Household Size (Distribution by Number of Persons)
        STF1: P27
    x Income
        Use: Nonfamily Household Income
    Percentage of All Households
        STF1: GenProfile
    Persons in Households x Household Relationship
        STF1: P15, P23
        STF3: P17, P18
    Poverty Status x Age of Householder
        STF3: P127
    x Race of Householder
        STF1: P19
        STF3: P20
    x Sex of Householder
        STF1: P16
    Total Number
        STF1: GenProfile
        STF3: GenProfile3
Nonfarm Rural Housing Units
    STF3: H5
Nonfarm Rural Population
    STF3: P6
Nonfarm Self-Employment Income
    See Also: Farm Self-Employment Income
    See Also: Household Income x Source of Income
    Aggregate Amount
        STF 3: P99
    Average (Mean) Household Income
        STF3: GenProfile3
    Households Receiving
        STF3: GenProfile3, P91
Noninstitutional Group Quarters Population
    See Also: Group Quarters Population
    See Also: Institutionalized Persons

Noninstitutional Group Quarters Population
    Age 17 or Younger
        STF1: P18, P21
        STF3: P41
    Age 65 or Older
        STF1: P23
        STF3: P18, P41
    x Age Group
        STF3: P41
    Income, Aggregate Amount
        STF3: P114
    Income, Per Capita
        STF3: P114B
    Total Persons
        STF1: GenProfile, P15
        STF3: P17
    x Type of Institution
        STF1: P28
        STF3: P40
Nonrelatives
    See Also: Household Relationship
    See Also: Relatives
    See Also: Unrelated Individuals
    Age 17 or Younger x Age
        STF1: P22
    Age 17 or Younger x Household Type
        STF1: P21
    Age 65 or Older x Household Type
        STF1: P23
        STF3: P18
    x Household Type and Relationship
        STF1: P15
        STF3: P17
    Households with Nonrelatives Present
        STF1: P26
    Poverty Status x Age Group
        STF3: P122
Norwegian Ancestry
    STF3: GenProfile1, P33, P34, P35
Not-For-Profit Workers
    STF3: P79
Number of Inhabitants
    Use: Total Population
Nursing Homes Population
    STF1: P28
    STF3: P40
    See Also: Group Quarters Population

-O-

Occasional Use Housing
   Use: Seasonal, Recreational, or Occasional Use Housing Units (Vacant Units)
Occupancy Status
   STF1: GenProfile, H2
   STF3: H4
   See Also: Occupied Housing Units
Occupation (Employment)
   See Also: Industry
   Imputation
      STF3: P164
   x Type
      STF3: GenProfile2, P78
Occupied Housing Units
   See Also: Owner Occupied Housing Units
   See Also: Renter Occupied Housing Units
   See Also: Vacant Housing Units
   x Bedrooms in Unit
      STF3: H33
   Condominium Status x Tenure and Mortgage Status
      STF3: H7
   Contract Rent
      Use: Contract Rent (Specified Renter Occupied Units)
   Gross Rent
      Use: Gross Rent (Specified Renter Occupied Units)
   Hispanic Origin of Householder x Race
      STF1: H10
      STF3: H11
      See Also: Housing Tenure x Hispanic Origin of Householder
   x Home Heating Fuel Type
      STF3: GenProfile4, H30
   Imputation
      STF1: H51
      STF3: H86
   x Mortgage Status
      Use: Mortgage Status
   Overcrowding (More Than 1 Person Per Room)
      STF1: GenProfile
      STF1B
      See Also: Persons Per Room
   Persons Living in Housing Units (Aggregate Persons)
      STF1: H19, H20
      STF1B
      STF3: H19
      See Also: Group Quarters Population

One-Person Households
  Use: Single-Person Households
Other Race (Racial Category)
  See Also: Race of Householder
  Age x Poverty Status
    STF3: P119
  Age x Sex
    STF1: P12
    STF3: P14I, P14J
  x Educational Attainment (Age 25 or Older)
    STF3: P58
  x Educational Attainment and Employment Status (Age 16-19)
    STF3: P62
  Employment Status x Sex (Age 16 or Older)
    STF3: P71
  x Employment Status and Educational Attainment (Age 16-19)
    STF3: P62
  x Hispanic Origin
    STF1: P10
    STF3: P12
  Imputation
    STF1: P34
    STF3: P132
  Income, Aggregate Amount
    STF3: P115
    See Also: Race of Householder x Household Income
  Income, Per Capita
    STF3: P115A
  Poverty Status x Age
    STF3: P119
  x School Enrollment
    STF3: P55
  x School Enrollment or Educational Attainment (Age 16-19)
    STF3: P62
  Sex x Age
    STF1: P12
    STF3: P14I, P14J
  Sex x Employment Status (Age 16 or Older)
    STF3: P71
  Total Persons
    STF1: GenProfile, P6
    STF3: P8
Other Type of Income
  See Also: Household Income x Source of Income
  Aggregate Amount
    STF3: P105
  Households Receiving
    STF3: P97

Owner Occupied Housing Units
    Aggregate Persons in Owner Occupied Units
        STF1: H20
        STF3: H19
    Aggregate Persons in Owner Occupied Units x Hispanic Origin of Householder
        STF3: H14
    Aggregate Persons in Owner Occupied Units x Race of Householder
        STF3: H15
    x Bedrooms in Unit
        STF3: H33
    Hispanic Origin of Householder x Race
        STF1: H11
        STF3: H12
    Household Income (Aggregate) x Mortgage Status
        STF3: H63
        See Also: Specified Owner Occupied Housing Units x Hispanic Origin
    x Mortgage Status and Aggregate Household Income
        STF3: H63
    Overcrowding (More Than 1 Person Per Room)
        STF1B
        See Also: Persons Per Room
    Percentage of All Occupied Units
        STF1: GenProfile
    x Persons Living in Owner Occupied Unit (Distribution by Number of Persons)
        STF1: H18
        STF3: H18
    Persons Per Unit
        STF1: GenProfile, H18A
    Persons Per Room
        STF1: H22
    Plumbing Facilities x Persons Per Room
        STF3: H69
    x Race of Householder
        STF1: H9
        See Also: Specified Owner Occupied Housing Units x Race of Householder
    x Race of Householder x Hispanic Origin
        STF1: H11
        STF3: H12
    Rooms (Aggregate)
        STF1: H15
    x Size (Number of Persons)
        STF1: H18
        STF3: H18
        See Also: Owner Occupied Housing Units -- Persons Per Unit
    x Telephone Availability
        STF3: H35
    Total Number
        STF1: GenProfile, H3

Owner Occupied Housing Units
    Total Number
        STF1B
        STF3: H8
    x Units in Structure
        STF3: H22
    Value (Aggregate) x Units in Structure
        STF1: H29
    x Value (Specified Owner Occupied Units)
        Use: Housing Value (Specified Owner Occupied Units)
    x Vehicles Available
        STF3: H37, 38
    x Year Householder Moved into Unit
        STF3: H29

-P-

Pacific Islander or Asian Languages Spoken
    Use: Asian or Pacific Islander Languages Spoken
Pacific Islanders (Race)
    STF1: P7
    STF3: P9
    See Also: Asians and Pacific Islanders (Racial Group)
    See Also: Race
Panamanians (Hispanic Origin)
    STF3: P11
    See Also: Hispanic Origin
Parents, Working
    Employment Status of Women x Presence of Own Children
        STF3: GenProfile2, P73
    Children Present in Household x Employment Status of Parents
        STF3: P74
Part-Time Workers
    STF3: P76
Per Capita Income
    See Also: Personal Income (Individuals)
    Group Quarters Population
        STF3: P114B
    x Hispanic Origin
        STF3: P116A
    x Race
        STF3: P115A
    x Total Population
        STF3: GenProfile3, P114A
Period of Military Service
    Use: Military Service Time Period
Personal Income (Individuals)
    See Also: Household Income
    See Also: Family Income

Polish Ancestry
    STF3: GenProfile1, P33, P34, P35
Polish Language Spoken
    STF3: P31
Polynesians (Race)
    STF1: P7
    STF3: P9
    See Also: Pacific Islanders
Population Count
    Use: Total Population
Portuguese Ancestry
    STF3: GenProfile1, P33, P34, P35
Portuguese Creole Language Spoken
    STF3: P31
Portuguese Language Spoken
    STF3: P31
Poverty Status (Households or Families)
    See Also: Poverty Status (Persons)
    Age of Householder x Household Type
        STF3: P127
    x Family Type and Presence and Age of Children
        STF3: P123
    Hispanic Origin x Family Type
        STF3: P125
    Race of Householder x Family Type and Children Present
        STF3: P124
Poverty Status (Persons)
    See Also: Poverty Status (Households or Families)
    x Age
        STF3: GenProfile3, P117
    Age x Hispanic Origin
        STF3: P120
    Age x Household Type and Relationship
        STF3: P122
    Age x Race
        STF3: P119
    Age x Sex
        STF3: P118
    Age 65 or Older
        STF3: GenProfile3, P117, P118, P119, P120, P122
    Hispanic Origin x Age
        STF3: P120
    x Household Type and Relationship
        STF3: P122
    Imputation
        STF3: P170
    Percentage of Persons Below Poverty Level
        STF3: GenProfile3

Poverty Status (Persons)
    Persons for Whom Poverty Status Is Determined
        STF3: GenProfile3
    x Race x Age
        STF3: P119
    Related Children Below Poverty Level
        STF3: GenProfile3
    x Ratio of Income
        STF3: P121
    Sex x Age
        STF3: P118
    Total Persons Below Poverty Level
        STF3: GenProfile3
    Unrelated Individuals Below Poverty Level
        STF3: GenProfile3, P122
Pre-School (Preprimary) Enrollment
    Use: School Enrollment -- Distribution (by Grade Level)
Preprimary School Enrollment
    Use: School Enrollment -- Distribution (by Grade Level)
Previous Residence
    Use: Residence in 1985
Price Asked (Specified Vacant Housing Units For Sale)
    Aggregate Amount
        STF1: H31
    Imputation
        STF1: H53
Private Household Occupations (Persons Employed)
    STF3: GenProfile2, P78
Private School Enrollment
    STF3: P54
Private Sector Workers (For-Profit and Nonprofit Employers)
    STF3: P79
Private Vehicle Occupancy
    Use: Vehicle Occupancy (Commuting)
Professional Specialty Occupations (Persons Employed)
    STF3: GenProfile2, P78
Protective Service Occupations (Persons Employed)
    STF3: GenProfile2, P78
Psychiatric Hospitals Population
    Use: Mental Hospitals Population
Public Administration Industries (Persons Employed)
    STF3: GenProfile2, P77
    See Also: Government Workers
Public Assistance Income
    See Also: Household Income x Source of Income
    Aggregate Amount
        STF3: P103
    Average (Mean) Household Income
        STF3: GenProfile3

Public Assistance Income
    Households Receiving
        STF3: GenProfile3, P95
    Persons in Households Receiving x Age
        STF3: 106
Public School Enrollment
    STF3: P54
Public Transportation (Mode of Travel to Work)
    STF3: GenProfile2, P49
Public Utilities and Communications Industries (Persons Employed)
    STF3: GenProfile2, P77
Puerto Rican Born Population (Place of Birth)
    STF3: P42
Puerto Ricans (Hispanic Origin)
    STF1: P9
    STF3: P11
    See Also: Hispanic Origin

-R-

Race
    See Also: Race of Householder
    Age x Poverty Status
        STF3: P119
    Age x Sex
        STF1: P12
        STF3: P14
    Distribution (by 5 Racial Groups)
        STF1: GenProfile, P6
        STF1B
        STF3: P8
    Distribution (by 25 Racial Groups)
        STF1: P7
        STF3: P9
    x Educational Attainment (Age 25 or Older)
        STF3: P58
    x Educational Attainment and Employment Status (Age 16-19)
        STF3: P62
    Employment Status x Sex (Age 16 or Older)
        STF3: P71
    x Employment Status and Educational Attainment (Age 16-19)
        STF3: P62
    Hispanic Origin x ...
        STF1: P10
        STF3: P12
    Imputation
        STF1: P34
        STF3: P132

Race of Householder
    Household Income x ... x Age of Householder
        STF3: P87
    x Household Type
        STF1: P19
    x Household Type and Presence of Children
        STF3: P20
    x Housing Tenure
        STF1: H9, H25, H34
        STF3: H10
    x Housing Tenure (Aggregate Persons in Unit)
        STF3: H14
    x Housing Tenure x Hispanic Origin of Householder
        STF1: H11
        STF3: H12
    x Housing Value (Aggregate)
        STF1: H26
    Monthly Owner Costs x Mortgage Status x ...
        STF3: H54
    x Mortgage Status x Monthly Owner Costs
        STF3: H54
    Owner-Occupied Housing Units (Specified) x ...
        STF1: H25
    Percentage x Housing Tenure
        STF1: GenProfile
    Persons in Unit (Aggregate) x ... x Tenure
        STF3: H14
    Plumbing Facilities x ...
        STF3: H66
    Poverty Status x ... x Family Type and Children Present
        STF3: P124
    Renter Occupied Housing Units (Specified) x ...
        STF1: H34
    x Vehicles Available
        STF3: H39
Ratios (Values Calculated)
    See Also: Averages (Values Calculated)
    Gross Rent to Household Income
        STF3: GenProfile4, H50, H51, H60
    Income to Poverty Level
        STF3: P121
    Monthly Owner Costs to Household Income
        STF3: GenProfile4, H58, H59, H60
Real Estate, Insurance, and Finance Industries (Persons Employed)
    STF3: GenProfile2, P77
Recreation Services and Entertainment Industries (Persons Employed)
    STF3: GenProfile2, P77
Recreational-Use Housing
    Use: Seasonal, Recreational, or Occasional Use Housing Units (Vacant Units)

Relatives
    x Household Type and Relationship
        STF1: P15
        STF3: P17
Relocation
    Use: Residence in 1985
Rent
    Contract Rent
        Use: Contract Rent (Specified Renter Occupied Units)
    Gross Rent
        Use: Gross Rent (Specified Renter Occupied Units)
    Meals Included
        STF1: H39
        STF3: H47, H48
    Utilities Included
        STF3: H49
Rent Asked (Specified Vacant Housing Units)
    STF1: H38
Rental Income
    Use: Interest, Dividend, or Net Rental Income
Renter Occupied Housing Units
    See Also: Housing Tenure
    See Also: Owner Occupied Housing Units
    See Also: Specified Renter Occupied Housing Units
    See Also: Vacancy Rate (Housing Units For Sale or Rent)
    x Age of Householder
        STF1: H12
        STF3: H13
    Aggregate Persons Living in Renter Occupied Units
        STF1: H20
        STF3: H19
    Aggregate Persons Living in Renter Occupied Units x Hispanic Origin of Householder
        STF3: H15
    Aggregate Persons Living in Renter Occupied Units x Race of Householder
        STF3: H14
    x Bedrooms in Unit
        STF3: H33
    x Contract Rent (Specified Renter Occupied Units)
        Use: Contract Rent (Specified Renter Occupied Units)
    x Gross Rent (Specified Renter Occupied Units)
        Use: Gross Rent (Specified Renter Occupied Units)
    Hispanic Origin of Householder x Race
        STF1: H11
        STF3: H12
        See Also: Specified Renter Occupied Housing Units x Hispanic Origin
    Household Income (Aggregate) x Mortgage Status
        STF3: H63

Renter Occupied Housing Units
    Imputation
        STF1: H51
        STF3: H85
    x Mortgage Status and Aggregate Household Income
        STF3: H63
    Overcrowding (More Than 1 Person Per Room)
        STF1B
        See Also: Renter Occupied Housing Units -- Persons Per Room
    x Persons Living in Renter Occupied Unit (Distribution by Number of Persons)
        STF1: H18
        STF3: H18
    Persons Per Room
        STF1: GenProfile, H22
    Persons Per Unit
        STF1: GenProfile, H18A
    Plumbing Facilities x Persons Per Room
        STF3: H69
    x Race of Householder
        STF1: H9
        See Also: Specified Renter Occupied Housing Units x Race of Householder
    Race of Householder x Hispanic Origin
        STF1: H11
        STF3: H12
    Rooms (Aggregate)
        STF1: H15
    x Size (Number of Persons)
        STF1: H18
        STF3: H18
        See Also: Renter Occupied Housing Units -- Persons Per Unit
    x Telephone Availability
        STF3: H35
    Total Number
        STF1: GenProfile, H3
        STF1B
        STF3: H8
    x Units in Structure
        STF3: H22
    x Vehicles Available
        STF3: H37, H38
    x Year Householder Moved into Unit
        STF3: H29
Residence Elsewhere
    Use: Usual Residence Elsewhere
Residence in 1985
    Abroad
        STF3: GenProfile1, P43, P44

Residence in 1985
    Distribution (by Former Residence)
        STF3: GenProfile1
    Imputation
        STF3: P143, P144
    x MSA/PMSA Level
        STF3: P44
    x State and County Level
        STF3: P43
Retail Trade Industries (Persons Employed)
    STF3: GenProfile2, P77
Retirement Income
    See Also: Household Income x Source of Income
    See Also: Social Security Income
    Aggregate Amount
        STF3: P104
    Average (Mean) Household Income
        STF3: GenProfile3
    Households Receiving
        STF3: GenProfile3, P96
Ride Sharing
    Use: Vehicle Occupancy (Commuting)
Romanian Ancestry
    STF3: GenProfile1, P33, P34, P35
Roommates
    Use: Nonfamily Households
Rooms in Housing Unit
    See Also: Bedrooms
    See Also: Persons Per Room (Occupied Units)
    Aggregate
        STF1: H14, H15, H16
        STF3: H17
    Distribution (by Number of Rooms)
        STF1: H13
        STF3: H16
    Imputation
        STF1: H50
        STF3: H87
    x Tenure (Aggregate Rooms)
        STF1: H15
    x Vacancy Status (Aggregate Rooms)
        STF1: H16
Rural Housing Units
    Farm/Nonfarm
        STF3: H5
    Total Number
        STF1: H4
        STF3: H5

Rural Population
    Farm Population
        STF3: GenProfile1, P6
    Nonfarm Population
        STF3: P6
    Percentage of Total Population
        STF3: GenProfile1
    Total Persons
        STF1: P4
        STF3: GenProfile1, P6
Russian Ancestry
    STF3: GenProfile1, P33, P34, P35
Russian Language Spoken
    STF3: P31

-S-

Salary Income
    Use: Wage or Salary Income
Salespersons (Occupation)
    STF3: GenProfile2, P78
Salvadorans (Hispanic Origin)
    STF3: P11
    See Also: Hispanic Origin
Samoans (Race)
    STF1: P7
    STF3: P9
    See Also: Pacific Islanders
Sample Count (Unweighted)
    Total Housing Units
        STF3: H2
    Total Population
        STF3: P2
Sampling Rates
    Housing Units
        STF3: H3A
    Persons
        STF3: P3A
Scandinavian Languages Spoken
    STF3: P31
School Enrollment
    See Also: Educational Attainment
    Distribution (by Type of School)
        STF3: GenProfile1, P54
    Employment Status and ... (Age 16-19)
        STF3: GenProfile2, P61, P62, P63
    x Hispanic Origin (Age 3 or Older)
        STF3: P56

Sex
    Imputation
        STF1: P32
        STF3: P130
    x Marital Status
        STF1: P14
        STF3: P27
    Mobility Limitation Status x Age
        STF3: P67, P68, P69
    Poverty Status x Sex x ...
        STF3: P118
    Race x Age
        STF1: P12
        STF3: P14
    Race x Employment Status
        STF3: P71
    Self-Care Limitation Status x Age
        STF3: P68, P69
    Usual Hours Worked x Weeks Worked in 1989
        STF3: P76
    Veteran Status x Age
        STF3: P64
    Weeks Worked in 1989 x Usual Hours Worked
        STF3: P76
    Work Disability Status x Age
        STF3: P66, P68
    x Work Status in 1989
        STF3: P75, P76
Shelters, Population in
    Use: Homeless Population (Emergency Shelters and Visible in Street Locations)
Single Fathers
    Householders
        Use: Male Householder, No Wife Present
    in Subfamilies
        STF3: P25
Single Houses
    Use: Units in Structure (Housing Units)
Single Mothers
    Householders
        Use: Female Householder, No Husband Present
    in Subfamilies
        STF3: P25
Single-Person Households
    See Also: Nonfamily Households
    Age 60 or Older
        STF1: P24
    Age 65 or Older
        STF1: GenProfile, P23, P25
        STF3: P18

Solar Energy (for Home Heating)
 STF3: GenProfile4, H30
Source of Household Income
 See Also: Household Income
 Aggregate Amount (by Source)
  STF3: P98, P99, P100, P101, P102, P103, P104, P105
 Distribution (by Source)
  STF3: P90, P91, P92, P93, P94, P95, P96, P97
Spanish Creole Language Spoken
 STF3: P31
Spanish Language Spoken
 See Also: Hispanic Origin
 x Ability to Speak English
  STF3: GenProfile1, P28
 Age x Ability to Speak English
  STF3: P28
 Age x Linguistic Isolation
  STF3: P30
 x Linguistic Isolation (Households)
  STF3: P29
 x Linguistic Isolation (Persons)
  STF3: P30
 Total Persons
  STF3: GenProfile1, P31
Spanish Origin
 Use: Hispanic Origin
Specified Owner Occupied Housing Units
 See Also: Owner Occupied Housing Units
 x Hispanic Origin of Householder
  STF1: H27
  See Also: Owner Occupied Housing Units x Hispanic Origin x Race
 x Race of Householder
  STF1: H25
  See Also: Owner Occupied Housing Units x Race of Householder
 Total Number
  STF3: GenProfile4
 x Value
  Use: Housing Value (Specified Owner Occupied Units)
Specified Renter Occupied Housing Units
 See Also: Renter Occupied Housing Units
 x Contract Rent
  Use: Contract Rent (Specified Renter Occupied Units)
 x Gross Rent
  Use: Gross Rent (Specified Renter Occupied Units)
 x Hispanic Origin of Householder (Paying Cash Rent)
  STF1: H36
  See Also: Occupied Housing Units -- Hispanic Origin x Race

Substitution Rates (Imputation Method)
    Persons
        STF1: P29
Swedish Ancestry
    STF3: GenProfile1, P33, P34, P35
Swiss Ancestry
    STF3: GenProfile1, P33, P34, P35

-T-

Tagalog Language Spoken
    STF3: P31
Technicians and Related Support Occupations (Persons Employed)
    STF3: GenProfile2, P78
Teenage Employment
    Employment Status x Educational Attainment (Age 16-19)
        STF3: GenProfile2, P61, P62, P63
    x Hispanic Origin
        STF3: P63
    x Race
        STF3: P62
Teenage Householder or Spouse
    STF1: P21, P22
Telecommuters
    Use: Working at Home (Number of Persons)
Telephone in Household
    x Age of Householder
        STF3: H36
    Households with No Telephone
        STF3: GenProfile4
    x Housing Tenure
        STF3: H35
    Imputation
        STF3: H82
Tenure
    Use: Housing Tenure
Thais (Race)
    STF1: P7
    STF3: P9
    See Also: Asians
Time Leaving Home to Go to Work
    Distribution (by Time Period)
        STF3: P52
    Imputation
        STF3: P157
Tongans (Race)
    STF1: P7
    STF3: P9
    See Also: Pacific Islanders

Total Population
 Complete Count
  STF1: GenProfile, Geographic Identifiers, P1
  STF1B
  STF3: Geographic Identifiers, P3
 Estimated
  STF3: GenProfile1, P1
 Farm Population
  STF3: GenProfile1, P6
 Nonfarm Rural Population
  STF3: P6
 Persons Substituted (Imputation Method)
  STF1: P29
 Persons with at Least One Item Allocated
  STF1: P30
  STF3: P128
 Rural Population
  STF1: P4
  STF3: GenProfile1, P6
 Sampling Rate
  STF3: P3A
 Unweighted Sample Count
  STF3: P2
 Urban Population
  STF1: P4
  STF3: GenProfile1, P6
 Urbanized Population
  STF1: P4
  STF3: P6
Trailers
 Use: Mobile Homes
Transportation and Material Moving Occupations (Persons Employed)
 STF3: GenProfile2, P78
Transportation Industries (Persons Employed)
 STF3: GenProfile2, P77
Transportation to Work (Mode of Travel)
 Imputation
  STF3: P155, P156
 x Mode of Transportation
  STF3: GenProfile2, P49
Travel-Time to Work
 Aggregate Time
  STF3: P51
 Average (Mean) Time (in Minutes)
  STF3: GenProfile2
 Distribution (by Time Spent)
  STF3: P50
 Imputation
  STF3: P157, P158

Travel-Time to Work
   Time Leaving Home
      STF3: P52

-U-

Unemployment Rate
   x Sex
      STF3: GenProfile2
   x Total Labor Force
      STF3: GenProfile2
Unemployment Status
   Use: Employment Status
Ukrainian Ancestry
   STF3: GenProfile1, P33, P34, P35
United States Ancestry
   STF3: P33, P34, P35
Units in Structure (Housing)
   Distribution (by Number of Units)
      STF1: GenProfile, H41
      STF3: H20
   Housing Tenure x ...
      STF1: H43, H44
      STF3: H22
   Imputation
      STF1: H49
      STF3: H88
   Inhabitants (Aggregate) x Housing Tenure x ...
      STF1: H44
   Plumbing Facilities x ...
      STF3: H70
   Single-Unit Structures
      STF1: GenProfile, H41
      STF1B
      STF3: H20
   Ten Units or More in Structure
      STF1: GenProfile
      STF1B
   Vacant Units x ...
      STF1: H42
      STF3: H21
   Value (Aggregate) x ...
      STF1: H29
Unpaid Family Workers
   STF3: GenProfile2, P79
Unrelated Individuals
   See Also: Nonrelatives

Unrelated Individuals
    Poverty Status
        STF3: GenProfile3
    Poverty Status x Age Group
        STF3: P122
    Total Persons
        STF3: GenProfile3
Urban Housing Units
    STF1: H4
    STF3: H5
Urban Population
    Percentage of Total Population
        STF3: GenProfile1
    Total Persons
        STF1: P4
        STF3: GenProfile1, P6
Urbanized Housing Units
    STF1: H4
    STF3: H5
Urbanized Population
    STF1: P4
    STF3: P6
Usual Hours Worked Per Week
    See Also: Weeks Worked in 1989
    See Also: Work Status
    Imputation
        STF3: P161
    x Sex x Weeks Worked
        STF3: P76
Usual Residence Elsewhere
    STF1: H7
    See Also: Seasonal, Recreational, or Occasional Use Housing
    See Also: Vacant Housing Units
Utilities Included in Rent
    STF3: H49

-V-

Vacancy Rates (Housing Units For Sale or Rent)
    STF1: GenProfile
Vacancy Status
    STF1: GenProfile, H2
    STF3: H4
    See Also: Vacant Housing Units
Vacant Housing Units
    See Also: Occupied Housing Units
    Aggregate Rooms
        STF1: H16

Vacant Housing Units
    x Bedrooms in Unit
        STF3: H32
    Boarded-Up Units
        STF1: H6
    x Condominium Status
        STF3: H6
    x Duration
        STF1: H40
    For Rent
        STF1: H5, H16, H30, H40
        See Also: Vacant Housing Units -- Specified For Rent
        See Also: Vacancy Rate (Housing Units For Sale or Rent)
    For Sale
        STF1: H5, H16, H30, H40
        See Also: Vacant Housing Units -- Specified For Sale
        See Also: Vacancy Rate (Housing Units For Sale or Rent)
    Imputation
        STF1: H47, H48
        STF3: H86
    Plumbing Facilities
        STF3: H65
    Price Asked, Aggregate (Specified Vacant For Sale)
        STF1: H31
    Rent Asked, Aggregate (Specified Vacant For Sale)
        STF1: H38
    Rooms (Aggregate)
        STF1: H16
    Specified For Rent
        STF1: H30, H38
        See Also: Vacant Housing Units -- For Rent
    Specified For Sale
        STF1: H30, H31, H53
        See Also: Vacant Housing Units -- For Sale
    Total Number
        STF1: GenProfile, H2
        STF3: H4
    x Type
        STF1: H5
        STF3: H6
    x Units in Structure
        STF1: H42
        STF3: H21
    Usual Residence Elsewhere
        STF1: H7
    Vacancy Rates (For Sale or For Rent Only)
        STF1: GenProfile
    Year Structure Built
        STF3: H26

-W-

Wage or Salary Income
> *See Also: Earnings*
> *See Also: Household Income x Source of Income*
> Aggregate Amount
>> STF3: P98
> Average (Mean) Household Income
>> STF3: GenProfile3
> Households Receiving
>> STF3: GenProfile3, P90

Water Source
> Imputation
>> STF3: H75
> x Type
>> STF3: GenProfile4, H23

Weeks Worked in 1989
> *See Also: Work Status*
> *See Also: Usual Hours Worked Per Week*
> Imputation
>> STF3: P162
> Sex x Usual Hours Worked Per Week x ...
>> STF3: P76

Welfare Income
> *Use: Public Assistance Income*

Welsh Ancestry
> STF3: GenProfile1, P33, P34, P35

West Indian Ancestry (excluding Hispanic Origin)
> STF3: P33, P34, P35

Whites (Race)
> *See Also: Race of Householder*
> Age x Poverty Status
>> STF3: P119
> Age x Sex
>> STF1: P12
>> STF3: P14A, P14B
> x Educational Attainment (Age 25 or Older)
>> STF3: P58
> x Educational Attainment and Employment Status (Age 16-19)
>> STF3: P62
> Employment Status x Sex (Age 16 or Older)
>> STF3: P71
> x Employment Status and Educational Attainment (Age 16-19)
>> STF3: P62
> x Hispanic Origin
>> STF1: P10
>> STF3: P12

Work Status in 1989
    Usual Hours Worked x Weeks Worked in 1989
        STF3: P76
Work Week
    Use: Usual Hours Worked Per Week
Workers (Persons Working During Reference Week)
    STF3: GenProfile2
    See Also: Employment Status
Workers, Class of
    Use: Class of Worker
Workers in Family
    Distribution (by Number of Workers)
        STF3: P112
    x Family Income (Aggregate)
        STF3: P113
Working at Home (Number of Persons)
    STF3: P49, P50, P52
Working Mothers
    Employment Status x Presence and Age of Children
        STF3: P73
    Children in Household x Age
        STF3: P74
Working Parents
    Employment Status of Women x Presence of Own Children
        STF3: GenProfile2, P73
    Children Present in Household x Employment Status of Parents
        STF3: P74
Working Teenagers
    Employment Status x Educational Attainment (Age 16-19)
        STF3: GenProfile2, P61, P62, P63
    x Hispanic Origin
        STF3: P63
    x Race
        STF3: P62
World War I Veterans
    Use: Military Service Times Period
World War II Veterans
    Use: Military Service Times Period

-Y-

Year Householder Moved into Unit
    Distribution (by Time Period)
        STF3: GenProfile4, H28
    x Housing Tenure
        STF3: H29
    Imputation
        STF3: H78

Part II
Section 5

Numerical List of Data Tables
STF 1 and *STF 3*

Numerical List of Data Tables, *STF 1* and *STF 3*

PART ONE: SUMMARY TAPE FILE 1A
(Note: Table structure is identical for all subfiles
except STF 1B)

Table Number	Title (Matrices) and Universe Measured	Number of data cells
P1.	Persons (1) Universe: Persons	1
P2.	Families (1) Universe: Families	1
P3.	Households (1) Universe: Households	1
P4.	Urban and Rural (4) Universe: Persons	4
P5.	Sex (2) Universe: Persons	2
P6.	Race (5) Universe: Persons	5
P7.	Race (25) Universe: Persons	25
P8.	Persons of Hispanic Origin (1) Universe: Persons of Hispanic origin	1
P9.	Hispanic Origin (5) Universe: Persons	5
P10.	Hispanic Origin (2) by Race (5) Universe: Persons	10
P11.	Age (31) Universe: Persons	31
P12.	Race (5) by Sex (2) by Age (31) Universe: Persons	310
P13.	Sex (2) by Age (31) Universe: Persons of Hispanic origin	62
P14.	Sex (2) by Marital Status (5) Universe: Persons 15 years and over	10
P15.	Household Type and Relationship (13) Universe: Persons	13
P16.	Household Size and Household Type (10) Universe: Households	10
P17.	Persons in Families (1) Universe: Persons in families	1

STF 1

P17A.　Persons per Family (1)　　1
　　　　Universe: Families

P18.　Age of Household Members (2) by
　　　Household Type (5)　　10
　　　Universe: Households

P19.　Race of Householder (5) by Household
　　　Type (8)　　40
　　　Universe: Households

P20.　Household Type (8)　　8
　　　Universe: Households with householder of
　　　Hispanic origin

P21.　Household Type and Relationship (9)　　9
　　　Universe: Persons under 18 years

P22.　Relationship and Age (37)　　37
　　　Universe: Persons under 18 years

P23.　Household Type and Relationship (12)　　12
　　　Universe: Persons 65 years and over

P24.　Age of Household Members (2) by Household Size
　　　and Household Type (3)　　6
　　　Universe: Households

P25.　Age of Household Members (2) by Household Size
　　　and Household Type (3)　　6
　　　Universe: Households

P26.　Household Type (2)　　2
　　　Universe: Households

P27.　Household Type and Household Size (13)　　13
　　　Universe: Households

P28.　Group Quarters (10)　　10
　　　Universe: Persons in group quarters

P29.　Persons Substituted (3)　　3
　　　Universe: Persons

P30.　Imputation of Population Items (2)　　2
　　　Universe: Persons not substituted

P31.　Imputation of Relationship (2)　　2
　　　Universe: Persons not substituted

P32.　Imputation of Sex (2)　　2
　　　Universe: Persons not substituted

P33.　Imputation of Age (2)　　2
　　　Universe: Persons not substituted

P34.　Imputation of Race (2)　　2
　　　Universe: Persons not substituted

P35.　Imputation of Hispanic Origin (2)　　2
　　　Universe: Persons not substituted

P36.　Imputation of Marital Status (3)　　3
　　　Universe: Persons 15 years and over

H1.　Housing Units (1)　　1
　　　Universe: Housing units

H2.　Occupancy Status (2)　　2
　　　Universe: Housing units

H3.　Tenure (2)　　2
　　　Universe: Occupied housing units

H4.　Urban and Rural (4)　　4
　　　Universe: Housing units

H5.　Vacancy Status (6)　　6
　　　Universe: Vacant housing units

H6.　Boarded-up Status (2)　　2
　　　Universe: Vacant housing units

H7.　Usual Home Elsewhere (2)　　2
　　　Universe: Vacant housing units

H8.　Race of Householder (5)　　5
　　　Universe: Occupied housing units

H9.　Tenure (2) by Race of Householder (5)　　10
　　　Universe: Occupied housing units

H10.　Hispanic Origin of Householder (2) by Race of
　　　Householder (5)　　10
　　　Universe: Occupied housing units

H11.　Tenure (2) by Race of Householder (5)　　10
　　　Universe: Occupied housing units with
　　　householder of Hispanic origin

H12.　Tenure (2) by Age of Householder (7)　　14
　　　Universe: Occupied housing units

H13.　Rooms (9)　　9
　　　Universe: Housing units

STF 1

H14. Aggregate Rooms (1)   1
      Universe: Housing units

H15. Aggregate Rooms (1) by Tenure (2)   2
      Universe: Occupied housing units

H16. Aggregate Rooms (1) by Vacancy Status (6)   6
      Universe: Vacant housing units

H17. Persons in Unit (7)   7
      Universe: Occupied housing units

H17A. Persons per Occupied Housing Unit (1)   1
      Universe: Occupied housing units

H18. Tenure (2) by Persons in Unit (7)   14
      Universe: Occupied housing units

H18A. Persons per Occupied Housing Unit by Tenure (2) 2
      Universe: Occupied housing units

H19. Aggregate Persons (1)   1
      Universe: Persons in occupied housing units

H20. Aggregate Persons (1) by Tenure (2)   2
      Universe: Persons in occupied housing units

H21. Persons per Room (5)   5
      Universe: Occupied housing units

H22. Tenure (2) by Persons per Room (5)   10
      Universe: Occupied housing units

H23. Value (20)   20
      Universe: Specified owner-occupied housing units

H23A. Lower Value Quartile (1)   1
      Universe: Specified owner-occupied housing units

H23B. Median Value (1)   1
      Universe: Specified owner-occupied housing units

H23C. Upper Value Quartile (1)   1
      Universe: Specified owner-occupied housing units

H24. Aggregate Value (1)   1
      Universe: Specified owner-occupied housing units

H25. Race of Householder (5)   5
      Universe: Specified owner-occupied housing units

H26. Aggregate Value (1) by Race of Householder (5) 5
      Universe: Specified owner-occupied housing units

H27. Hispanic Origin of Householder (2)   2
      Universe: Specified owner-occupied housing units

H28. Aggregate Value (1) by Hispanic Origin of House-
      holder (2)   2
      Universe: Specified owner-occupied housing units

H29. Aggregate Value (1) by Units in Structure (6)   6
      Universe: Owner-occupied housing units

H30. Vacancy Status (3)   3
      Universe: Vacant housing units

H31. Aggregate Price Asked (1)   1
      Universe: Specified vacant-for-sale-only housing
      units

H32. Contract Rent (17)   17
      Universe: Specified renter-occupied housing units

H32A. Lower Contract Rent Quartile (1)   1
      Universe: Specified renter-occupied housing units
      paying cash rent

H32B. Median Contract Rent (1)   1
      Universe: Specified renter-occupied housing units
      paying cash rent

H32C. Upper Contract Rent Quartile (1)   1
      Universe: Specified renter-occupied housing units
      paying cash rent

H33. Aggregate Contract Rent (1)   1
      Universe: Specified renter-occupied housing units
      paying cash rent

H34. Race of Householder (5)   5
      Universe: Specified renter-occupied housing units
      paying cash rent

H35. Aggregate Contract Rent (1) by Race of House-
      holder(5)   5
      Universe: Specified renter-occupied housing units
      paying cash rent

H36. Hispanic Origin of Householder (2)   2
      Universe: Specified renter-occupied housing units
      paying cash rent

H37. Aggregate Contract Rent (1) by Hispanic Origin of
      Householder (2)   2
      Universe: Specified renter-occupied housing units
      paying cash rent

STF 1

H38.   Aggregate Rent Asked (1)   1
       Universe: Specified vacant-for-rent housing units

H39.   Age of Householder (2) by Meals Included
       in Rent (3)   6
       Universe: Specified renter-occupied housing units

H40.   Vacancy Status (3) by Duration of Vacancy (3) 9
       Universe: Vacant housing units

H41.   Units in Structure (10)   10
       Universe: Housing units

H42.   Units in Structure (10)   10
       Universe: Vacant housing units

H43.   Tenure (2) by Units in Structure (10)   20
       Universe: Occupied housing units

H44.   Aggregate Persons (1) by Tenure (2) by Units
       in Structure (10)   20
       Universe: Persons in occupied housing units

H45.   Housing Units Substituted (2)   2
       Universe: Housing units

H46.   Imputation of Housing Items (2)   2
       Universe: Housing units not substituted

H47.   Imputation of Vacancy Status (3)   3
       Universe: Vacant housing units

H48.   Imputation of Duration of Vacancy (3)   3
       Universe: Vacant housing units

H49.   Imputation of Units in Structure (2)   2
       Universe: Housing units not substituted

H50.   Imputation of Rooms (2)   2
       Universe: Housing units not substituted

H51.   Imputation of Tenure (3)   3
       Universe: Occupied housing units

H52.   Imputation of Value (3)   3
       Universe: Specified owner-occupied housing units

H53.   Imputation of Price Asked (3)   3
       Universe: Specified vacant-for-sale-only housing
       units

H54.   Imputation of Contract Rent (4)   4
       Universe: Specified renter-occupied housing units

H55.   Imputation of Meals Included in Rent (4)   4
       Universe: Specified renter-occupied housing units

PART TWO: SUMMARYTAPE FILE 3A
(Note: Table structure is identical for all STF 3 subfiles)

Table Number	Title (Matrices) and Universe Measured	Number of data cells
P1.	PERSONS (1) Universe: Persons	1
P2.	UNWEIGHTED SAMPLE COUNT OF PERSONS (1) Universe: Persons	1
P3	100-PERCENT COUNT OF PERSONS (1) Universe: Persons	1
P3A.	PERCENT OF PERSONS IN SAMPLE (1) Universe: Persons	1
P4.	FAMILIES (1) Universe: Families	1
P5.	HOUSEHOLDS (1) Universe: Households	1
P6.	URBAN AND RURAL (4) Universe: Persons	4
P7.	SEX (2) Universe: Persons	2
P8.	RACE (5) Universe: Persons	5
P9.	RACE (25) Universe: Persons	25
P10.	PERSONS OF HISPANIC ORIGIN (1) Universe: Persons of Hispanic origin	1
P11.	HISPANIC ORIGIN (16) Universe: Persons	16
P12.	HISPANIC ORIGIN (2) BY RACE (5) Universe: Persons	10
P13.	AGE (31) Universe: Persons	31

STF 3

STF 3

STF 3

STF 3

STF 3

STF 3

FAMILY TYPE AND PRESENCE AND AGE OF CHILDREN (12)   60
Universe: Families with income in 1989 below poverty level

P125.   POVERTY STATUS IN 1989 (2) BY FAMILY TYPE AND PRESENCE AND AGE OF CHILDREN (12)   24
Universe: Families with householder of Hispanic origin

P126.   POVERTY STATUS IN 1989 (2) BY FAMILY TYPE AND AGE (9)   18
Universe: Related children under 18 years

P127.   POVERTY STATUS IN 1989 (2) BY AGE OF HOUSEHOLDER (3) BY HOUSEHOLD TYPE (5)   30
Universe: Households

P128.   IMPUTATION OF POPULATION ITEMS (3)   3
Universe: Persons

P129.   IMPUTATION OF RELATIONSHIP (2)   2
Universe: Persons in households

P130.   IMPUTATION OF SEX (3)   3
Universe: Persons

P131.   IMPUTATION OF AGE (3)   3
Universe: Persons

P132.   IMPUTATION OF RACE (3)   3
Universe: Persons

P133.   IMPUTATION OF MARITAL STATUS (3)   3
Universe: Persons 15 years and over

P134.   IMPUTATION OF HISPANIC ORIGIN (3)   3
Universe: Persons

P135.   IMPUTATION OF GROUP QUARTERS (2) 2
Universe: Persons in group quarters

P136.   IMPUTATION OF PLACE OF BIRTH (3)   3
Universe: Persons

P137.   IMPUTATION OF CITIZENSHIP (3)   3
Universe: Persons

P138.   IMPUTATION OF YEAR OF ENTRY (3)   3
Universe: Foreign-born persons

P139.   IMPUTATION OF SCHOOL ENROLLMENT (3)   3
Universe: Persons 3 years and over

P140.   IMPUTATION OF EDUCATIONAL ATTAIN-MENT (3)   3
Universe: Persons 18 years and over

P141.   IMPUTATION OF EDUCATIONAL ATTAIN-MENT (3)   3
Universe: Persons 25 years and over

P142.   IMPUTATION OF ANCESTRY (3)   3
Universe: Persons

P143.   IMPUTATION OF MOBILITY STATUS (3) 3
Universe: Persons 5 years and over

P144.   IMPUTATION OF RESIDENCE IN 1985 (5) 5
Universe: Persons 5 years and over

P145.   IMPUTATION OF LANGUAGE STATUS (3) 3
Universe: Persons 5 years and over

P146.   IMPUTATION OF LANGUAGE SPOKEN AT HOME (4)   4
Universe: Persons 5 years and over

P147.   IMPUTATION OF ABILITY TO SPEAK EN-GLISH (4)   4
Universe: Persons 5 years and over

P148.   IMPUTATION OF VETERAN STATUS (2) 2
Universe: Persons 16 years and over

P149.   IMPUTATION OF PERIOD OF MILITARY SERVICE (3)   3
Universe: Civilian veterans 16 years and over

P150.   IMPUTATION OF WORK DISABILITY STA-TUS (3)   3
Universe: Civilian noninstitutionalized persons 16 years and over

P151.   IMPUTATION OF MOBILITY LIMITATION STATUS (3)   3
Universe: Civilian noninstitutionalized persons 16 years and over

P152.   IMPUTATION OF SELF-CARE LIMITATION STATUS (3)   3
Universe: Civilian noninstitutionalized persons 16 years and over

STF 3

STF 3

H10. TENURE (2) BY RACE OF HOUSE-
HOLDER (5)   10
Universe: Occupied housing units

H11. HISPANIC ORIGIN OF HOUSE-
HOLDER (2) BY RACE OF
HOUSEHOLDER (5)   10
Universe: Occupied housing units

H12. TENURE (2) BY RACE OF HOUSE-
HOLDER (5)   10
Universe: Occupied housing units with
householder of Hispanic origin

H13. TENURE (2) BY AGE OF HOUSE-
HOLDER (7)   14
Universe: Occupied housing units

H14. AGGREGATE PERSONS (1) BY
TENURE (2) BY RACE OF
HOUSEHOLDER (5)   10
Universe: Persons in occupied housing units

H15. AGGREGATE PERSONS (1) BY
TENURE (2)   2
Universe: Persons in occupied housing units with
householder of Hispanic origin

H16. ROOMS (9)   9
Universe: Housing units

H17. AGGREGATE ROOMS (1)   1
Universe: Housing units

H18. TENURE (2) BY PERSONS IN UNIT (7)   14
Universe: Occupied housing units

H19. AGGREGATE PERSONS (1) BY
TENURE (2)   2
Universe: Persons in occupied housing units

H20. UNITS IN STRUCTURE (10)   10
Universe: Housing units

H21. UNITS IN STRUCTURE (10)   10
Universe: Vacant housing units

H22. TENURE (2) BY UNITS IN
STRUCTURE (10)   20
Universe: Occupied housing units

H23. SOURCE OF WATER (4)   4
Universe: Housing units

H24. SEWAGE DISPOSAL (3)   3
Universe: Housing units

H25. YEAR STRUCTURE BUILT (8)   8
Universe: Housing units

H25A. MEDIAN YEAR STRUCTURE BUILT (1)   1
Universe: Housing units

H26. YEAR STRUCTURE BUILT (8)   8
Universe: Vacant housing units

H27. TENURE (2) BY YEAR STRUCTURE
BUILT (8)   16
Universe: Occupied housing units

H28. YEAR HOUSEHOLDER MOVED INTO
UNIT (6)   6
Universe: Occupied housing units

H29. TENURE (2) BY YEAR HOUSEHOLDER
MOVED INTO UNIT (6)   12
Universe: Occupied housing units

H30. HOUSE HEATING FUEL (9)   9
Universe: Occupied housing units

H31. BEDROOMS (6)   6
Universe: Housing units

H32. BEDROOMS (6)   6
Universe: Vacant housing units

H33. TENURE (2) BY BEDROOMS (6)   12
Universe: Occupied housing units

H34. BEDROOMS (4) BY GROSS RENT (7)   28
Universe: Specified renter-occupied housing units

H35. TENURE (2) BY TELEPHONE IN HOUSING
UNIT (2)   4
Universe: Occupied housing units

H36. AGE OF HOUSEHOLDER (4) BY TELEPHONE
IN HOUSING UNIT (2)   8
Universe: Occupied housing units

H37. TENURE (2) BY VEHICLES AVAILABLE (6) 12
Universe: Occupied housing units

H38. AGGREGATE VEHICLES AVAILABLE (1) BY
TENURE (2)   2
Universe: Occupied housing units

STF 3

H39. RACE OF HOUSEHOLDER (5) BY VEHICLES
AVAILABLE (2) 10
Universe: Occupied housing units

H40. VEHICLES AVAILABLE (2) 2
Universe: Occupied housing units with householder
of Hispanic origin

H41. AGE OF HOUSEHOLDER (2) BY VEHICLES
AVAILABLE (2) 4
Universe: Occupied housing units

H42. KITCHEN FACILITIES (2) 2
Universe: Housing units

H43. GROSS RENT (17) 17
Universe: Specified renter-occupied housing units

H43A. MEDIAN GROSS RENT (1) 1
Universe: Specified renter-occupied housing units
paying cash rent

H44. AGGREGATE GROSS RENT (1) 1
Universe: Specified renter-occupied housing units
paying cash rent

H45. RACE OF HOUSEHOLDER (5) BY GROSS
RENT (7) 35
Universe: Specified renter-occupied housing units

H46. HISPANIC ORIGIN (2) BY GROSS RENT (7) 14
Universe: Specified renter-occupied housing units

H47. MEALS INCLUDED IN RENT (2) 2
Universe: Specified renter-occupied housing units
paying cash rent

H48. AGGREGATE GROSS RENT (1) BY MEALS
INCLUDED IN RENT (2) 2
Universe: Specified renter-occupied housing units
paying cash rent

H49. INCLUSION OF UTILITIES IN RENT (2) 2
Universe: Specified renter-occupied housing units

H50. HOUSEHOLD INCOME IN 1989 (5) BY GROSS
RENT AS A PERCENTAGE
OF HOUSEHOLD INCOME IN 1989 (6) 30
Universe: Specified renter-occupied housing units

H50A. MEDIAN GROSS RENT AS A PERCENTAGE
OF HOUSEHOLD INCOME
IN 1989 (1) 1
Universe: Specified renter-occupied housing units
paying cash rent

H51. AGE OF HOUSEHOLDER (2) BY GROSS RENT
AS A PERCENTAGE OF
HOUSEHOLD INCOME IN 1989 (6) 12
Universe: Specified renter-occupied housing units

H52. MORTGAGE STATUS AND SELECTED
MONTHLY OWNER COSTS (21) 21
Universe: Specified owner-occupied housing units

H52A. MEDIAN SELECTED MONTHLY OWNER
COSTS AND MORTGAGE STATUS (2) 2
Universe: Specified owner-occupied housing units

H53. AGGREGATE SELECTED MONTHLY OWNER
COSTS (1) BY MORTGAGE
STATUS (2) 2
Universe: Specified owner-occupied housing units

H54. RACE OF HOUSEHOLDER (5) BY MORT-
GAGE STATUS AND SELECTED
MONTHLY OWNER COSTS (11) 55
Universe: Specified owner-occupied housing units

H55. MORTGAGE STATUS AND SELECTED
MONTHLY OWNER COSTS (11) 11
Universe: Specified owner-occupied housing
units with householder of Hispanic origin

H56. AGGREGATE SELECTED MONTHLY
OWNER COSTS (1) BY MORTGAGE
STATUS (2) 2
Universe: Owner-occupied mobile homes or trailers

H57. AGGREGATE SELECTED MONTHLY
OWNER COSTS (1) BY MORTGAGE
STATUS (2) 2
Universe: Owner-occupied condominium housing
units

H58. MORTGAGE STATUS (2) BY SELECTED
MONTHLY OWNER COSTS ASA PERCENT-
AGE OF HOUSEHOLD INCOME
IN 1989 (6) 12
Universe: Specified owner-occupied housing units

STF 3

STF 3

H82.   IMPUTATION OF TELEPHONE IN
        HOUSING UNIT (2)   2
        Universe: Occupied housing units

H83.   IMPUTATION OF VEHICLES
        AVAILABLE (2)   2
        Universe: Occupied housing units

H84.   IMPUTATION OF MORTGAGE
        STATUS (2)   2
        Universe: Specified owner-occupied housing units

H85.   IMPUTATION OF TENURE (2)   2
        Universe: Occupied housing units

H86.   IMPUTATION OF VACANCY
        STATUS (2)   2
        Universe: Vacant housing units

H87.   IMPUTATION OF ROOMS (2)   2
        Universe: Housing units

H88.   IMPUTATION OF UNITS IN
        STRUCTURE (2)   2
        Universe: Housing units

H89.   IMPUTATION OF VALUE (2)   2
        Universe: Specified owner-occupied housing units

H90.   IMPUTATION OF MEALS INCLUDED IN
        RENT (2)   2
        Universe: Specified renter-occupied housing units
        paying cash rent

H91.   IMPUTATION OF GROSS RENT (2)   2
        Universe: Specified renter-occupied housing units

H92.   IMPUTATION OF MORTGAGE STATUS
        AND SELECTED MONTHLY OWNER
        COSTS (4)   4
        Universe: Specified owner-occupied housing units

Part II
Section 6

List of Tables Containing Special Population or Housing Universes

List of Tables Containing Special Population or Housing Universes

THE FOLLOWING GUIDE lists *STF 1* and *STF 3* tables according to the Universe (domain) covered in the table. Many population tables cover the entire population, but others are limited to a subgroup of the population. For example, the data in Table P61 of *STF 3* pertain to persons age 16 to 19 years only. Likewise, some housing tables pertain to all Housing Units, but others are restricted to a particular subgroup, such as Owner-Occupied Units.

The Universes shown in Census tables are often determined by definitions established by the Bureau of the Census. For example, Poverty Status is not measured for all persons. Excluded from the definition of Poverty are Unrelated Individuals under the age of 15, plus persons living in Institutions, college dormitories, or military barracks. Therefore, the Universe for most Poverty tables is limited to "Persons for Whom Poverty Status is Determined." Similarly, the Census Bureau does not ask small children questions about spoken language, so many language tables are limited to "Persons Age 5 and Older."

Another reason for using different Universes is to provide detailed information about particular segments of the population, such as teenagers, working mothers, the elderly, or Hispanics.

The listings below provide an alphabetical index to the population and housing Universes used in *STF 1* and *STF 3*. Users of *Summary Tape Files* on CD-ROM should always be careful to identify the pertinent Universe before turning to a particular Census table. The Universe for each table can also be seen in the numerical list of tables shown in Part II, Section 5.

Age — Persons 3 Years and Over
    STF3: P54, P55, P139
Age — Persons 5 Years and Over
    STF3: P28, P30, P31, P43, P44, P143, P144, P145, P146, P147
Age — Persons 15 Years and Over
    STF1: P14, P36
    STF3: P27, P114, P115, P133, P166

Age — Persons 16 to 19 Years
STF3: P61, P62
Age — Persons 16 Years and Over
STF3: P64, P70, P71, P75, P76, P148, P159, P160, P161, P162
Age — Persons Under 18 Years
STF1: P21, P22
Age — Persons 18 Years and Over
STF3: P60, P140
Age — Persons 25 Years and Over
STF3: P57, P58, P141
Age — Persons 65 Years and Over
STF1: P23
STF3: P18
American Indian, Eskimo, or Aleut Females
STF3: P14F
American Indian, Eskimo, or Aleut Households
STF3: P87C
American Indian, Eskimo, or Aleut Males
STF3: P14E
Asian and Pacific Islander Females
STF3: P14H
Asian and Pacific Islander Households
STF3: P87D
Asian and Pacific Islander Males
STF3: P14G
Black Females
STF3: P14D
Black Households
STF3: P87B
Black Males
STF3: P14C
Civilian Noninstitutionalized Persons 16 Years and Over
STF3: P66, P67, P68, P69, P150, P151, P152
Civilian Veterans 16 Years and Over
STF3: P65, P149
Condominium Units, Owner Occupied
Use: Owner-Occupied Condominium Housing Units
Employed Persons 16 Years and Over
STF3: P77, P78, P79, P163, P164, P165
Families
STF1: P2, P17A
STF3: P4, P22, P107, P107A, P108, P109, P112, P113, P123, P168
See Also: Persons in Families
Families with Householder of Hispanic Origin (Above and Below Poverty Level)
STF3: P125
Families with Income in 1989 Above Poverty Level
STF3: P124A
Families with Income in 1989 Below Poverty Level
STF3: P124B

Occupied Housing Units
    STF1: H3, H8, H9, H10, H12, H15, H17, H17A, H18, H18A, H21, H22, H43, H51
    STF3: H7, H8, H9, H10, H11, H13, H18, H22, H27, H28, H29, H30, H33, H35, H36, H37, H38,
        H39, H41, H63, H66, H68, H69, H71, H78, H79, H82, H83, H85
Occupied Housing Units with Householder of Hispanic Origin
    STF1: H11
    STF3: H12, H40, H67
    See Also: Households with Householder of Hispanic Origin
    See Also: Specified Owner-Occupied Housing Units with Householder of Hispanic Origin
Other Race Females
    STF3: P14J
Other Race Households
    STF3: P87E
Other Race Males
    STF3: P14I
Own Children Under 18 Years
    STF3: P23
    See Also: Related Children Under 18 Years
Own Children Under 18 Years in Families and Subfamilies
    STF3: P74
Owner-Occupied Condominium Housing Units
    STF3: H57
Owner-Occupied Housing Units
    STF1: H29
    See Also: Specified Owner-Occupied Housing Units
Owner-Occupied Mobile Homes or Trailers
    STF3: H56
Persons (Total)
    STF1: P1, P4, P5, P6, P7, P9, P10, P11, P12, P15, P29
    STF3: P1, P2, P3, P3A, P6, P7, P8, P9, P11, P12, P13, P17, P32, P33, P34, P35, P37, P42, P114A, P114B,
        P115A, P128, P130, P131, P132, P134, P136, P137, P142
Persons by Age Group
    Use: Age — Persons...
Persons for Whom Poverty Status is Determined
    STF3: P117, P118, P119, P121, P122, P170
Persons in Families
    STF1: P17
    See Also: Families
Persons in Group Quarters
    STF1: P28
    STF3: P40, P41, P135
Persons in Households
    STF3: P106, P129
    See Also: Households
    See Also: Persons in Occupied Housing Units
Persons in Occupied Housing Units
    STF1: H19, H20, H44
    STF3: H14

Part III

Glossary of Commonly Misunderstood Census Terms

Compiled by Michael Lavin

Glossary of Commonly Misunderstood Census Terms

Terms are listed in alphabetical order. Words or phrases which appear in bold can also be found in the Glossary under their own entries.

Users who wish to read more detailed definitions should consult the *1990 Census of Population and Housing Guide: Part B. Glossary*, published by the Bureau of the Census in 1993. Partial glossaries can also be found in "Appendix B" of any printed Census report or any CD-ROM disc. Readers may also wish to explore *Understanding the Census*, published by Epoch books in 1996. The latter work provides in-depth discussions of Census terms and explains their relationships to one another.

ABILITY TO SPEAK ENGLISH

All persons age five or older who speak a language other than English in the home are asked to identify their level of English proficiency. Respondents choose one of the following levels: very well; well; not well; or not at all. The Census Bureau also measures **Household** ability to speak English as **Linguistic Isolation**.

ADULT CHILD

A **Child** age 18 or older who is living with one or more parents.

AGGREGATE

The sum of all individual responses for a specific characteristic. For example, the aggregate **Income** for a city would be the sum of all incomes received by every person in that city. The Census provides aggregate values to enable users to calculate averages (means) or to perform similar statistical analyses.

ALLOCATION

An **Imputation** method where the Census Bureau assigns partial characteristics to a person or Housing Unit for which incomplete answers were received. A more detailed description of the Allocation process can be found in Chapter 10 of *Understanding the Census*.

AMERICAN INDIAN, ESKIMO, OR ALEUT

One of the five basic categories of Race reported by the Census. Tabulation is based on self-identification by the respondent. Some Census tables subdivide this category into its three component parts. Special subject reports tabulate the Native American population by tribe.

ANCESTRY

The ethnic origin, heritage, or "roots" with which a person most closely identifies. Ancestry can be the person's **Place of Birth**, his/her parents' place of birth, or that of his/her ancestors. Respondents can identify a single ancestry group (e.g., Irish) or two ancestry groups (e.g., German and Irish). For persons of **Hispanic Origin**, their ethnic background is tabulated under "detailed Hispanic Origin," not Ancestry. For persons of **Asian or Pacific Islander** ancestry, their ethnic background is recorded under "detailed Race."

ASIAN OR PACIFIC ISLANDER

One of the five basic categories of Race reported by the Census. Tabulation is based on self-identification by the respondent. Some Census tables subdivide this category into more detailed breakdowns, such as Japanese, Vietnamese, or Hawaiian.

BEDROOM

A room is counted as a bedroom if it was designed for that purpose, regardless of its use by the Housing Unit's current occupants. The room is defined as it would be if the house or apartment were listed for sale or rent.

BLACK

One of the five basic categories of Race reported by the Census. Tabulation is based on self-identification by the respondent.

CHILD

A son or daughter of the **Householder**, by birth, marriage, or adoption, regardless of the Child's age. Children are tabulated under Household relationship in the following two categories: natural born or adopted child; and step-child. The Census Bureau also tabulates data for more specialized definitions known as **Own Child** and **Related Child**.

CHILDREN EVER BORN
See: Fertility.

CIVILIAN LABOR FORCE

All persons in the **Labor Force** except persons currently serving in the armed forces.

CLASS OF WORKER

Employed persons are subdivided by the sector of the economy in which they are employed, according to the following categories: government employee; private sector employee (wage or salary earning); self-employed; or **Unpaid Family Worker**. The Bureau also classifies **Employed** Persons by Industry and by Occupation.

COMPLETE COUNT DATA

Also called 100% data. Tabulations are based on responses from all Census Questionnaires, both short-form and long-form. The decennial Census also tabulates results based on **Sample Data**.

CONDOMINIUM

A condominium is a type of property ownership which allows a person to own an apartment or a house in a development of similarly owned units, while at the same time holding joint or common ownership to shared areas in the development, such as land, hallways, swimming pool, etc.

CONGREGATE HOUSING
See: Meals Included in Rent.

CONTRACT RENT

The monthly rent agreed to or contracted for between landlord and tenant, regardless of any additional services included in the fee. Contract Rent can include money for utilities, meals, maintenance, or other services, if they are part of the monthly payment. Contract Rent for Vacant Units is tabulated as "Rent Asked." **Renter Occupied Units** where the tenant lives "rent free" may be tabulated separately as "No Cash Rent." The Census Bureau also tabulates data for **Meals Included in Rent**. Another measure of rental costs is **Gross Rent**.

DISABILITY STATUS

The 1990 Census reports three types of disability, each of which is self-identified by the respondent: **Mobility Limitation**, **Self-Care Limitation**, and **Work Disability**.

EARNINGS

A **Source of Income** which includes wages or salary received for work performed as an employee, as well as any net income received from self-employment.

EMERGENCY SHELTERS AND VISIBLE IN STREET LOCATIONS

An enumeration category which tabulates persons who were counted during the Census Bureau's special "Shelter and Street Night" operations on March 20-21, 1990. The sum of the two categories-- **Emergency Shelters for Homeless Persons** and **Visible in Street Locations** -- may be considered an estimate of the 1990 homeless population, though the data are subject to many limitations.

EMERGENCY SHELTERS FOR HOMELESS PERSONS

Counts persons who stayed at temporary emergency facilities, including city missions, flophouses, and Salvation Army centers overnight on "Shelter Night" (March 20-21, 1990).

EMPLOYED

Persons age 16 or older who were at work in one of the following categories: as paid employees in the **Civilian Labor Force** or in the armed forces; as self-employed business people, professionals, or farmers; or as **Unpaid Family Workers** who worked 15 hours or more in the family business. The Employed category also includes persons who had jobs during the **Reference Week** but were temporarily absent due to illness, vacation, or similar reasons.

EMPLOYMENT STATUS

Persons age 16 years or older who are in the **Labor Force** during the Reference Week are tabulated as either **Employed** or **Unemployed**.

ENGLISH LANGUAGE PROFICIENCY
See: Ability to Speak English.

EXPERIENCED UNEMPLOYED

Unemployed persons who have worked at some time in the past.
The Experienced Labor Force consists of all **Employed** Persons plus all Experienced Unemployed.

FAMILY

A **Household** in which one or more members is related to the **Householder** by birth, marriage, or adoption. Also known as a Family Household. Families are subdivided into three categories: **Married-Couple Families; Female Householder, No Husband Present**; and Male Householder, No Wife Present. The key element in defining families and family type is the Householder and the relationship of other Household members to this person. **Nonrelatives** living with a family are members of the Household, but not members of the Family. Some members of a Family can also comprise a **Subfamily**.

FAMILY INCOME

The sum of all **Income** received in 1989 by Family members age 15 or older. A subset of **Household Income**.

FAMILY RELATIONSHIP
See: Household Relationship.

FARM

Any **Housing Unit** situated on one acre or more of land and which sold $1,000 or more of agricultural products in 1989. By definition, a Farm must be located in a **Rural** territory. All persons living on a Farm in a Rural area constitute the Farm Population. Persons living in **Group Quarters** or in multi-unit buildings are excluded from the Farm Population.

FEMALE HOUSEHOLDER, NO HUSBAND PRESENT

Any **Family** Household whose **Householder** is female and is either not married or whose husband does not live in the **Household**. Such Households can consist of a mother and her child (or children), or they can consist of a female Householder who lives with other family members, such as a sister or a parent. Excluded from this category are single-person Households and other **Nonfamily Households** with a female Householder (e.g., two female roommates).

FERTILITY

Also known as Children Ever Born. The total number of children born to any woman during her lifetime, including children who died at some point after birth or who no longer live with their mother. Stillborn babies and adopted children are excluded from this tabulation.

This question is asked of all females age 15 or older, regardless of **Marital Status**.

GROSS RENT

Contract Rent plus the estimated monthly cost of utilities and heating fuels, if these are paid for by the tenant. Gross Rent is designed to eliminate the difference between a Contract Rent which includes the cost of utilities and a Contract Rent which does not.

GROUP QUARTERS

Any living quarters which are not counted as **Housing Units** are classified as Group Quarters. The decennial Census does not count the actual number of Group Quarters, but it does tabulate the number of persons living in Group Quarters. Group Quarters are classified into two types: **Institutions**, and **Noninstitutional Group Quarters**. The distinctions between these categories can be subtle, and data users are encouraged to consult more detailed Census definitions.

HISPANIC ORIGIN

Persons born in a Spanish-speaking country or descended from persons born in a Spanish-speaking country. All persons are counted as either Hispanic or Non-Hispanic. In some tables, Hispanic Origin is subdivided by specific country, such as Mexican, Cuban, Puerto Rican, etc. Tabulation is based on self-identification of the respondent. Hispanic Origin is not a racial category, because persons of Hispanic Origin can be of any **Race**.

HOMELESS POPULATION

See: Emergency Shelters and Visible in Street Locations.

HOUSEHOLD

All persons living in an **Occupied Housing Unit** comprise a Household. In **Complete-Count** tabulations, the number of Households equals the number of Occupied Housing Units in a given geographic area. Households are divided into two types: Family Households, and **Nonfamily Households**. Households are also classified according to various characteristics of the Householder, such as age, sex, **Race**, or **Hispanic Origin**.

HOUSEHOLD INCOME

The sum of all **Income** received in 1989 by all persons in the **Household** age 15 or older, whether they were related to the **Householder** or not. Because many

Households consist of one person only, median **Family Income** is usually greater than **median** Household Income.

HOUSEHOLD RELATIONSHIP

Household members are defined by their relationship to the **Householder**. In **Family** Households, members are classified as spouses, natural-born or adopted children, step-children, nephews, etc. Persons not related to the Householder are classified as **Nonrelatives**, whether they live in a Family Household or a **Nonfamily Household**.

HOUSEHOLDER

Each **Household** has one Householder, defined as the person who fills in column one of the Census questionnaire. Usually this is the person in whose name the **Housing Unit** is owned or rented. Households are classified according to various characteristics of the Householder. Other Household members are defined by their relationship to the Householder.

HOUSING TENURE

All **Occupied Housing Units** are classified according to Tenure, as either **Owner Occupied Housing Units** or **Renter Occupied Housing Units**.

HOUSING UNIT

A Housing Unit is a house, an apartment, a mobile home, a room, or a group of rooms that is intended as a separate living quarters. Members of the Housing Unit must live and eat separately from other persons in the building, and they must have direct access to the Unit from the outdoors or through a common hallway, otherwise the living quarters cannot be tabulated as a separate Housing Unit. By definition, 10 or more **Unrelated Individuals** living together constitute a **Group Quarters**, not a Housing Unit. Housing Units are subdivided into **Occupied Housing Units** and **Vacant Housing Units**.

HOUSING VALUE

The market value (as identified by the owner) of **Owner Occupied Housing Units**, or the price asked for Units that are **Vacant** and For Sale. Value includes the lot and all buildings on the lot, except in the case of **Condominium** Units.

Housing Value is tabulated separately for Owner Occupied Housing Units, and for Vacant-For-Sale Housing Units, as well as for **Specified Owner Occupied Housing Units** and Specified Vacant-For-Sale Housing Units.

IMPUTATION

A technique used by the Census Bureau to complete missing information on questionnaires. The Census Bureau creates fictitious responses by assigning characteristics from a similar person or **Housing Unit**. Two types of Imputation are employed: **Allocation** and **Substitution**. Detailed statistics on the amount of Imputation which occurred in 1990 are available for every geographic entity and every major population or housing characteristic. Imputation tables are found on all *STF 1* and *STF 3* CD-ROM discs.

INCOME

The sum of all money received in 1989 by persons age 15 or older from each of the eight **Sources of Income** tabulated by the Census. Sources of Income exclude numerous exceptions: noncash benefits (such as food stamps or employer contributions to retirement funds); money received from the sale of property; borrowed funds; money withdrawn from bank accounts; gifts; insurance settlements; and similar lump-sum payments. Income may be tabulated as **Personal Income, Family Income,** or **Household Income.**

INDIVIDUAL INCOME

See: Personal Income.

INSTITUTION

Group Quarters in which the patients or inmates are under the care and supervision of trained staff. Institutionalized persons are generally restricted to the Institution's building or grounds, and they have limited interactions with their surrounding community. Examples include correctional facilities, mental hospitals, and nursing homes.

JOURNEY TO WORK

Journey to Work comprises a series of Census questions measuring commuting patterns. The Journey to Work questions include Place of Work, the time leaving home for work, travel time (the duration of the trip), the means of transportation used, and for personal vehicles, the **Private Vehicle Occupancy.**

KITCHEN FACILITIES

The 1990 Census differentiates between **Housing Units** with complete kitchen facilities and those lacking complete facilities. Housing Units have Complete Kitchen Facilities if they include all of the following: a sink with piped water, an oven (microwave or convection); a range, cook top, or stove; and a refrigerator.

LABOR FORCE

The Labor Force consists of all persons age 16 or older who are **Employed** or **Unemployed,** including those in the armed forces. Persons outside the Labor Force include full-time students, homemakers, retired persons, and persons who are out of work but no longer seeking a job. A subcategory is the **Civilian Labor Force.**

LANGUAGE SPOKEN AT HOME

Each person in the **Household** was asked whether they sometimes or always spoke a language other than English in the home. Excluded from this category are persons who speak a foreign language at school only, or who only know a few words of the foreign language.

LINGUISTIC ISOLATION

A **Household** in which all persons age 14 or older speak a language other than English in the home, and no person speaks English "very well."

MARITAL HISTORY

Tabulated for females only, as a **Fertility** characteristic. Responses are classified into two categories: Never Married, and Ever Married. The latter grouping includes persons currently married, as well as persons who are widowed or divorced.

MARITAL STATUS

All persons age 15 or older are classified into one of the following categories: Never Married (including Separated); Married; Divorced; and Widowed.

MARRIED COUPLE FAMILY

A **Family** Household in which the **Householder** and spouse live together. Married Couple Families are subdivided into two categories: with children present, and no children present.

MEALS INCLUDED IN RENT

Housing Units for which the **Contract Rent** includes

the cost of meals provided. This item is intended to measure "congregate housing," where rent includes meals and other services, such as transportation to shopping. Such Housing Units are generally designed for the elderly population not living in **Group Quarters**.

MEDIAN
A type of average. The middle value in a ranked list of responses.

MOBILITY LIMITATION
A mental or physical health condition lasting six months or longer which restricts the respondent's ability to leave the home alone (i.e., to perform such tasks as shopping or visiting a doctor). One of three types of **Disability Status** tabulated by the 1990 Census.

MONTHLY OWNER COSTS
See : Selected Monthly Owner Costs.

NATIVITY
See: Place of Birth.

NONFAMILY HOUSEHOLD
A **Household** consisting of one person living alone, or two or more **Unrelated Individuals** living together. Unrelated individuals may be roommates, or they may share a more personal relationship as an **Unmarried Couple** or as **Unmarried Partners**.

NONINSTITUTIONAL GROUP QUARTERS
Group Quarters consisting of ten or more **Unrelated Individuals** who are not inmates of an **Institution**. Examples include college dormitories, military barracks, and **Emergency Shelters for the Homeless**.

NONRELATIVE
Any **Household** member who is not related to the Householder. "Nonrelative" is one component of the broader category of **Unrelated Individual**.

OCCUPIED HOUSING UNIT
A **Housing Unit** which is the **Place of Usual Residence** for the persons living in it at the time of the Census. This includes Housing Units whose inhabitants are temporarily away due to vacation or similar absence. In **Complete-Count** tabulations, the number of Occupied Housing Units equals the number of **Households**. Occupied Housing Units are subdivided into **Owner**

Occupied Housing Units and **Renter Occupied Housing Units**.

100% DATA
See: Complete Count Data.

OTHER RACE
One of the five basic categories of **Race** reported by the Census. Persons are counted in this category when they did not identify one of the other four racial groups in their response. The majority of persons tabulated in the "Other Race" category mistakenly indicated **Hispanic** as their racial group. Tabulation is based on self-identification by the respondent.

OWN CHILD
A son or daughter of the **Householder** (by birth, marriage, or adoption) who is age 17 years or younger. Own Child is a subset of **Child**.

OWNER COSTS
See: Selected Monthly Owner Costs.

OWNER OCCUPIED HOUSING UNIT
A **Housing Unit** inhabited by its owner. For certain tabulations, the Census Bureau also defines a special category called **Specified Owner Occupied Housing Units**.

PER CAPITA INCOME
The **Aggregate** amount of **Income** for a population group, divided by the total population for that group (i.e., the Income per person for every man, woman, and child).

PERSONAL INCOME
Income received in 1989 by any individual age 15 or older who lives in a **Household** or in a **Noninstitutional Group Quarters**. Other measures used in the Census are **Family Income** and **Household Income**.

PLACE OF BIRTH
Persons are classified as Natives or Foreign Born. Natives are persons born in the United States, Puerto Rico, or an outlying area of the United States, or who are born abroad but have at least one American parent. Foreign Born persons are subdivided into Natural Citizens and "Not a Citizen."

PLACE OF USUAL RESIDENCE

The address at which a person lives for the majority of the year. Persons are counted by the Census at their Place of Usual Residence, regardless of their actual location at the time of the Census.

PLUMBING FACILITIES

The 1990 Census differentiates between **Housing Units** with complete plumbing facilities and those lacking complete facilities. Housing Units have Complete Plumbing Facilities if they include all of the following: hot and cold piped water; a flush toilet; and a bathtub or shower.

POVERTY STATUS IN 1989

Persons or Families whose **Income** falls below a specified threshold are said to be "Below the Poverty Level." Poverty thresholds are based on an "economy food plan" originally devised by the Department of Agriculture in 1964. These thresholds reflect the cost of providing a minimum level of nutrition to a family or individual. Figures are based on the size of the **Family** and the number of children present. Levels are adjusted for inflation annually, based on the Consumer Price Index. Specific Poverty thresholds used in the 1990 Census can be found in Appendix B of any printed or CD-ROM report which contains Poverty data, or in Chapter 5 of *Understanding the Census*. Poverty Status is determined for **Unrelated Individuals** and for Families and Family Members. Poverty Status is not determined for **Households** or for persons living in **Institutions**.

PRIVATE VEHICLE OCCUPANCY

For persons who travel to work via private vehicles (cars, trucks, minivans, etc.), the Census Bureau tabulates the number of persons riding in the vehicle. In this way, transportation planners can determine how many people commute alone and how many carpool.

RACE

The Census divides the population into five racial groups, based on regulations established by the U.S. Office of Management and Budget. The five categories are listed as follows: **White; Black; American Indian, Eskimo, or Aleut; Asian or Pacific Islander;** and **Other Race.** In some detailed tables, certain of the five categories are subdivided into more specific categories, such as Eskimos, Chinese, or Koreans. Tabulation is based on

self-identification by the respondent. **Hispanic Origin** is not a racial category because Hispanics can be of any Race.

REFERENCE WEEK

The calendar week preceding the date on which an individual respondent completed the census questionnaire. The Reference Week is used to determine **Labor Force** status and **Journey to Work** data.

RELATED CHILD

A broader definition than **Child** or **Own Child**. A Related Child is any **Family** member age 17 or younger who is related to the **Householder** in any way. This includes Own Children as well as nieces, nephews, or other young relatives living with the Family.

RELATIVE

A household member related to the **Householder** by marriage, birth, or adoption.

RENTER OCCUPIED HOUSING UNIT

A **Housing Unit** inhabited by a tenant. For some tabulations, the Census Bureau defines a special subcategory for **Specified Renter Occupied Housing Units**.

RURAL

All territory, population, and **Housing Units** that are not **Urban**. Rural territory comprises all land lying outside an **Urbanized Area** and which is not a Place (Incorporated or Census Designated) with population of 2,500 or greater. The Rural population is divided into Rural **Farm** and Rural Nonfarm.

SAMPLE DATA

Estimated numbers generated from responses to the long-form Census questionnaire, which was received by approximately 17% of United States households. Where available, users should consult **Complete Count Data** first.

SEASONAL, RECREATIONAL, OR OCCASIONAL USE HOUSING

Vacation homes, hunting cabins, time-sharing **Condominiums**, and other **Housing Units** intended for occasional use. By definition, Units in this category are counted as **Vacant Housing Units**, even if someone is temporarily inhabiting the Unit at the time of the

Census. This is because all persons are counted at one location only--their **Place of Usual Residence**.

SELECTED MONTHLY OWNER COSTS

The sum of monthly payments for mortgages of all types, real estate taxes, fire, hazard, and flood insurance on the property, utilities, and heating fuels. **Condominium** fees and mobile home fees are included where appropriate. Some tables report Selected Monthly Owner Costs for all **Owner Occupied Housing Units**, while others are limited to **Specified Owner Occupied Housing Units** only.

SELF-CARE LIMITATION

A mental or physical health condition lasting six months or longer which restricts the respondent's ability to care for their personal needs unassisted. Examples include the ability to bathe or dress. One of three types of **Disability Status** tabulated by the 1990 Census.

SINGLE-PERSON HOUSEHOLD

A **Nonfamily Household** consisting of one individual living alone.

SOURCE OF INCOME

The means by which **Income** is received. This topic is tabulated by the following eight categories: Wage or Salary; Self-Employment Income (Nonfarm); Farm Self-Employment Income; Interest, Dividend, or Net Rental Income; Social Security; Public Assistance; Retirement or Disability; and All Other Income. The latter category includes alimony, child support, gambling winnings, etc.

SPECIFIED OWNER OCCUPIED HOUSING UNIT

A subset of **Owner Occupied Housing Units** restricted to single-Unit houses situated on fewer than 10 acres of land, with no business or medical offices on the premises. Mobile homes are excluded from the "Specified" category, as are multi-Unit structures. The purpose of this designation is to provide an alternate measure of **Housing Value** which does not include commercial property, houses situated on large tracts of land, or other **Housing Units** which tend to distort the average price of a home.

SPECIFIED RENTER OCCUPIED HOUSING UNIT

A subset of **Renter Occupied Housing Units** which excludes single-Unit homes situated on 10 or more acres of land. The purpose of this designation is to provide an alternate measure of **Contract Rent** which is not distorted by rental homes situated on large acreage.

SUBFAMILY

A group of people who would constitute a **Family** if they lived on their own, but instead are living with another Family to whom they are related. For example, if a divorced daughter and her children moved in with the woman's parents, the daughter and her children would constitute a Subfamily. Subfamilies are not counted as Families, but the individuals in the Subfamily are counted as members of the larger Family to which they are related.

SUBSTITUTION

An **Imputation** method where the Census Bureau assigns a complete set of characteristics to a person or Housing Unit because no Questionnaire was returned to the Bureau. Substitution is used only when all other methods of obtaining the data have failed. A more detailed description of the Substitution process can be found in Chapter 10 of *Understanding the Census*.

TELEPHONE AVAILABILITY

A telephone must be available within the house or apartment to be classified as a **Housing Unit** with telephone available.

TENURE

See: Housing Tenure.

UNEMPLOYED

Persons age 16 or older who were without a job during the Reference Week, but who were looking for work and willing and able to accept employment. Out-of-work persons who have given up job-seeking are neither **Employed** or Unemployed, and thus are not members of the **Labor Force**.

UNEMPLOYMENT RATE

The number of **Unemployed** Persons divided by the total number of persons in the **Labor Force**.

UNITS IN STRUCTURE

The number of **Housing Units** located in a given building. Single-Unit structures are classified as detached or attached (e.g., townhouses or row houses), while multi-units structures are tabulated according to the number of units in the building. Mobile Homes and Trailers are listed under Units in Structure as a separate tabulation category.

UNMARRIED COUPLE

Two people of the opposite sex who live together and share an intimate relationship.

UNMARRIED PARTNERS

Two persons of the same sex who live together and share an intimate relationship.

UNPAID FAMILY WORKER

A person who worked 15 or more hours during the **Reference Week** for their family business or farm, but who received no money income for this employment.

UNRELATED INDIVIDUAL

This is a special category used to tabulate **Personal Income** and the **Poverty Status** of individuals. Unrelated Individuals consist of the following three groups: **Householders** living alone or with **Nonrelatives** only; Household members who are not related to the Householder (i.e., Nonrelatives); and persons living in **Noninstitutional Group Quarters.**

URBAN

All territory, population, and Housing Units located within an **Urbanized Area**, plus all Places (Incorporated or Census Designated) with a population of 2,500 or greater. By definition, Minor Civil Divisions located outside an Urbanized Area are not classified as Urban, regardless of their population size. All territory in the United States is either Urban or **Rural.**

URBANIZED AREA

A large Place (usually a city), together with its most densely populated surrounding territory, called the Urban Fringe. Urbanized Areas must have a minimum total population of 50,000. Generally speaking, the Urban Fringe is comprised of all contiguous Census Blocks which combine to create a density of 1,000 persons per square mile. Urbanized Areas do not follow traditional political boundaries and are difficult to identify without a Census map. All Urbanized territory is **Urban**, but not all Urban territory is Urbanized.

USUAL RESIDENCE ELSEWHERE

Persons who indicate that their address at the time of the Census is not their **Place of Usual Residence.** This category would include persons on vacation, away on extended business trips, or otherwise away from home at the time of the Census.

VACANT HOUSING UNIT

A **Housing Unit** which is not listed as someone's **Place of Usual Residence.** A Vacant Housing Unit can have people living in it at the time of the Census, but only if it is not their Place of Usual Residence. For example, **Seasonal, Recreational, and Occasional Use Housing Units** are Vacant by definition. Vacant Housing Units are subdivided into the following categories: Vacant, For Sale; Vacant, For Rent; Awaiting Occupancy; Seasonal, Recreational, and Occasional Use; For Migrant Workers; and Other Vacant.

VALUE

See: Housing Value.

VEHICLE OCCUPANCY

See: Private Vehicle Occupancy.

VEHICLES AVAILABLE

The number of functioning passenger cars, vans, and light trucks kept at home and available for use by **Household** members. Leased vehicles are included, as are employer-owned vehicles which are kept at home and used for nonbusiness purposes.

VISIBLE IN STREET LOCATIONS

Counts persons who were seen on the street on March 21, from 2:00 AM to 4:00 AM at locations identified by local officials as places where the homeless congregate at night. This category also includes persons seen exiting boarded-up buildings from 4:00 AM to 8:00 AM on that night. Together with **Emergency Shelters for the Homeless**, this serves as a measure of the Homeless population.

WAGE OR SALARY INCOME

See: Source of Income.

WHITE

One of the five basic categories of **Race** reported by the Census. Tabulation is based on self-identification by the respondent.

WORK DISABILITY

A mental or physical health condition lasting six months or longer which limits the amount or type of work a person can perform at a job. This includes limitation in the choice of jobs and limitation to part-time jobs, as well as complete inability to accept employment. Work Disability is subdivided into "Prevented from Working," and "Not Prevented from Working." One of three types of **Disability Status** tabulated by the 1990 Census.

WORK STATUS IN 1989

Persons age 16 or older who worked at least one week in 1989. Respondents also provided data on the number of weeks worked, and the usual hours worked per week.

WORKER

Employed Persons who actually worked during the **Reference Week**. Excluded from this category are persons who were absent from their job due to illness, vacation, or similar reason. The total number of Workers is the universe from which **Journey to Work** data are tabulated.

—————— **Also Available from Epoch Books** ——————

Understanding the Census: A Guide for Marketers, Planners, Grant Writers, and Other Data Users

by Michael R. Lavin. ISBN 0-9629586-1-1. Softcover, 530 pp. $49.95

Understanding the Census explains the complexities of the decennial Census in an easy-to-read narrative format. It contains a wealth of detail about Census methodology, concepts, and geography, as well as offering descriptive guides to the Bureau's decennial publications in print, CD-ROM, online, and other electronic formats. A separate chapter takes the reader on a step-by-step exploration of the Bureau's EXTRACT software package. *Understanding the Census* is a valuable resource for experienced Census users and for novices alike.

Understanding the Census offers numerous special features to guide readers through the complex world of Census data. More than 150 exhibits are provided, including sample tables from print and electronic publications and many comparative charts compiled specifically for this book. "Q&A" sections explore frequently asked questions about the decennial Census. *Understanding the Census* contains several hundred additional sidebars comparing the 1990 Census to its 1980 predecessor and offering tips on finding and understanding Census data. This unique book also offers a variety of case studies explaining how to locate and use Census information correctly and efficiently.

What reviewers are saying about *Understanding the Census*:

"An encyclopedic guide to the U.S. Census... Its clear and concise explanations can be understood by people who do not have survey backgrounds, while being instructive to those with years of experience. Serves as a useful desk reference for anyone working with census data."
Government Finance Review

"Clearly written... Difficult ideas are made understandable through the use of illustrations, text boxes, and the thoughtful organization of text. *Understanding the Census* guides census information seekers through simple and complex ideas and makes data easier to use and understand. This book should be in libraries of all types."
Business Information Alert

"The organization of the text is masterful... the discussion is clear and concise. The author weaves 160 figures and 350 sidebars in appealing and appropriate fashion. An excellent guide."
APA Journal (American Planning Association)

"Census methodology, rationale, and processes are explained thoroughly. Lavin's book could be used as a textbook, or as a very detailed reference book for Census users."
Choice: Books for College Libraries

"A clear and comprehensive introduction to using Census data. Highly recommended."
The Information Advisor

"Provides readers with copious examples, case studies, figures, tables, and helpful hints... The book's design and page format contribute greatly to its success. A valuable reference source."
RQ

Order Form

Subject Index to the 1990 Census of Population and Housing
    by Michael Lavin, Jane Weintrop, and Cynthia Cornelius
        ISBN 0-9629586-2-X   261 pages

Understanding the Census: A Guide for Marketers, Planners, Grant Writers, and Other Data Users
    by Michael Lavin
        ISBN 0-9629586-1-1   545 pages

Order both books and receive a 25% discount on the retail price

	Price	Quantity	Total
Subject Index to the 1990 Census	$39.95	_____	$ _____
Understanding the Census	$49.95	_____	$ _____
Special Discount for Dual Order	$67.50	_____	$ _____
New York State residents add	8% sales tax	_____	$ _____
Shipping and handling (see rates below)		_____	$ _____
Total Amount of Order			$ _____

Book Rate: (allow 2-3 weeks for delivery)
    $4.00 for the first book
    $1.00 for each additional book

Air Mail: $5.40 per book

    Do not send cash.
    Make checks payable to:

EPOCH BOOKS, INC.
22 Byron Avenue - Suite A6
Kenmore, NY 14223
(716) 837-4341

Name_____

Address _____

City _____

State_____ ZIP _____